CHILD DEVELOPMENT AND THE BRAIN
From Embryo to Adolescence

Second Edition

Rob Abbott and Esther Burkitt

First edition published in Great Britain in 2015
Second edition published in Great Britain in 2023 by

Policy Press, an imprint of
Bristol University Press
University of Bristol
1–9 Old Park Hill
Bristol
BS2 8BB
UK
t: +44 (0)117 374 6645
e: bup-info@bristol.ac.uk

Details of international sales and distribution partners are available
at policy.bristoluniversitypress.co.uk

British Library Cataloguing in Publication Data
A catalogue record for this book is available from the British Library

ISBN 978-1-4473-5567-0 paperback
ISBN 978-1-4473-5568-7 ePub
ISBN 978-1-4473-5608-0 ePdf

Cover design: Nicky Borowiec
Front cover image: iStock/DrAfter123
Bristol University Press and Policy Press use environmentally responsible
print partners.
Printed and bound in Great Britain by CPI Group (UK) Ltd, Croydon, CR0 4YY

FSC
www.fsc.org
MIX
Paper | Supporting
responsible forestry
FSC® C013604

Contents

Contents

List of tables and figures

About the authors

Rob Abbott is an experienced lecturer in early childhood, having taught for many years at the University of Chichester. He currently teaches with the Open University and works as a counsellor and clinical supervisor. Rob is a Fellow of the Higher Education Academy. He is the clinical director of the Arun Counselling Centre in Littlehampton in Sussex. He lives in Poole in Dorset.

Esther Burkitt is a Professor of Developmental Psychology with the University of Chichester and has held lecturing posts in a range of national and international universities. Esther has Chartered Psychologist and Chartered Scientist status with the British Psychological Society. She is an Associate Fellow of the British Psychological Society and is a Fellow of the Higher Education Academy.

Acknowledgements

Many thanks to Regina Karousou, Chris Downs, Charlie Bell and Marianne Parish for their feedback on chapters in the book.

Introduction to the second edition

Who the book is for

The book is written for everyone who is interested in neuroscience and how it has changed our understanding of how children develop. As such, it will be attractive to students and teachers in subjects such as teacher training, psychology, social work, counselling and childhood studies. It will also be of interest to parents, grandparents, aunties, uncles, prospective parents and the general reader.

What this book is about

This book begins by introducing the reader to some basic ideas about the brain, how it is structured and how it develops from a tiny cluster of cells into a complex dynamic structure that controls every aspect of our very existence.

Each chapter in this book covers a different aspect of development. It provides an overview of what we know and then explores the ways in which neuroscience has extended, or sometimes changed, this understanding.

This is a book that encourages learning

The aim of this book is to provide a readable text for the non-scientist. Wherever possible we have put what are often complicated ideas into accessible language. We have also explained the jargon and technical language of neuroscience.

We have tried to design the book so that however you go about your learning you will be able to get something from it. We have:

- highlighted our key terms and added them to a glossary at the back of the book;
- pulled out key ideas;
- explored supplementary ideas in separate boxed sections;
- set out the contents of each chapter in bulleted lists;
- given summaries at the end of each chapter;
- provided revision questions;
- provided discussion questions with ideas on how we would answer such questions;
- offered suggestions for further reading at the end of each chapter;
- provided illustrations where these are helpful;
- referenced all the ideas closely and provided a full references section at the end of the book.

How we explore knowledge

Exploring disagreement

Where there is disagreement (and there is plenty) we explore the areas of contention. For example, in Chapter 5 we explore whether we have our emotions in place when we are born or whether these develop during the first months or even years of life. We don't sit on the fence; we show which ideas are most plausible, and which ones are best supported by the evidence, but we also explain why these issues are still contentious.

Exploring areas where more evidence is needed

Where there is still an absence of knowledge, we show the aspects that are known and describe what is unknown. For example, in looking at gender differences in language development, we show that while there is much hot debate about the difference between male and female brains, there is still considerable uncertainty about it.

Where it seems to us that conclusions have been drawn that go beyond what is known, we show why this is problematic. For example, the idea that we can produce dramatic images in a scanner that show the effects of deprivation is problematic. We show in Chapter 6 why these scans are misleading and why such evidence needs to be held up to scrutiny. Deprivation in its many forms undoubtedly leads to huge problems in brain development, but misleading images, however beguiling they appear, do not help us understand the how and why of such issues.

Critiquing fake knowledge

Where an absence of knowledge has led to ideas that are wrong, we also call out these errors. We explore throughout the book many neuromyths and show how these ideas are false. The idea, for example, that we only use 10% of our brain is just plain daft: why would we carry around a heavy brain if we didn't use 90% of it? What a waste of effort!

Animal studies versus human studies

Much of what we know about the brain comes from animal experiments. For example, quite a lot of our knowledge about the workings of the neuron comes from experiments with sea slugs. There are always issues about applying research findings from animal experiments to human subjects. Issues around animal welfare and the ethics of conducting experiments on animals often create strong feelings. There are also problems around whether findings from such research can be translated to humans. For example, in Chapter 6 we explore the way in which studies of how cortisol affects behaviour rely heavily on animal research and explain why this is misleading.

Taking a position

We argue for the importance of experience in the development of effective brains and functional human beings. We show how poverty, deprivation, abuse and neglect have a terrible and long-lasting effect on brain development. Poverty, for example, leads to malnutrition and this in turn, as we explore in Chapter 4, affects the way the brain develops. Babies and young children who do not get enough to eat, or do not get enough of the right food at the right time, do not develop their full quota of neurons and fail to develop the same number of synaptic connections as children who receive adequate nutrition. This leads to both cognitive delay and long-term cognitive deficiencies. What is most terrible about this is that such poverty is avoidable. There is enough food for us to feed the world and enough resources for us to distribute these foods around the globe. What stops this happening are the huge inequalities that beset humankind and the lack of political will to solve these problems.

The structure of the book

A mostly chronological approach

This book covers development from the first stages of brain development through to the teenage years. Often it makes sense to do this chronologically, beginning with early development and proceeding towards adolescence. On other occasions, for example when looking at trauma, this structure does not work and so we look holistically at both childhood and adolescence.

The chapters

Chapter 1 introduces the structure and workings of the brain. We look at the ways in which the outer part of the brain, the cerebral cortex, can be divided up, and we introduce some of the main parts of the lower or subcortical brain as well as the way in which neurons and other cells work within the central nervous system. We also provide a guide to the terms used to describe the geography of the brain, explaining terms such as 'caudal', 'rostral' and 'medial'. Finally, in this chapter we look at the way in which images of the brain are captured. We critique ideas around brain imaging and show how these images are manipulated to make them easier to read but also easier to misinterpret.

Chapter 2 explores how brains develop. We look at how brains grow from a few cells into a fully functioning human being. Central to this is that amazing property of the brain: plasticity. We explore the difference between experience-expectant plasticity and experience-dependent plasticity, showing how both operate to control and steer development. We also look at what happens in adolescence and critique ideas around gender and brain development.

In Chapter 3 we look at the development of thinking, focusing on how neuroscience has built on and changed the understanding that grew from the work of Jean Piaget. We explore, for example, his ideas on object permanence and consider this in terms of what we now know about cognitive processing and short-term memory. We also look at more contemporary theories of cognitive processing and examine how knowledge about the frontal cortex is changing our understanding of cognitive development. We conclude this chapter by considering the huge cognitive changes that occur during adolescence.

Chapter 4 focuses on health. We look at what helps brains grow well and what disturbs this growth. We begin with food and consider what food babies and mothers need to produce healthy infants with healthy brains. We look at drugs of all sorts, both medicines and recreational drugs, and consider their impact on the brain of the developing foetus. We also consider how cigarettes, alcohol and other drugs can affect the brains of adolescents.

Chapter 5 examines emotional and social development. We consider ideas about how emotions develop and the timescale over which this happens. We critique the evidence on whether we are born with a set of basic emotions or whether these develop because of experience. We explore social development from the sensitivity of babies to human faces through the development of smiling, and we conclude with a study of how teenagers are particularly susceptible to social influences.

Chapter 6 is about attachment and how trauma can damage our capacity to form steady, loving and fulfilling human relationships. We begin with the work of John Bowlby and critique ways in which neuroscience adds, or fails to add, to this model of development. We then explore how emotional, physical and sexual abuse can lead to trauma in children and teenagers. We explore three key brain areas: the amygdala, the hippocampus and the hypothalamic-pituitary-adrenocortical axis. We conclude the chapter with a brief study of the impact of abuse on Romanian orphans who were provided with inadequate care under the Ceaușescu regime.

Chapter 7 explores aspects of language development. It reviews the work of 20th-century theorists and then considers the ways in which neuroscience is changing our understanding of how babies and children process the language sounds they hear around them. We critique ideas about multilingualism and consider the advantages of speaking more than one language. While most of the significant developments in language occur in early childhood, we also consider what neuroscience is telling us about later language development. Lastly, in this chapter we look at the thorny issue of gender and language development. Are girls better at language than boys or is this just a myth?

Chapter 8 considers what we know about the development of literacy and numeracy. We look at the process of reading from decoding the letters on the page to understanding and analysing meaning. We look at the areas of the brain that process written text and critique how neuroscience is adding to our understanding of dyslexia. In a similar way we look at how we process numbers. Our brains deal differently with big numbers and small numbers, and we consider how neuroscience is adding to our understanding of how each of these is processed. We also critique what we know and what we don't yet know about the neuroscience of dyscalculia.

Chapter 9 probes our understanding of how memory works. It looks at the different types of memory and how these develop during childhood and adolescence. It considers how memory is stored in the brain, particularly the workings of the hippocampus. In the second part of the chapter, we look at how our knowledge about learning is changing. We conclude this chapter by discussing some common neuromyths: false ideas about learning and the brain that have gained popular currency in recent years.

In Chapter 10 we look at some neurodevelopmental disorders. We present an account of our current knowledge of each of these conditions and then consider how brain science is adding to this knowledge. In this chapter we also give the names of organisations where you can find out more about the conditions discussed.

More materials on our website

We hope you enjoy the book and want to explore some further ideas on our website. This can be found at:

https://policy.bristoluniversitypress.co.uk/child-development-and-the-brain/companion-website

Included in these materials there is:

- advice about how to read this book: https://policy.bristoluniversitypress.co.uk/child-development-and-the-brain/companion-website/general-introduction
- ideas on how to read difficult academic articles: https://policy.bristoluniversitypress.co.uk/child-development-and-the-brain/companion-website/how-to-read-difficult-academic-papers
- how to find more information about brain development: https://policy.bristoluniversitypress.co.uk/child-development-and-the-brain/companion-website/finding-materials-about-brain-development
- a glossary of terms used in brain development (also to be found at the end of this book): https://policy.bristoluniversitypress.co.uk/child-development-and-the-brain/companion-website/glossary

1

Getting to know the human brain

This chapter:

- describes what the brain looks like;

- introduces the different parts of the brain;

- helps you to find your way around the brain;

- identifies the different types of brain cells and shows how our knowledge of these is growing;

- shows how brain imaging helps us to see inside the brain and explores the problems around interpreting these images.

Introduction

In this chapter we begin by exploring the central nervous system and introduce you to some of its important elements. We begin with the outer crinkly layer, the cerebral cortex, and describe the main divisions. We then look at the subcortical brain and introduce the different parts of this such as the cerebellum, the amygdala and the hippocampus. We spend some time explaining the terms used to describe navigation through the brain. Terms such as 'up', 'down', 'top' and 'bottom' are not sufficient to describe human brains: something might be at the top when we stand up but would be somewhere else when we lie down!

We explore the different types of cells that are found in the brain such as neurons, dendrites, oligodendrocytes and astrocytes. Finally, we take a critical look at the process of picturing the brain. Many people assume that these wonderful, coloured images we see are photographs of the brain. We show this is far from the truth and consider the limitations of our abilities to really see what is happening inside our heads and, of course, the heads of children.

The amazing human brain

The human brain is quite amazing! We spend all our time living inside it, we understand the world we live in because of it, we hear, speak, see, smell and feel because of its ability to process information. We laugh, cry and fall in love because of its capacity to generate and process feelings. We are self-aware because of this strange quality called consciousness that goes on somewhere inside our brain. We have written this text and you are reading it because the brain is able to translate these squiggles on the page and turn them into a meaningful language. And as we move through the 21st century, we are slowly adding to our knowledge of how this incredible organ works and, just as important, develops. The focus of this book is this developmental process in which the brain grows from a small cluster of cells to the brain of a functional adult. However, we first need to introduce the brain and the central nervous system.

Introducing the nervous system

The brain and the spinal cord form the **central nervous system (CNS)**. The spinal cord begins just beneath the brain itself and continues down through the spine. It contains large numbers of neurons or nerve cells. Some of these nerve cells in the spine belong to the CNS, while others belong to the **peripheral nervous system (PNS)**. The PNS comprises the nerves and the associated fibres that lie beyond the brain and connect the CNS to the rest of the body. The PNS also controls functions such as breathing and digestion.

The brain itself is made up of two symmetrical hemispheres (Figure 1.1). These are joined together by a thick layer of neural fibres, called the **corpus callosum**.

The left hemisphere receives and sends out signals mostly to the right side of the body and the right hemisphere deals in the same way with the left side of the body. There is much debate over the extent to which the right and left hemispheres are functionally different. Ideas that the right hemisphere of the brain is creative and the left more rational have been proved to be totally wrong. We use both sides of our brains for most of what we do. Regions of the brain are connected by many billions of neurons so that each part of the brain is in constant communication with other regions.

The corpus callosum is a large bundle of nerves situated just below the cerebral cortex. It connects the left and right sides of the brain and allows for communication between these two parts of the brain. The corpus callosum's main function is to integrate information between the two hemispheres. It is also involved in processing sensory information as well as having a role in language laterisation, memory and attention.

The cerebral cortex

The physical appearance of the brain is far from impressive. Maria Robinson describes it as having the shape of a walnut, its colour is of uncooked liver and its consistency is that of firm jelly (Robinson, 2008). The **cerebrum** is covered in a wrinkled layer of tissue that is 2–4 mm (0.08–0.16 inches) thick. This is the cerebral cortex. If you were to lay flat the cerebral cortex of an average adult, it would be about 1570 cm^2 in size, although two-thirds of this is hidden inside the folds that give it its wrinkled appearance (Hurdal et al, 2001). Think of a

Figure 1.1: The brain from above

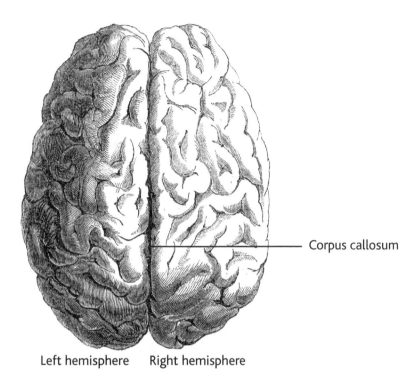

Corpus callosum

Left hemisphere   Right hemisphere

sheet of foam plastic measuring about 3 mm × 40 cm × 40 cm that is crammed inside a large coconut!

The hills and valleys that are formed by the scrunching up of the cerebral cortex are called sulci and gyri. They are usually referred to in the singular form, so each hill is called a **gyrus** (Greek = ring or circle) and each valley is called a **sulcus** (Latin = furrow)

> If you ironed the cerebral cortex flat, it would be a thin 3 mm sheet measuring 40 cm × 40 cm

These folds divide the cerebral cortex into four sections or lobes (Figure 1.2): the frontal lobe, the parietal lobe, the temporal lobes and the occipital lobe. Most of these folds are formed by 28 weeks after conception, although they will continue to develop in complexity after birth. The valleys formed by these main folds are called the primary sulci. The biggest of these, the central sulcus, divides the frontal lobe from the parietal lobe.

It was once thought that the folds in the brain were simply about an increasing number of synaptic connections in the developing brain. However, recent research has shown that how the brain folds is related to the amount of surface area and the thickness of the cortices. You can try this yourself with a few sheets of paper. Take one sheet of A4 paper and crumple it up. Next, lay five sheets

Figure 1.2: The hills and valleys of the cerebral cortex

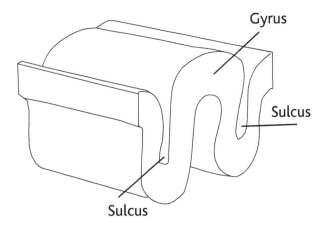

together and then crumple these. You can see for yourself that the result looks very different. The example and the mathematical way in which this works is the work of Mota and Herculano-Houzel (2015). They put it this way:

> stacking sheets before crumpling displaces the curves to the right ... but leaves their slope largely unaltered, resulting in similar-looking but less folded paper balls. (2015, p 76)

It is the same in the brain. What is important here, though, is that this seems to happen predictably, and it can be mapped according to a formula. If you are mathematically minded, then we suggest you read the original paper, which is available online. For the rest of us it might be enough to say that how the brain folds is the result of multiplying the cortical surface area with the square root of cortical thickness.

Most areas of the cortex are structured into six layers. The upper layers are mostly made up of neuronal cells or **neurons** and fibres that connect with each other, while the lower layers contain neurons that communicate with subcortical areas of the brain, that is, the layers of the brain that lie beneath the cortex.

It might be helpful to understand parts of the brain in a physical way, so we suggest that as you read the next part you use your hands to locate the four lobes of the brain (Figure 1.3). Place the palm of your hand flat on your forehead and stretch your fingers towards the back of your head. Your hand is now over the **frontal lobe**, which is the largest lobe of the brain. This part of the brain is involved in a great number of higher functions. Of significance is the front (anterior) part, which is called the **prefrontal cortex**. This is the executive area of the brain. It is

> The prefrontal cortex is the part of the brain that we use for decision making as well as regulating our emotions

Figure 1.3: The lobes of the brain

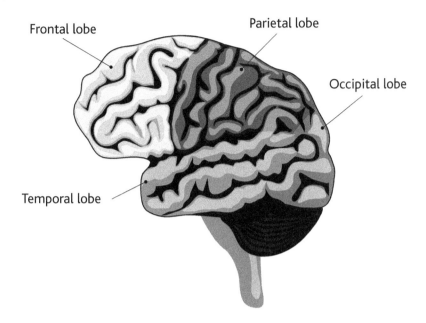

Frontal lobe

Parietal lobe

Occipital lobe

Temporal lobe

involved in planning, memory, personality and decision making and is also the area where emotional reactions are thought through. If you now move your hand upwards, until it is on top of the centre of your head, then you will be above the **parietal lobe**. This area of the brain deals with a lot of sensory information as well as controlling aspects of movement.

Now place each of your hands around your ears. The **temporal lobes** are beneath the parietal lobe at about the level of your ears: there are two of these, one on each side of your head. These play a role in the processing of sound. The temporal lobe in the left hemisphere is where most people process speech. The temporal lobe also contains a part of the brain called the **hippocampus**, which plays a role in memory. Lastly, move your hand to the back of your head, just above where your neck begins. This area is called the **occipital lobe**. This is where a lot of visual processing takes place.

The subcortical brain

Beneath the cerebral cortex are the subcortical areas of the brain. If we were to slice the brain in two from top to bottom down the middle of the head (technically we would say it has been hemisected in the midsagittal plane), then we could see the structures that make up the areas beneath the cortex.

The structure at the base of the cerebrum is the **brain stem**. The brain stem plays an important function in regulating reflex activities such as heart rate, blood sugar levels and breathing. The brain stem also plays a role in relaying

Figure 1.4: The subcortical brain

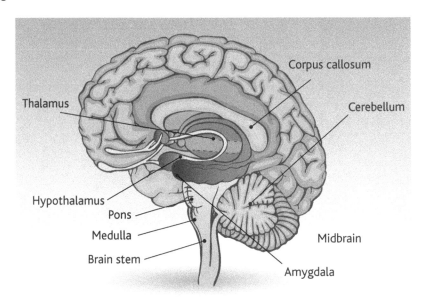

information between the brain and the spinal cord. The brain stem is sometimes called the reptilian brain and, in evolutionary terms, is the oldest part of the brain. The **medulla, pons** and **midbrain** form the brain stem and also play a role in regulation and the relay of information (Figure 1.4).

Next to this is the **cerebellum**, sometimes called the 'little brain'. This is involved in planning and controlling movement, although damage to this region also affects language use and decision-making abilities, so it clearly has many functions. Astonishingly, the cerebellum contains about 80% of all the neurons in the human brain (Azevedo et al, 2009).

The **thalamus** sits on the top of the brain stem and also has a relay function, receiving and processing signals from most of the sensory receptors in the body and then relaying them to the appropriate parts of the cortex. Just below this is the **hypothalamus**, which plays a role in regulating behaviours such as eating, sleeping and sexual activity. It partially achieves this by regulating hormones, which are released from the nearby **pituitary gland**.

The **limbic system** sits around the thalamus (Latin = limbus, meaning ring or circle). Exactly which parts of the brain are included in the limbic system is open to debate. However, it is often used to mean the **amygdala, insula, hippocampus** and **cingulate cortex**. Pinel (2011, p 69) writes that the limbic system controls the four Fs of motivation: 'fleeing, feeding, fighting and sexual behaviour' – an old joke, he admits, but a good one!

The hippocampus is essential to the processing of memory, particularly the transference of experiences from short-term into long-term memory. We look at this in more detail in Chapter 9.

Figure 1.5: Navigating the brain

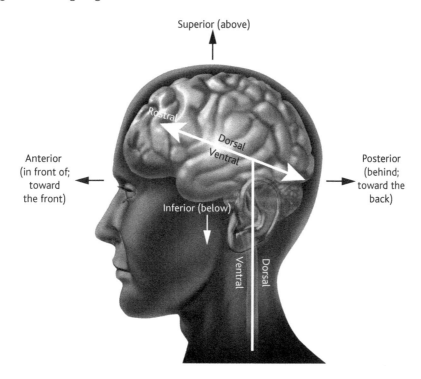

The amygdala is involved in the processing of emotions. It interacts with the **orbitofrontal** and prefrontal cortex to generate and regulate emotions.

Finding your way around the brain

It is often quite difficult to understand the language of neuroscience. Some of the most puzzling terms to the non-scientist are the ones used to navigate the anatomy of the brain. Science has always been very reluctant to use straightforward language. While 'up', 'down', 'left' and 'right' might not be quite sufficient when describing the anatomy of the brain, the use of terms such as *caudal*, *rostral*, *medial* and *lateral* causes much confusion for the non-specialist reader (see Figure 1.5). This confusion is not helped by the fact that different Latin terms are often used to refer to the same thing. Biologists and neuroscientists describe the relative positions of different parts of the body in relation to the spine.

Caudal and rostral

Caudal here means the tail (Latin caudum = tail) and rostral the nose (Latin rostrum = beak). The brain develops in stages. This can be seen as a hierarchical process. In the neuroscience literature you will sometimes see this described as caudal to rostral development, which simply means that brain development starts at the bottom and works its way up. The inner parts of the brain, the subcortical regions, develop first, while the cortical regions, the outer parts, develop later.

Superior and inferior

Superior means above, while inferior means below.

Anterior and posterior

Anterior means in front or towards the front and posterior means behind or towards the back.

You can remember this by thinking about how you sit on your posterior!

Dorsal and ventral

Dorsal means towards the surface or the top of the head, while ventral means towards the surface of the chest or bottom of the head. If you imagine a dolphin swimming in the water, the dorsal area will be where the fins are, and the ventral area will be where the breast of the animal is located. Again, these terms are best illustrated in a diagram (Figure 1.6).

Medial and lateral

Medial means towards the middle, while lateral means further away from the middle.

Types of cells in the brain

The cells which make up the central nervous system can be broadly divided into two different types: neurons and glia or glial cells.

Figure 1.6: Understanding the language of navigation

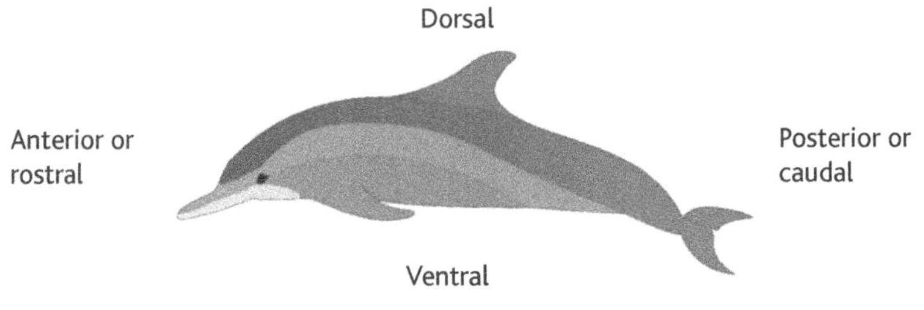

Dorsal

Anterior or rostral

Posterior or caudal

Ventral

Neurons

Understanding how neurons work is an important part of learning how brains function. We know that there are on average 86 billion neurons in the human brain (Herculano-Houzel, 2017): almost all of them have been produced while the baby is still in the womb. In the adult brain these neurons are not distributed equally. On average, about 16 billion of these neurons are in the cerebral cortex, 69 billion of them are in the cerebellum and about 1 million of them are in the rest of the brain. Each neuron can fire an electrical signal and will do so if it is suitably stimulated by signals from other neurons or by input from the senses.

Neurons come in three different shapes and sizes: multipolar neurons, bipolar neurons and unipolar neurons. As well as a central cell body with a nucleus at its centre, the neuron has two types of processes, called **dendrites** and **axons**, which extend away from the cell body (see, for example, Figure 1.7). Dendrites are bushy, tree-like fibres whose job is to receive information from other neurons. These are the listening devices of the neuron.

Multipolar neurons make up most of the neurons in the brain. These have a single axon and many dendrites, in some cases as many as 200,000 dendrites per neuron. Bipolar neurons have a single axon at one end and a single dendrite at the other. A unipolar neuron has a single branch that extends from the cell body. This then divides into two branches. The axon terminals extend from one end of the branch and the dendrites from the other.

While dendrites can often appear like the branches of an old tree, axons can be very long, sometimes up to several feet or tens of centimetres in length. There is a great deal of variety in the size, structure and appearance of neurons. Some neurons will have one axon, while others will have two axons; some will have no axons, while others will have many. Neurons fire a very brief electrical charge (called an **action potential**) within the length of the axon. These action potentials fire when the neuron receives enough stimulation either from other neurons or from sense receptors such as those in the skin that respond to contact or those in the eye that respond to light.

The dendrites of one neuron are not in direct contact with the axon terminals of another neuron and so, in this sense, do not quite touch. There is a very small gap measuring less than a millionth of an inch, called a **synaptic cleft**, between the end of one neuron and the dendrites of the receiving neuron. The synapse converts the electrical activity into a chemical signal. When the action potential (or electrical signal) reaches the axon terminals at the end of the neuron (referred to as the presynaptic cell), it stimulates the release of chemical messengers in the form of molecules called neurotransmitters. The neurotransmitter travels across the synaptic cleft to the receiving neuron (referred to as the postsynaptic cell), where it binds to receptors, creating small electrical changes in the postsynaptic neuron. If this neuron receives enough stimulation, then it too will fire an action potential, thus passing the signal on and enabling communication with the next neuron in the chain.

There are numerous neurotransmitter chemicals in the brain. They each form different pathways and have different functions. Serotonin, for example, plays

Figure 1.7: Structure of a neuron

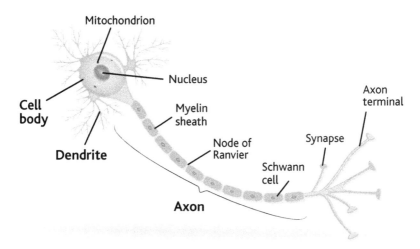

a part in determining mood as well as affecting hunger and sleep. Dopamine is important in movement as well as in learning. Acetylcholine plays an important role in muscle control.

Glial cells

BOX: How to count the number of neurons in the brain

For many years we were told that there are about 100 billion neurons in the brain. However, this figure was, at best, just a guess. The task of counting all these neurons is quite a problem. First of all, how do you separate out all the neurons from all the other stuff (that is, other brain cells and blood vessels), and if you manage to do this, how on earth do you count them all? Susana Herculano-Houzel (2017) solved the problem a few years back: you take a whole brain and then dissolve it using a strong detergent. This destroys the cell membranes but leaves the nuclei of the neurons intact. It produces what Herculano-Houzel calls 'brain soup'. By sampling a small amount of this, her team were then able to count the number of neurons in this tiny amount of brain and multiply it up to arrive at a number representing the number of neurons in the brain as a whole. It turns out that we humans have about 86 billion neurons in our brains. This compares with 257 billion in the much larger elephant brain. So why aren't elephants three times more intelligent than humans? We'll answer this question in the chapter on learning.

The other types of cells in the brain are called glial cells, usually just called **glia** (Greek = glue). It was once thought that there are more than ten times as many glial cells in the brain as there are neurons. We now know this to be wrong, although you still find this figure in many books and on many websites. We now know that there are about the same number of glial cells as there are neurons (Azevedo et al, 2009).

Glia have a whole range of different functions. They support the process of neurotransmission – that is, the sending of electrical and chemical signals from one neuron to the next; they have a maintenance role, particularly in balancing the concentration of ions in the spaces between neurons; and they act to insulate longer neurons to speed up communication. New research also shows that they have an important role in the processing of information during brain development and in later life.

Glial cells in the brain come in several different types:

- **oligodendrocytes** and **Schwann cells**
- **microglia**
- **astrocytes**

Oligodendrocytes and Schwann cells

These surround the axons in the central nervous system and form a myelin sheath. This provides a layer of fatty insulation that increases the speed at which electrical signals can travel down the length of the neuron. The process of covering the body of the neuron with insulation is called **myelination**. The role performed by oligodendrocytes in the central nervous system is done by Schwann cells in the peripheral nervous system.

Myelinated cells appear white. These are also referred to as **white matter**. White matter is the name given to neurons where the axon has been myelinated. **Grey matter**, on the other hand, is a mix of unmyelinated axons, blood vessels, and the synaptic connections between neurons and glial cells.

The insulation provided by the process of myelination greatly speeds up the action potential as it travels down the axon. The myelin does not cover all the axon. There are gaps in the covering which occur about once every millimetre. These gaps contain what we might think of as booster stations known as **nodes of Ranvier**. With the help of the myelin layer and the nodes of Ranvier, action potential can travel down the axon at speeds of up to 120 metres per second – that's over 260 mph!

Microglia

As you might guess from their name, microglia are smaller than other glial cells. They respond to injury or disease in the brain and act as the first line of defence by multiplying and wrapping around damaged neurons and other bits of debris in the brain. They also play a role in pruning unused synaptic connections. They have been described as the 'professional phagocytes of the brain' (Wolf et al, 2017, p 621), meaning they eat up the unwanted matter within the brain.

Given that about half of all the cells that are produced during development are later eliminated, this is clearly a significant developmental function. The pruning process appears to be vital to the survival of functioning and used brain cells – so without glia performing their cleaning role, these cells might not survive.

Astrocytes

These are so named because they are star shaped (Greek *astron* = star). They have also perhaps been, until recently, the overlooked stars of the brain! They keep the brain running by providing energy and the underlying structure to facilitate neurotransmission. When neurons start to fire, it is the astrocytes which signal to the blood vessels that more oxygenated blood is needed. They order up, if you like, the blood and the glucose it carries to the regions of the brain that are active. They also play an important role in neurotransmission. Once neurotransmitters have been secreted by the neuron and have carried their signal to an adjoining neuron, astrocytes turn off the neurotransmitter action and help to reabsorb the neurotransmitter back into the neuron. They have the capacity to communicate with each other and with neurons.

Astrocytes also have a developmental role. They are known, for example, to contribute towards the process of forming synapses in the postnatal brain (Clarke and Barres, 2013). It is also now known that they have a role in some degenerative diseases (Khakh et al, 2017), although work here has so far only focused on animal models and there is much more to be studied in humans.

Picturing the brain

> Developments in brain imaging have revolutionised the way we can study the brain

Before the 1970s it was impossible to obtain images of the living brain. Most of what we knew about brains at that time was from post-mortem examinations of adults and children. X-rays had been around for most of the 20th century but were almost useless when it came to imaging the soft tissue organs such as the brain. Some methods of measuring brain activity were also developed early in the 20th century; electroencephalography, for example, was first used on humans in 1924. However, developments in brain imaging in the early 1970s completely revolutionised the way in which we can study the brain by allowing us to produce images of it in vivo, that is, within the living body.

A recent study of a decade of neuroimaging studies of infants (Azhari et al, 2020) shows some revealing trends. The most imaged periods of infant development occur just after birth and at 12 months, with another peak at 24 months, suggesting a lack of information about the periods in between and a tendency towards describing development in terms of milestones, whereas, in reality, there may just be steady development. The vast majority of the infants studied by imaging came from North America, although there have been similar numbers of such studies in the United States and Japan, perhaps because the manufacturers of much of the equipment, for example Shimadzu and Hitachi, are based in Japan. This results in a geographical bias, with some populations of the planet, for example those in parts of South-East Asia, South America and Europe, being underrepresented.

Types of imaging

Electroencephalography (EEG) measures electrical signals in the brain by means of electrodes placed on different areas of the scalp. These electrodes are connected to a machine which then produces a printout from each of the electrodes and gives a direct measure of the electrical activity in particular parts of the brain. There are lots of advantages to EEGs: they are non-invasive (you do not need to be injected with anything); they do not require the subject to sit or lie still; they are not scary or noisy. They can tell researchers a lot about the electrical signals that fire in the brain as a result of a particular stimulus, for example, seeing something, doing something or touching something. We can, for example, present a child with a particular stimulus and then measure the neural activity in response to this. These signals are called event-related potentials (ERPs). These can be measured very accurately in milliseconds as well as in real time. The disadvantages of EEGs are that they only measure signals that are near the scalp, and they are not all that accurate in telling us where the signal originates.

Magnetoencephalography (MEG) requires the person to sit with their head inside what looks like a large and highly sophisticated hairdryer. It measures the very small magnetic fields that are generated every time a neuron fires. As the earth itself also generates a magnetic field, MEG requires super-sensitive detectors called superconducting quantum interference devices or SQUIDs for short. The advantage of this is that it has high temporal and spatial resolution, that is, it can both tell researchers where in the brain the signal comes from and measure it as it happens. MEG allows us to measure the rapid changes that happen in the communication between dendrites and neurons.

Images from **computerised tomography**, often just called CT scans, were developed in the 1950s. They are still used today but typically in hospitals and other clinical settings, where they are used for diagnosis of, for example, brain tumours or haemorrhaging. In order to have a CT scan you lie with your head inside what looks like a large doughnut. The doughnut allows for several X-rays to be taken and the computer is then used to build up a three-dimensional picture of the brain. However, passing X-rays through the brains of healthy people, particularly healthy children, is clearly a health hazard and one which would most certainly prohibit repeated scans, even if such procedures are necessary for diagnosis.

Positron emission tomography, usually called PET, came into use in the second half of the 20th century and has today largely been replaced by fMRI.

Before the scan takes place, a person needs to be injected with a small amount of a radioactive tracer. In the bloodstream this releases a particle called a positron. These then collide with electrons, which in turn release photons that can be detected by the scanner.

> MRI (and fMRI) allows for repeated images to be made of the same brain and so can show how the structure changes over time

Magnetic resonance imaging (MRI) provides a much better means of letting us image the brains of healthy children and adults without the concomitant health risks. MRI also gives much clearer pictures of the brain; it can distinguish, for example, between white matter and grey matter in the brain. This technology has also allowed for repeated scans of the same brain and so given us the ability to see how they develop over time.

One critical factor in MRI technology is the graininess of the image. This is measured in a unit called a voxel. The size of the voxel determines how clear or how grainy the eventual picture will be. The best and smallest voxels can only be obtained at the cost of making the patient lie still for a long period of time. This is clearly a problem with children. Most paediatric MRI (Figure 1.8) studies require the patient to lie still for between five and 20 minutes. As everyone who works with children will tell you, getting them to lie still even for reasonably short periods of time can be extremely difficult!

Functional magnetic resonance imaging (fMRI) scans are used to produce what are called functional images of the brain, that is, images which show us the moment-by-moment activity of the brain as the person does things such as reading or thinking. fMRI is now used extensively in medicine for

Figure 1.8: Brain scanner

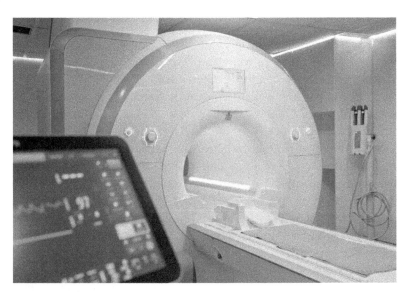

Source: Shutterstock Photo ID: 1586726968

diagnosis but is also widely used in all branches of neuroscience. It works on the principle that active areas of the brain take up more oxygenated blood than they use. Such oxygenated blood has magnetic properties which can be recorded within the scanner. In technical terms the signal that is recorded by the fMRI scanner is called the BOLD (blood-oxygen-level-dependent) signal. It is important to remember when you look at these sorts of scans that what you are seeing is not neural activity but a BOLD signal.

> fMRI is very useful for telling us where neural activity in the brain is taking place; it is not good, however, at showing exactly when this happens

That is, you are seeing oxygenated blood, not the firing of neurons. There is not a straightforward relationship between the BOLD signal that you get from the scanner and the amount of neural activity that might be going on in the brain. fMRI scans have another problem as well. The images take several seconds to be produced. This means that it is not possible to capture the very quick firing of neurons. fMRI is very good at giving us a picture with good spatial resolution but not so good when it comes to temporal resolution. In other words, it is good at showing us *where* things are in the brain and *what* they are doing, but it is not so good at showing us *when* they are happening. fMRI takes a snapshot of the brain about every two seconds. In contrast, neuron firing is measured in milliseconds. It is about 1,000 times too slow to follow neural activity (Slotnick, 2013).

Resting state functional magnetic resonance imaging (RsfMRI) is a new type of fMRI scan which maps interactions between different regions of the brain while subjects are not involved in a task.

Diffusion MRI (also called diffusion tensor imaging or DTI) is a relatively new technique based around the process of diffusion (the moving of molecules) and is used to detect changes in diffusion of water in both white and grey matter in the brain.

We also have to be very careful about cause and effect when using any of these scanning techniques in experimental work with children. If, for example, we are measuring a child's reaction to a particular stimulus, we cannot be absolutely sure that the BOLD signal from the scanner is showing us a picture of this reaction in the brain. There might be other explanations.

One way of overcoming this difficulty is to use another technique called transcranial magnetic stimulation or TMS.

Transcranial magnetic stimulation (TMS) involves placing a large electronic magnet next to the skull; the resulting magnetic field turns off particular areas of the brain. This sounds rather crude and there are quite a lot of questions still to be answered about ethics and safety. However, it does overcome some of the difficulties about determining cause and effect.

Near-infrared spectroscopy (NIRS) is another means of measuring the blood oxygen level in the brain. Rather than magnets, however, it uses light in the infrared spectrum. Such light will reflect differently from blood vessels depending on how much oxygen they are carrying. Skullcaps are fitted with arrays of little infrared lights which penetrate the skull and are then reflected back from the surface of the brain. The relative thinness of the infant's skull means this technique is particularly effective in looking at the developing brain. This technique has allowed neuroscientists to look at the brains of very young children and even babies as it is much more tolerant of head movement than techniques such as fMRI. **Functional near-infrared spectroscopy** (fNIRS) allows neuroscientists to see the processing of activity in the brain. It is particularly good at establishing a relationship between two parts of the brain even when these locations are physically separated. Because this method is based on changes in blood composition, it is relatively slow, so although it is sometimes described as visualising changes 'moment by moment', we must understand that this is measured in seconds rather than milliseconds. Growth in this aspect of neuroimaging has been exponential, with the number of papers published based on studies using fNIRS doubling every three and a half years (Pinti et al, 2020).

Looking critically at brain images

Brain images are not like photographs. They are based on statistical analysis and are manipulated in order to make them understandable

We are all used to looking at images of every sort. We take photos on our phones; we watch moving and still pictures on our computer screens. We make lots of assumptions about what we see even though we know that pictures can be manipulated and that what we are looking at might not be an exact reproduction of any sort of reality. How about brain scans, though? Surely we can rely on those? The truth is that brain scans are not photographs. Each of the technologies we discussed previously collects data in a different way, but all of them collect numbers rather than images. They are statistical methods of understanding the brain. Once the numbers have been gathered, they need to be processed and manipulated to let us understand (and in most cases see) the brains they are measuring. Here are just three ways in which data is manipulated to make it more understandable.

Stereotactic normalisation

In the process of **stereotactic normalisation**, the data from each individual brain is mapped onto a standard reference brain. You may remember that in fMRI and other imaging methods the information gathered by the technology is measured in voxels. A voxel is a point in three-dimensional space which can be mapped by three coordinates: x, y and z. These measurements need to be either squashed or stretched around agreed landmarks so that they can be mapped onto something resembling a standard atlas. Brains are in fact all sorts of different shapes and sizes, but if we want to compare one brain with another, we need to adjust our measurements so that they look much the same. Infant brain atlases are used for the mapping of the brains of babies. For example, the University of North Carolina IDEA Group has produced a set of templates for neonates, one-year-old and two-year-old infants. You can view these online: www.med.unc.edu/bric/ideagroup/software/unc-infant-0-1-2-atlases.

Cognitive subtraction

Another part of the process is called cognitive subtraction. Brain scans suggest that one bit of the brain is active while the rest is silent. In reality, this is not the case; in a physical sense brains are always active, and all the brain is always active all the time, unless that part has died, for example after a stroke. If we want, for instance, to look at which bits of the brain are active when reading compared with when we are just looking at stuff, then we must measure quite a few brains in which people are reading and quite a few in which they are just looking. If we then take the data from the reading people and subtract from it the data from those who were just looking, we should, in theory, have some idea of what regions are involved in reading. Simple, eh?

Of course, the problem is that it is assumed that the parts that are active in both the lookers and the readers do not matter too much. Clearly, this may not be the case and the parts that are used in both reading and looking might matter a great deal. Subtraction is important in helping us to visualise areas of cognitive activity, but we need to keep in mind that what we are seeing has been manipulated and is not a true representation of what is really happening in the brain.

Colourisation

The third way in which brain data is manipulated is through the process of colourisation. Colour is used in presenting data from brain scans as a way of emphasising differences. They do not come out of the scanner in pretty colours: these are added by the researchers before publication. The choice of colour is quite critical. Bright yellow or red for regions that are active and relevant for the study stand out clearly from blue regions that are not perhaps so significant, or through subtraction are not seen as important.

Conclusion

In this chapter we have given an account of the structure of the human brain and described the primary functions of different parts of the brain. However, it is important to remember that the brain is a highly complex organ and that the regions of the brain are connected by many millions of neurons. We have also given an account of how brain imaging works and shown that the images we see in research are not photographs, but rather are manipulated to make it possible to compare activity in one brain with that in another.

Summary

- The brain is divided into two symmetrical hemispheres. Although it was once thought that these two halves were functionally different, we now know that most of what we do involves both sides of the brain.

- The brain can be visually divided into four lobes: frontal, parietal, temporal and occipital.

- The subcortical brain contains both the brain stem and several other parts of the brain that are usually associated with controlling unconscious aspects of human behaviour.

- The brain contains neurons, which fire electrical signals called action potentials, and glial cells, which perform other functions such as repair and maintenance.

- Neuroimaging techniques allow us to visualise brain activity, although we need to remember that these images are produced statistically and are not the same as photographs.

Test your knowledge
1. What part of the subcortex is known as the 'little brain'?
2. What parts of the brain make up the limbic system?
3. What does the hippocampus do?
4. What's the name of the bushy, tree-like fibres whose job it is to receive information from other neurons?
5. What transformation is carried out in the synaptic cleft?
6. What's the difference between grey matter and white matter?
7. Is the anterior at the front or the back?
8. What are the disadvantages of signals from an electroencephalograph?
9. What's the name of the very brief electrical charge produced by neurons?
10. What's stereotactic normalisation?

Discussion questions
(a) Why do you think the brain has developed the ability to form folds in the cerebral cortex – what does this achieve?
(b) Why don't neurons touch each other? Surely it would be much more efficient if neurons were connected rather than relying on chemical neurotransmitters to signal across tiny gaps?
(c) What do you think is the impact of colouring brain images?

Our answers

(a) The folding of the cerebral cortex happens as a result of the brain expanding in size. The folding of the thin layer of neurons in the brain allows for a vastly increased surface area. In simple terms, it allows for more neurons to be squeezed into a relatively small space, resulting in increased cognitive ability.

(b) Some neurons do communicate directly by touch – the big motor neurons, for example. But most neurons don't touch. The advantage of this is that is allows for flexibility. The synaptic cleft, that is, the gap between each neuron, is tiny, and communication across that gap is by means of a neurotransmitter chemical. There are lots of different neurotransmitters and each has its own receptor. This means that there is local control over communication between neurons. It also allows for one-way transmission: there is a sending side and a receiving side to neurotransmission.

(c) On the one hand, it is a useful thing to do as it makes the image clearer and differentiates between areas that are active and important as opposed to areas that are less active and of less relevance. On the other hand, in popular science spectacular colourisation often gives a misleading picture (pun intended) of what is actually happening in the brain. It also feeds into the myth that what we are looking at is similar to a photograph rather than a highly processed and manipulated image.

Further reading

For an introduction to brain structure see:

Burnett, D. (2016) *The Idiot Brain: A Neuroscientist Explains What Your Head Is Really Up to*, London: Guardian Faber.

Eagleman, D. (2020) *Livewired: The Inside Story of the Ever-Changing Brain*, Edinburgh: Canongate Books.

Ward, J. (2015) *The Student's Guide to Cognitive Neuroscience* (3rd edn), Hove: Psychology Press.

For accounts of brain imaging see:

Azhari, A. et al (2020) 'A decade of infant neuroimaging research: What have we learned and where are we going?', *Infant Behavior and Development*, 58: 101389.

Passingham, R. E. (2015) *A Short Guide to Brain Imaging: The Neuroscience of Human Cognition*, Oxford: Oxford University Press.

On our website

You can find lots more material on our website at https://policy.bristoluniversitypress.co.uk/child-development-and-the-brain/companion-website

You might be interested in our article about the development of developmental neuroscience: https://policy.bristoluniversitypress.co.uk/child-development-and-the-brain/companion-website/developmental-neuroscience

2

How brains develop

This chapter:

- tells the story of how the brain is formed and then develops in the womb;

- describes the changes that take place in the brain during later childhood and adolescence;

- explores the process by which experience drives both the connecting of neurons and how these connections are pruned;

- looks at issues around health and early brain development.

Conception

The development of the human brain begins very soon after conception and continues beyond adolescence into the late 20s or early 30s. While much of the development takes place within the womb, humans are unique in that a great deal of the brain develops postnatally, that is, after birth. Changes in brain structure occur throughout the lifespan, even into old age.

Life begins with the joining of a sperm and an egg. This leads to the creation of a two-celled organism that is called a **zygote** (meaning joined or yoked).

These two cells begin to divide (Figure 2.1) and then divide again until after about a week there are approximately 100 cells (Figure 2.2). This cluster of cells is called a **blastocyst** (meaning bud or sprout). The cluster having got to this stage, a complicated set of changes begins to occur that leads to the formation of the different layers that eventually form parts of the body. The inner layer, which is called an **embryoblast**, will form the embryo, while the outer part, which is called the **trophoblast**, will form the external supporting tissues such as the placenta, umbilical cord and amniotic sac.

> The neural tube, which develops into the brain, is almost completely developed by three to four weeks after conception

The inner layer, the **embryoblast**, now begins another transformation, which results in three layers: an inner layer, a middle layer and an outer layer. The inner layer will develop into parts of the body such as the thymus, liver and pancreas. The middle layer will develop into bones, muscles, heart, blood vessels, kidneys and genitals, among others. However, it is the outer layer that interests us.

27

Figure 2.1: A zygote

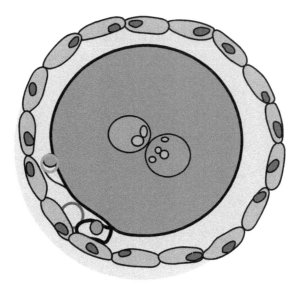

Figure 2.2: An embryoblast

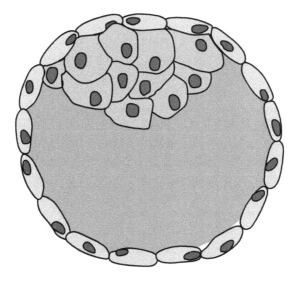

This will give rise to the central nervous system, which includes the brain and spinal cord, as well as the peripheral nervous system, parts of the nose, ears and eyes, as well as the skin, hair and nails and a number of other parts of the body.

From this outer region, a thin layer of tissue begins to form that eventually develops into a thicker layer of tissue that is known as the neural plate. This plate is the foundation of the human brain. About 22 days after conception the neural plate will begin to fold inwards, transforming itself into a tube known as the neural tube. This process usually takes about four days. The frontal (rostral) part of the tube will form the brain, while the rear (caudal) part will form the spinal cord. At first the tube will be open at both ends, but it will eventually close. The neural tube is almost completely developed by three to four weeks after conception.

BOX: Neural stem cells

These begin to develop in the very early stages of brain formation, prior to the formation of the neural tube. Like all stem cells, they have the ability both to produce new copies of themselves and to produce new cells in the organs with which they are associated. Neural stem cells can therefore produce more neural stem cells as well as other cells found in the central and peripheral nervous systems, such as neurons, astrocytes and oligodendrocytes. These are different from embryonic stem cells, which have the capacity to produce all tissues and cell types within the body.

Because of their astonishing ability to replicate, stem cells offer considerable hope to those who have suffered damage to the brain because of disease or injury. It is hoped that one day the use of neural stem cells can be applied to a range of degenerative conditions such as Parkinson's disease, Alzheimer's and Huntington's. There has been quite a lot of work on mice and rats, but there are still many problems that need to be overcome before these treatments become a reality.

Early brain development

The front (rostral) end of the tube now begins to subdivide into sections that will eventually form the forebrain (**prosencephalon**), midbrain (**mesencephalon**) and hindbrain (**rhombencephalon**) (Figure 2.3). At this stage the embryo looks like a worm that is bent at one end, or perhaps a walking stick with a crook.

The rear (caudal) part of the tube continues to develop into the spinal cord. The three sections that are developing into the brain continue to develop through a series of folds. Once the three initial brain regions are formed, they go through several other stages of division, and it is here that we start to see the very beginnings of the adult brain as we know it. The forebrain, which is at the head of the crook, forms and splits into two parts. The first of these is called the **telencephalon**. This will develop into the cerebral cortex and the hippocampus as well as other bits of the brain, including the basal ganglia, basal forebrain nuclei and the olfactory bulb. The second part is called the **diencephalon** and will

Figure 2.3: The early embryo

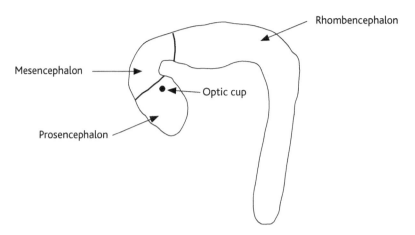

develop into the thalamus and hypothalamus. The **mesencephalon** continues to develop into the midbrain, which exerts a significant influence on things such as vision and hearing as well as motor control, alertness and temperature regulation. The hindbrain (**rhombencephalon**) develops into various other parts of the brain, including the pons, cerebellum and medulla. It is also at this point that the first stages of the eyes begin to develop with two little pockets called the optic cups.

The rostral part of the neural tube, which forms the primitive parts of the brain, grows larger and divides further as development continues. Within this the neural cells are born, and through a process of migration these travel to parts of the developing brain where they continue to change into the different types of cells that make up the human brain.

> New neurons can be produced at the rate of 250,000 per minute

The brain continues to grow rapidly as the baby develops in the womb. The most rapid period of brain growth is during the third trimester, when it can grow at the rate of 22 ml per week (Hüppi et al, 1998). A recent study showed that during the third trimester the cerebellum shows the greatest relative maturation rate of 12.87% per week, showing a volume increase of 384% between 25 to 36 weeks of pregnancy. In comparison, total brain volume increases by 230% over the same period (Clouchoux et al, 2012).

BOX: The miracle baby

On 6 March 2012 a baby boy weighing 9 lb 7 oz was born by means of caesarean section. He had already been diagnosed with spina bifida. This is a condition where the baby's spine does not develop sufficiently in the womb, causing a gap in the spine. He was given almost no chance of survival. Soon after birth he underwent a five-hour operation to close the spina bifida. The spina bifida had resulted in hydrocephalus, also called 'water on the brain'. It was then discovered that the hydrocephalus had put pressure on the developing brain, filling his head with spinal fluid. An MRI scan revealed that Noah had been born with just 2% of his brain. There was a midbrain and a brain stem but no cerebral cortex (Pereira and Reddy, 2018). Yet despite these seemingly insurmountable problems the baby survived, and now, some years later, Noah Wall is alive and well and living in Cumbria. It's hard not to use words such as 'miracle' when describing how Noah managed to grow 80% of his brain postnatally and gain an amazing amount of capacity.

You can follow Noah's journey via quite a few social media channels. Just do a Google search for Noah Wall.

Myelination

Myelin is the fatty substance that grows around the axons of neurons as they develop (Figure 2.4). It is formed by oligodendrocytes (see Chapter 1). This insulates the body of the neuron and so speeds up transmission of signals along the axon. It develops in different regions staring with the brain stem at about 29 weeks. It tends to happen from inferior to superior and posterior to anterior; without the jargon, that means it happens from bottom to top and from the back areas to the front (see Chapter 1 for an explanation of how to navigate the brain). Myelination occurs mostly during childhood but in some areas continues into adolescence and even beyond (for more on myelination see Giedd et al, 1999; Dubois et al, 2014).

Growing neurons

The process of producing new neurons is called **neurogenesis**. It begins around the fifth week after conception and reaches a peak at around the third and fourth month after conception. These cells are produced at an astonishing rate. For example, during the peak period neurons can be produced at the rate of 250,000 a minute. With a few exceptions, almost all the 86 billion neurons that form the adult human brain are formed in the embryo stage. We are born with most of the brain cells we will ever possess. We have only relatively recently understood that a few regions of the brain can produce new neurons after birth. These regions include the olfactory bulb, which controls our ability to smell, and the dentate region of the hippocampus, which plays a part in the formation of new memories.

Figure 2.4: Myelin sheath

Neurogenesis

Neurogenesis begins in inner portions of the neural tube in what are called the proliferative zones. The most significant of these is the ventricular zone, which is next to the fluid centre of the neural tube. The first kind of cells that are produced are called progenitor cells. Progenitor cells are a bit like stem cells in that they can produce other cells. However, unlike stem cells, they can produce only a limited number of other cells for a limited time. It is within the proliferative zones that the neurons that will form the brain are born. From here they will travel outwards, often passing through neurons that have already been created. Some cells reach their destination simply by what is called passive migration, that is, by being pushed outwards by new neurons as they are created in the proliferation zones. The thalamus and parts of the hippocampus are formed in this way. Other neurons will actively migrate, pushing their way through neural cells that have already been created. The neurons that form the six layers of the cerebral cortex are created by active cell migration.

Our description here of how the brain develops sounds as if it is almost mechanical, with one process automatically following on from another. Nowakowski and Hayes (2002, p 59) describe development occurring as a 'cascade of events', with each event having the potential to influence the one that follows. Yet in building the brain there are a lot of complex elements that interact with each other. Genetic encoding may determine the sequence of events, but there is also quite a complex interaction with the environment, that is, the mother.

Birth

Figure 2.5: The brain doubles in size in the first year of life

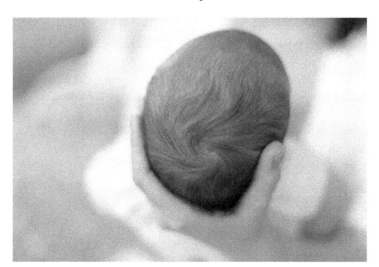

Source: Shutterstock, photo ID 1251233560

At birth the human brain weighs on average about 350 g (Figure 2.5) – that's about a third of the average adult brain, which weighs about 1,300–1,400 g (Holland et al, 2014).

We are also born with considerable brain functioning, although much less than that of many of other mammals, some of whom can walk from moments after birth. The postnatal brain is an unfinished project. The baby at birth has been described as an 'external foetus' (Bostock, 1962, p 1033), which gives a sense of the vulnerability and the dependency of the baby. A huge amount of development will take place in the first few years of life; for example, Gilmore and colleagues (2007) suggest that the brain increases in volume by 100% in the first year of life. But even after infancy the project is not finished. Brains continue to grow and change in function and structure until we are at least at the end of our 20s.

> By the age of two we have twice as many connections in our brains as we will have as an adult

---

Measuring brains

There are many ways that brains are measured. One of these is by volume. Volume simply means the amount of space that the brain takes up. This is usually measured in cubic millilitres. It can also be measured by weight. Another measure is by the number of neurons in the brain or the number of synaptic connections. The surface area of the cortex can also be used as a measurement. It is known, for example, that the surface area of the cerebral cortex increases by almost 115% during the first two years of postnatal development (Lyall et al, 2015).

Connecting up the brain

Although most neurons are produced while we are still in the womb, the connection of these neurons, known as synaptogenesis, occurs postnatally. This happens at different speeds in different parts of the brain. The visual cortex, for example, gets wired together pretty quickly and achieves its maximum synaptic density (that is, the most connections it will ever have) by about four months. On the other hand, the prefrontal cortex does not get to its maximum density until the child is about four years old. The other strange thing that happens to the connections in the brain is that we produce far more of them than we need. By about the age of two years we have about 50% more connections in our brains than we typically have as an adult (Huttenlocher, 1979).

As the connections in the head develop, so the size of the head itself needs to grow. It expands by about 14 cm on average during the first two years of life outside the womb and then by a further 7 cm during early childhood and adolescence (Dubois et al, 2014).

Johnson and de Haan (2010) point out that the most obvious signs of this postnatal brain development are the astonishing changes in size and complexity of the dendritic tree. These structures develop many hundreds or even thousands of tiny branches. Their growth also means that there is a concomitant rise in the number of connections between neurons. The areas of the brain that seem to see the most synaptic development are those in the cerebral cortex. The brain is wired together in response to the environment. This adaptability is usually known as plasticity.

Plasticity

Plasticity is the ability of the brain to change and adapt to circumstances. While we maintain a reasonable degree of plasticity throughout life, the brains of infants and young children are highly plastic. Greenough and colleagues (2002) distinguish between two types of plasticity, which they call experience-expectant and experience-dependent.

Experience-expectant plasticity

Experience-expectant plasticity is an evolutionary strategy designed to allow humans (although other animals also have this capacity) to take advantage of their environments. Genes are seen to give a general template of how neurons might connect up, but it is the environment that does the fine tuning. During sensitive periods of development, the brain is waiting for something to happen. Both our visual systems and our language systems, for example, have periods of sensitivity. Being denied sight or language during those periods has a heightened impact on our ability to develop these faculties.

This theory may account for the overproduction of synaptic connections in the early developmental stages. Overproduction during the initial stages of development allows for a broad range of different possibilities (Figure 2.6). As muscles begin to be used, for example, the neurons that connect to these muscles' fibres are substantially overproduced. Gradually, however, as muscle usage begins to develop a more systematic pattern, the neurons that are not being used are pruned away, leaving an organised system in which one set of neurons deals with the movements of a particular set of muscles. It is experience-expectant, as, in the normal course of development, the genes have pre-programmed the muscles to develop in response to movement, but the exact way in which they do so is left to experience.

> The more different possibilities for patterns of neural connection that the child explores, the greater chance of finding the very best one for the job in hand. (Thornton, 2002, p 14)

Figure 2.6: Baby playing

Source: Shutterstock, Photo ID: 182516240

We are born with the capacity to become specialists. Overproduction of synaptic connections allows us to explore many different possibilities before we hit upon the one that works best. It makes us extremely adaptable, as synaptic overproduction allows us a very broad range of possibilities. We can see this clearly in the area of language development. There seems to be an innate ability to categorise the sounds we hear into recognisable phonemes. Yet the languages we end up speaking are dependent upon those that we hear. The processes of categorical speech perception are explored more fully in Chapter 7.

Experience-dependent plasticity

Experience-dependent plasticity involves the storage of information that is based on experiences that are unique to an individual. This relates to the ability of the infant to learn and remember events. While the processes of learning and memory are still not very well understood, we know that memory storage does require the generation of new synaptic connections. The abilities of the brain to learn and of individuals to change the way in which they behave are perhaps the most graphic illustrations of brain plasticity.

Synaptic pruning

While there is a great deal of synaptogenesis during the first few years of life, there is also a considerable amount of synaptic pruning. As with many aspects of brain development, we do not fully understand all the mechanisms involved in this process of growth and pruning. Pruning would seem to be an essential part of shaping the brain. Initial overproduction of synaptic connections means that those that are not needed are cut away. This process seems to occur most strongly at various stages of development. Quite a lot of pruning occurs during early childhood. Those connections that are used become stronger, while those that are not die away. There is a further and intense period of synaptic pruning of the cerebral cortex during adolescence, when the brain is extensively reshaped.

Asymmetry

Brains do not grow in a symmetrical fashion. Different parts of the brain grow at different rates and at different times. It is thought that this begins in the prenatal brain and continues during postnatal and later development. As early as 15 weeks into foetal development there is a preference for moving the right arm and sucking the right thumb (Hepper et al, 1991). Which thumb is sucked as a foetus also seems to be a reasonably good indicator of whether in later life the adult will be left-handed or right-handed. In a study by Hepper and colleagues (2005), of a group of 75 foetuses studied, 60 who sucked their right thumbs in the prenatal stage went on to be assessed as right-handed when they were aged 10–12. Left-handedness seems not to be quite so predictable: of the 15 who sucked their left thumbs, only ten were assessed as left-handed later in life.

One of the most significant asymmetrical differences concerns the different development patterns between the right and left hemispheres of the brain. This feeds into the discussion around ideas of hemispheric specialisation, that is, whether some skills are more dependent on one hemisphere or the other. This could potentially affect language acquisition, emotional development and handedness.

After the first five years

There are many studies of the early development of the brain, and there is a burgeoning field which explores the changes in brain structure and function during adolescence. There has also been research interest in several specific functions in the years between early childhood and adolescence. For example, Castro-Caldas and Reis (2003) have shown that the development of literacy, which in the minority (or developed) world usually takes place around the age of four-plus, affects the interparietal region of the corpus collosum. It is also accepted that the prefrontal region of the brain develops later than most other areas of the brain. This area is known to play a key role in behaviour, language and thinking. In the adult brain it also accounts for as much as one-third of the total cortex. The grey matter in this area reaches its maximum volume at some point between four and 12 years of age. In contrast, the white matter increases throughout childhood and adolescence and into adulthood (Fuster, 2002; Teffer and Semendeferi, 2012).

By the age of five the brain is about 90% of the size of the adult brain (Dekaban and Sadowsky, 1978). However, there is still a lot of development to take place. Human brains continue to grow until we are around 30 years old. fMRI studies have helped to see what happens after the age of five. Brains are at their biggest when boys are aged 14 and a half and girls are aged 11 and a half (Giedd et al, 1999).

Adolescence: rearranging the brain

Adolescence is a period in life that is defined both biologically and socially. Biologically it begins with the onset of puberty, while socially and culturally, in Western societies at least, it ends with a level of independence (Lerner and Steinberg, 2009). It is a time when there are many changes in the structure and functioning of the brain. These changes include an increase in the amount of white matter and lower levels of grey matter in the parietal and frontal cortices. White matter, you will recall, is where the axon is covered with a fatty insulating layer of myelin. One explanation for these changes is that there is an increase in the growth of synapses at puberty and then a gradual pruning away of unwanted cortical connections during adolescence (Blakemore, 2012). A relatively large-scale study by Tamnes and colleagues (2017) showed that cortical volume is at its highest in early childhood and then gradually declines over time. There is an irregular decline in cortical volume and thickness from childhood through adolescence and beyond into our late 20s and even into our 30s.

The prefrontal cortex

The prefrontal cortex is probably the area that changes the most during adolescence. In Chapter 1 we explained that this area of the brain is essential for reasoning, planning and control of behaviour. It is also seen as being essential for reward-related learning, that is, the human tendency to engage in behaviour that leads to positive reinforcement (O'Doherty, 2004). It is also a part that matures much later than other areas of the brain, typically not fully maturing until the mid- to late 20s. There is relatively rapid development of the pathways that connect the frontal regions of the brain with the basal ganglia, particularly the striatum, which is seen as an important element of the brain's motor and reward system. These pathways affect movement, emotion, motivation as well as higher-order thinking (Reichelt and Rank, 2017). We can think of these pathways as being 'rewired' by means of pruning and progressive myelination. The slow maturation of the frontal areas and the much earlier maturation of subcortical areas of the brain, particularly the limbic system, is one of the theories put forward to suggest why some adolescents are more prone to risk taking than those in other age groups.

One of the many unanswered questions about adolescent neurodevelopment is whether or not this is a sensitive period for brain plasticity. Fuhrmann and colleagues (2015) suggest that this is a period when the brain expects particular types of interaction with the environment and that it is pre-tuned for this to happen. Memories, for example, seem to be gathered with more intensity during the period from ten to 30 years of age than at any other period in life. This includes both autobiographical memories and cultural memories. It's called the 'reminiscence bump', and there's more about this in Chapter 9. So, when someone says that the music of a particular era was far better than that of any time before or since, they are probably referring to their own sensitive period for memory.

Gender and brain development

There have been a lot of studies and a great deal of controversy over how and where the brains of men differ from those of women, and it is far too easy to step into the men are from Mars and women are from Venus level of debate. The brains of young boys and girls have also been intensely studied and the differences disputed. According to Rippon, the million-dollar question is 'are the brains of baby girls different from the brains of baby boys?' (2019, p 146). On the surface at least, this question matters because it feeds into the ongoing nature–nurture debate of whether males and females are different because of genetic and biological factors or due to cultural and environmental factors. The technical term for the dispute is **sexual dimorphism** – the idea that males and females of the same species differ in parts of their bodies beyond the sexual organs. In this view the gonads within the embryo secrete hormones which act on the developing brain to create differences in volume and structure in the brains of boys and girls.

We know that during foetal development genetic sex, the presence of the XX chromosomes in females and the XY chromosomes in males, produces the sexual organs, whether they be ovaries or testes. The question is whether this sexual biological process affects other parts of the body – specifically here the brain. In theory it should now be possible to inch towards answering Rippon's question. In the past the only way to answer it was to slice up the brains of babies who had died and physically examine the differences post-mortem. New brain imaging techniques have started to provide images of the brains of living newborn babies. However, perhaps not surprisingly, this new capability seems to have caused even more disagreement rather than providing definitive answers. Let's look at some of the evidence here.

Evidence for sexual dimorphism

A recent fMRI study of 39 newborn boys and 48 newborn girls showed no difference in whole brain volume between the sexes (Holland et al, 2014). After 90 days the brains of the boys had grown more rapidly than those of the girls, but not by much – 66% for the boys compared with 63% for the girls. The cerebellum showed a higher growth rate and a larger difference – 113% for the boys compared with 195% for the girls. This suggests that boys and girls may be born without too many differences and it is the environment that drives the differences.

In contrast, an earlier study (Gilmore et al, 2007) of 40 male and 34 female neonates showed that there were significant differences in brain volume between the two genders at birth. The authors state very firmly that '[s]exual dimorphism is present in the neonatal brain' (2007, p 1258). As well as brain volume differences, they found that the baby boys had 10% more cortical grey matter and 6% more cortical white matter than the baby girls.

A 2015 study has shown a greater rate of connectivity in the frontoparietal region for boys than for girls (Gao et al, 2015). The authors suggest that there might be advantages here for boys in terms of executive control.

A 2018 study of 77 girls and 72 boys (Dean et al, 2018) showed that the boys had a significantly larger brain volume than girls. The boys also had a larger amygdala, insula and hippocampus. The girls, meanwhile, had larger volumes of several subcortical organs including the anterior and middle cingulate gyrus, caudate and parahippocampal gyrus. They also had an 8.7% larger corpus callosum by volume.

Rippon concludes that once differences such as birth weight and head size have been taken into account, 'there are very few, if any, structural sex differences in the brain at birth' (2019, pp 153–154). Overall, on the surface at least, the evidence seems to be against this claim. Dean and colleagues' work would seem to be at odds with this. They state that '[p]atterns of sexual dimorphism suggest that processes underlying brain structure maturation differ between males and females' (2018, p 14). There are issues here that arise partly because of technological limitations and because of the assumptions behind the questions.

It is still expensive and difficult to image babies' brains in MRI scanners. Babies move around quite a lot; such studies can only be done while they are sleeping. This means that the number of babies included in these studies is statistically very low. Differences between male and female brains that are discovered in small-scale studies are often refuted when larger numbers of subjects are studied (see, for example, Bishop and Wahlsten, 1997, on supposed differences in the male and female corpus callosum). There are also issues around sampling. Most of the babies are White Caucasian. The Dean and colleagues (2018) study, for example, had only three Black African American babies, all of them female. Another point to bear in mind is that volume and functionality are separate and do not correlate. Bigger does not mean better. Sperm whales have huge brains, but they are not seen as cognitively comparable to humans.

On a broader level, the idea that sex and gender can be simply divided into two binary camps, male and female, is now hotly contested within the social sciences, although it is still often seen as a binary division in neuroscience

(Jordan-Young and Rumiati, 2012). If we look more closely at the studies, we can see that while there are clear differences in volume between the brains of baby girls and those of baby boys, there are also substantial differences within the two sexes. In the study by Dean and colleagues (2018), for example, there is a greater difference in brain volume within the range of both boys and girls sampled than there is between the two sexes.

Summary

- An early cluster of cells develops into several different layers to produce an embryo and an outer, supporting trophoblast.

- The embryo transforms into three layers to produce different parts of the body.

- Almost all neurons are produced during the embryonic stage of development.

- Both genetic encoding and environmental factors determine development.

- Postnatal synaptogenesis, plasticity and the pruning of little-used connections all make the brain a highly adaptable and experience-dependent organ.

- The brain undergoes another significant set of changes during adolescence.

- The idea that brains are sexually dimorphic remains controversial. There are differences here between the neuroscience view of sex/gender and that discussed within the social sciences.

Test your knowledge
1. When does the brain develop at the fastest rate?
2. What is the purpose of myelin?
3. What is plasticity and what role does it play in development?
4. What is the role of neural stem cells?
5. What's the difference between neurogenesis and synaptogenesis?
6. What's the difference between experience-expectant and experience-dependent plasticity?
7. What do you think are the advantages for humans of being born with an unfinished brain?
8. What are the advantages of the overproduction of synaptic connections?
9. What are the main changes that take place within the adolescent brain?
10. According to neuroscience studies, what are the differences between the brains of baby boys and baby girls?

Discussion questions

(a) Male brains are on average 9% larger than female brains. This is still seen as statistically significant even when this is adjusted for difference in weight and height. What do you think? Are these differences deterministic?

(b) What are the advantages of being born with a brain that still has a huge amount of growing to do?

(c) What are the advantages of having a brain that produces lots of synaptic connections and then goes through a period of synaptic pruning?

Our answers

(a) As you will see from the preceding chapter, there is still a huge amount of argument over this question. The technical limitations of scanning together with issues around babies moving their heads in the scanner, plus problems with study design, all contribute towards the controversy. In many countries the social identification of individuals as male or female is being reframed and with this also come questions about biological gender. The simple division of a population into two camps, male and female, is now being challenged. This means that the question of differences in brain sizes between two putative genders is itself becoming a less meaningful question.

(b) Having a small brain that still has lots of connecting up to do means that we have a huge capacity to learn by experience. While the process of synaptogenesis is biologically determined, exactly what connections are made will be determined on the basis of the lives that we lead, with the early years being particularly significant.

(c) Overproduction of synapses means that we are prepared for many different eventualities. It makes us remarkably adaptable. This plasticity of the brain gives us many advantages. It means we can reorganise our neural networks in response to what we experience. For example, at a basic level it means that if we have an injury to our brain, we can reorganise our neural networks and make what often seems a remarkable recovery, particularly if the injury happens when we are very young.

Further reading

Blakemore, S.-J. (2019) *Inventing Ourselves: The Secret Life of the Teenage Brain*, London: Black Swan.

Johnson, M.H. and de Haan, M. (2010) *Developmental Cognitive Neuroscience* (3rd edn), Hoboken, NJ: Wiley-Blackwell.

Keenan, T., Evans, S. and Crowley, K. (2016) 'The Biological Foundations of the Changing Brain', in *An Introduction to Child Development* (3rd edn), London: SAGE, pp 115–132.

Klingberg, T. (2012) *The Learning Brain: Memory and Brain Development in Children* (illustrated edn), Oxford: Oxford University Press.

Rippon, G. (2019) *The Gendered Brain: The New Neuroscience that Shatters the Myth of the Female Brain*, London: Bodley Head.

On our website

You can find lots more material on our website at https://policy.bristoluniversitypress.co.uk/child-development-and-the-brain/companion-website

This includes:

The development of developmental neuroscience: https://policy.bristoluniversitypress.co.uk/child-development-and-the-brain/companion-website/developmental-neuroscience

How to grow a good brain: https://policy.bristoluniversitypress.co.uk/child-development-and-the-brain/companion-website/grow-a-good-brain

3

The development of thinking

This chapter:

- provides an overview of some of the key underpinnings of select milestones of cognitive development in childhood and adolescence;

- considers the development of an emerging understanding of object permeance, decision making and the critical role of the prefrontal cortex;

- examines matters of cortical control and the basis of emergent increases in working memory.

The emergence of object permanence

Developing an awareness that the physical world exists beyond our own senses is a major development in infant cognition. Early theories of child cognition based a large part of their research on trying to understand how infants begin to learn about their physical world. It is a large task to begin to comprehend a three-dimensional world through sensory processing. Infants have sensory systems and motor skills to enable them to explore the physical world. Through singular and combined sensory input and motor exploration, they gradually learn about various physical properties around them such as the solidity of objects and that the three-dimensional physical world exists outside of themselves. A key topic in infant cognition is how children learn object permanence, namely that a psychical world exists in space and time independently from themselves.

To understand this, infants need to develop the ability to perceive objects and realise that an object is the same even when it is moving in space. **Shape constancy** is this tendency to perceive the shape of an object as constant despite differences in the viewing angle (and consequent differences in the shape of the pattern projected on the retina of the eye).

Modern research (Westermann and Mareschal, 2004; Ward, 2010) has recast our thinking on how children perceive objects, and new techniques have allowed us to better understand the basic mechanisms of object perception in infancy. Object perception is thought to be mediated by two separable cortical regions and visual pathways, the ventral and dorsal pathways. The ventral pathway comes from the primary visual cortex to parts of the temporal lobe, while the dorsal pathway extends from the primary cortex to the parietal cortex. The pathways are thought to process different kinds of visual information. The ventral route is argued to process information that helps us to understand what an object is (Moore and Price, 1999; Westermann and Mareschal, 2004), while the dorsal pathway is thought to process location and action information, namely where something is and how it is moving (Moore and Price, 1999; Johnson and de Haan, 2010; Rauschecker and Scott, 2015).

Object permanence

> Object permanence is our ability to understand that an object remains the same even if it changes shape or position

Object permanence is the ability to perceive and understand that an object exists as the same object even if it changes place or appearance, for example, a piece of play dough that has been squashed from a round to a flat shape. Object permanence has received extensive attention, not only in the realm of cognitive development but also in that of perceptual development. The cognitive studies about this will be discussed later. Using infant gaze to measure object permanence has shown that when objects in motion which are partially hidden are used (Johnson and Aslin, 1995), infants as young as two months of age show perception of object permanence, and infants as young as two weeks can perceive complete shapes behind occluding objects (Kawabata et al, 1999).

Research (e.g., Slater et al, 1990) has suggested that newborns as young as two days of age have the capacity to perceive depth and properties of objects using shape constancy. Babies were shown a patterned cube at a fixed distance until their interest was observed to fade. At this point similarly patterned cubes of different sizes were introduced at different distances. It was found that newborns preferred to look at the new cubes even when the retinal image was the same shape as the original cube. The capacity for depth perception was thus demonstrated at this age.

Infants' abilities to detect depth have also been studied using subjective contours, such as the Kanizsa cube (Zeki, 2004) (Figure 3.1).

Subjective contours are additional lines which the brain adds to optical illusions such as the Kanizsa cube in order to try to make sense of what is seen. They appear when we see relationships between figures which arise from the positioning of shapes rather than there actually being foreground or background hidden shapes. Since the classic work of Kellman and Spelke (1983), we have seen that an understanding of figure–ground relations is apparent in young infants. The use of subjective contours as stimuli assumes an understanding of the continuity of hidden objects. Kellman and Spelke (1983) habituated three-month-old infants to a training phase in which a grey bar was seen moving across a blue bar, potentially showing one object hidden behind another, creating either a view of subjective contours or a sequence of broken blue bars as the grey bar moved across it. Three-month-old infants showed a preference for the broken bar in a test phase, which was taken as the perception of a novel object

Figure 3.1: Kanizsa cube

and not one they had seen before in the training phase. Comparative research (e.g., Felleman and Van Essen, 1991) has shown that areas in the visual cortex V1 and V2 are stimulated in infant macaque monkeys when subjective contours are presented.

Very young infants respond to illusions in rotation that are designed to rotate and expand and contract. Yoshino and colleagues (2010) have named these moving stimuli as the rotational dynamic illusion, and it has been used to investigate whether movements of the square preserving its properties can be perceived even by very young infants. For example, it has been found (Yoshino et al, 2010) that three- to eight-month-old infants can perceive the Kanizsa square through rotational space, yet using a fixed trial familiarisation method, where stimuli are presented over a fixed period to familiarise infants to stimuli, they find it difficult to extract the expansion–contraction motion. Similarly demonstrating early capacities for depth perception, Corrow and colleagues (2012) used concave half frame wire cubes to show that infants as young as five months of age use line junction information when reaching for expected shapes in a cube (Figure 3.2).

As Johnson and de Haan (2010) argue, such findings indicate (Bhatt and Quinn, 2011) that the human perceptual system quickly develops to perceive one kind of invariance – namely, that the shape of an object does not change even when it is partially hidden from view or seen against different backgrounds.

Neuroscientific research has shown areas that are responsible for perception of object permanence. The functions of the ventral and dorsal pathways that enable the perception of such invariance have been systematically investigated. Mareschal and colleagues (1999) argued that a lack of integration between the two pathways is responsible for a discrepancy between when infants are able to

Figure 3.2: Concave half frame wire cubes

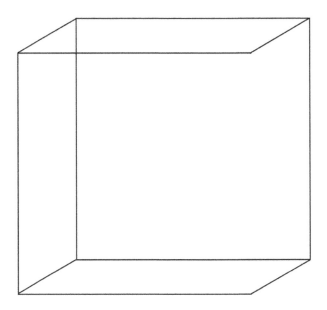

perceive invariance and when they are able to reach for an object that they may know is invariant yet will still not reach for it in behavioural studies (Baillargeon, 1993). Others have suggested that the systems become increasingly separate with maturation (Jacobs et al, 1991). A systematic review (Kaufman, Mareschal and Johnson, 2003) showed that when objects are seen to be graspable, it is the dorsal pathway that is more likely to be activated. Here it is size, shape and distance properties that are important, rather than texture or colour. Conversely, when objects are too far away to be grasped, infants may process object-related information such as surface features using their ventral pathways. Recent advances in methodology where EEG activity is measured during various object processing tasks in infancy have indicated areas that are activated when infants begin to integrate the separate features of objects to compose a whole object (Tallon-Baudry et al, 1998; Johnson et al, 2008; Perone et al, 2008). Kaufman, Csibra and Johnson (2003) found increased gamma activity though EEG readings in temporal regions of six-month-olds' brains while viewing an occlusion event and when an infant expected an object, in this case a train, to been seen when an occluding object was removed, namely when it passed through a tunnel. This activation was regarded as a representation of the hidden object. As Johnson and de Haan (2010) observe, the roles of the ventral and dorsal pathways continue to be investigated using EEG activation methods. For example, Perry and Fallah (2014) reviewed neuropsychological evidence examining the roles of both pathways in object identification and motion and proposed that the dorsal pathway integrates data from both pathways into an object representation utilised by decision-making processes, and that the ventral stream, while processing object features for recognition, also processes data for making selection- and action-related decisions. Moreover, abilities related to understanding object occlusion and object permanence based on motion cues when a static object is obscured by a moving one, have been found, namely that while global motion sensitivity is detected principally in the dorsal stream, static stimuli are mainly processed by the ventral stream (Ionta, 2021).

Piaget's theory of cognitive development

Jean Piaget (Piaget and Inhelder, 1969) gave us one of the most, if not the most, influential theories of cognitive development. He argued that cognitive operations proceed through consistent stages of qualitatively different kinds of thought processes in which infants and children progress to adult types of thought, in particular abstract logical thought. He proposed four main stages of development, each specifying qualitatively different kinds of cognitive operations. Each stage is characterised by an overall structure and a sequence of development that occurs within this structure. According to Piagetian theory, these structures consist of 'schemas', which are essentially ways of mentally organising experience. As we will see, there have been quite a few challenges to Piaget's theory, as well as some general objections to stage theories; nonetheless, his contribution has spurred a wealth of research into understanding the processes involved in children's cognitive development.

Piaget's stage theory argued that children pass through each stage in the same order, one stage necessitating progression to the next, meaning that no stage can be missed. The two mechanisms of learning that Piaget proposed were the complementary processes of **assimilation** and **accommodation**. In the

Table 3.1: Piaget's stages of development

Stage	Age range	Main characteristics
Sensorimotor stage	0 to 2 years	Move from responding to the environment wholly responsively to the beginnings of being able to think and use basic symbols. The development of object permanence.
Preoperational stage	2 to 7 years	Development of the ability to represent objects using language and other symbols.
Concrete operational stage	7 to 12 years	The ability to think by using mental operations.
Formal operational stage	12 years onwards	Develop the ability to reason in abstract ways.

process of assimilation, new information about the world is incorporated into existing schemas. A **schema** can be understood as the knowledge structure or metaphorical framework we have about something. Piaget argued that the assimilation of new knowledge occurred without changing the structure of existing schemas. However, when new learning cannot simply be assimilated in this way, the second process, of accommodation, allows for the schema to restructure itself in order to absorb new information. Piaget maintained that the cognitive system is driven towards consistency of internal and external information by a process he called **equilibration**. This means that new schemas emerge on the basis of the system accommodating and assimilating conflicting information to strive for consistency.

Challenges to Piaget

Piaget's theory of cognitive development and the key features of his specific stages have been challenged by extensive experimental research, and neuroscientific findings have challenged his conception and mechanisms of learning. For example, Donaldson (1978) demonstrated that many of Piaget's experiments did not show that young children were less able than older children but, rather, that they had simply misunderstood what Piaget was asking them to do.

Researchers (e.g., Siegal, 1997) have progressed from Piaget's stage theory and have highlighted huge variability in the types of thought and abilities children have across childhood and adolescence, thus challenging the characterisation of cognitive development as stage-like. Others (e.g., Wason and Johnson-Laird, 1972) have argued that taking formal operations as a sign of mature adult thinking is inaccurate, given that not all adults display these abilities, and that Piaget's theory gave no explicit account of how social learning can occur. Experimental evidence, reviewed later in this chapter, has challenged claims about the age ranges in which Piaget claimed a host of cognitive skills are developed, and criticism has also been levelled at the vagueness of the processes of accommodation and assimilation as testable mechanisms of learning. The focus of the present chapter is to draw on our increasing understanding of cognitive development and how this may interface with key aspects of cognitive functioning as highlighted in Piagetian theory.

Piaget's evidence and beyond

Piaget's main method of data collection involved careful observation of children's behaviour while they were engaged in a range of problem-solving tasks. Alongside this Piaget would interview children using non-standardised interviews. His cognitive theory was also developed by observation of infant behaviours in a range of reaching tasks, while older children were observed while engaged in various problem-solving tasks and usually subsequently interviewed about their experience and learning.

As previously discussed, the appreciation of object permanence is a key learning milestone combining perceptual and conceptual schemas. Piaget argued that a key feature of the sensorimotor stage was an infant's realisation of object permanence. Piaget used a reaching **paradigm** to explore infants' understanding of object permanence, in which infants would see an object hidden under a blanket and then see it being moved so that it was hidden under another. The test was which blanket the infant would reach for (Figure 3.3).

Figure 3.3: Object permanence

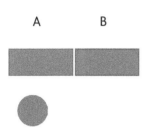

Infant sees ball hidden under blanket A and reaches there to retrieve it

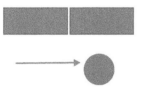

Infant sees ball moved under blanket B

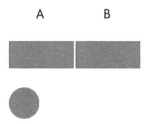

Infant still reaches to blanket A to retrieve the ball

Most infants aged between eight and 12 months would reach out to find the object under the first blanket, ignoring the fact that they had seen it hidden under the second. This common response was taken as an indication that the infant had not yet reached a stage where they had realised that the object existed beyond where the infant could reach. This lack of reaching for an object in the new location is called the *A not B error* and was also taken as a sign of an infant's solipsism, that is, a tendency to not comprehend that an objective reality exists beyond the infant's mind.

Experimental challenges have shown that perhaps these tasks underestimated the abilities of young infants. Younger infants than Piaget proposed have also been shown to have a permanent notion of the movement of objects, as demonstrated by Baillargeon and colleagues (1985), who found that five-month-olds were surprised to see a plank close over an object, having been habituated to a plank that swings, implying that they understood that the solid plank could not pass through the solid object.

The A not B error

Researchers showed that four-month-olds who have seen two toys placed behind a screen and then see one apparently being removed by the experimenter show surprise when the two screens are lifted and the two objects can still be seen (Wynn, 1992). This challenges the notion of solipsistic thought, in that the infants were aware that the two objects existed and showed that they understood that this impossible event could not occur in the objective world. Such evidence suggests that infants younger than Piaget proposed understand that there is an objective world that is not always visible to them.

The *A not B error* has been investigated for what it might actually be measuring and which parts of the developing brain control successful reaching in these tasks. Infants below the age of approximately seven months fail to reach in the correct location for a hidden object after a short delay if the object has been moved from the location from where it had previously been successfully retrieved. There is evidence that by nine months infants manage to perform well on this task, with delays of between one and five seconds (Diamond, 2001). When performing a visual version of the task that does not involve reaching for the object, infants as young as five months have been found to succeed, with performance on both the visual and reaching versions of the task levelling out at around eight months (Cuevas and Bell, 2010) in association with a developing prefrontal cortex.

Towards the end of the first year of postnatal life the infant's prefrontal cortex matures at a fast rate	## Impacts of neuroscientific insights on Piaget's ideas Piaget did not have access to any of the neuroimaging techniques that scientists have today. He could work only with the more abstract concept of the mind, rather than look directly

into the brain and see which areas of brain activity correlate with particular actions and behaviours, for example when considering the role of memory in developing an awareness of object permanence and where an object may move between places. In recent years neuroscientific methods have begun to show us that maturational changes (that is, changes that happen as the brain matures) can account for Piaget's observations on object permanence and other related tasks. Towards the end of the first year of postnatal life the infant's prefrontal cortex matures at a fast rate. This maturation of the prefrontal cortex has been argued to be responsible for infants' success in object-permanence tasks (Diamond, 1991, 2002; Cuevas and Bell, 2010). Johnson and de Haan (2010) have observed that, while there are currently no universally agreed theories about the lower and higher cognitive functions of the prefrontal cortex overall, evidence from case studies and clinical trials (e.g., Milner, 1982; Eslinger et al, 2004) shows that injuries to this area reduce the cognitive function, that is, the ability to think and to process information. We also know that the planning and implementation of sequential action, the ability to keep information in short-term working memory and the ability to switch between contexts to generate appropriate actions are served by this region in adults (e.g., Schwartz, 2006).

Does object permanence exist?

Johnson and de Haan (2010) reviewed evidence that has cast doubt on the notion that object permanence reveals any kind of scientific reasoning. Johnson and colleagues (2010) have identified areas responsible for object permanence that are active from an earlier age than was supposed by Piaget and has also cast doubt on Piaget's idea that object permanence reveals processes akin to cognition. Electroencephalogram studies of areas of the brain used for working memory have shown that prefrontal cortex activity occurs during the phase when infants need to remember the new location of an object (e.g., Bell and Fox, 1992). When infants are required to reach for an object, near-infrared spectroscopy studies have shown a correlation between success in this task and increased blood oxygenation in the prefrontal cortex (Baird et al, 2002).

A maturational perspective

Some researchers (e.g., Diamond, 1991) have argued that a maturational view of developing competency between five and 12 months with object-permanence tasks accounts for the evidence for maturation of the dorsolateral area of the prefrontal cortex. This part of the brain is seen as central to a range of processes, including the development of short-term memory. Diamond (1991) proposed that this region aids the retention of information over time delays and mediates the tendency of infants to respond naturally – for example when learning not to reach for an object – when these responses have been reinforced by experimental trials. In their review, Johnson and de Haan (2010) describe the evidence for this position showing that, indeed, before the age of seven and a half months, infants fail to retrieve hidden objects when there is a delay between hiding the object and its retrieval. This evidence indicates that the same parts of the brain might be used both for the sorts of tasks infants are asked to do in object-permanence experiments and when they reach and retrieve objects. As Johnson and de Haan (2010) observed, this body of evidence supports Diamond's maturational perspective. By the age of eight years, posterior brain regions controlling working functions such as recognition memory have been found to have matured.

The early development of working memory

> Working memory is used to keep small amounts of information accessible for short periods of time

Working memory is sometimes referred to as **short-term memory**. We will discuss other types of memory more fully in Chapter 9. Working memory is used to keep small amounts of information accessible for short periods of time. It stores both speech and visual and spatial information (Baddeley and Hitch, 1975). Working memory improves with age. Rose and colleagues (2001) have shown that this type of memory improves from about six months onwards. Half of the babies in the study by Rose and colleagues were able to hold three or four items in their short-term memories by the age of 12 months.

fMRI studies have shown that improved working-memory capacity is correlated with more activity in the frontoparietal network. The amount of activity in this area increases with age (Klingberg et al, 2002). fMRI studies have revealed that the capacity of working memory increases throughout childhood and adolescence. Klingberg (2006) describes fMRI studies conducted while participants are engaged with tasks requiring working memory in which older children and adolescents have been found to have greater brain activity in the intraparietal cortex and in the posterior part of the superior frontal sulcus.

White-matter maturation

Klingberg (2006) also presents a full review of studies that have demonstrated the structural maturation of **white matter**. This study used diffusion tensor imaging (DTI), which permits the non-invasive mapping of how molecules diffuse in the brain. This approach has revealed several regions in the frontal lobes where white-matter maturation is correlated with the development of working memory. These areas include the superior frontoparietal white-matter region that is located near to the grey matter regions that are also used in the development of working memory. Furthermore, Klingberg presents evidence to show that the degree of white-matter maturation is positively correlated with the degree of brain activation in the frontal and parietal regions. This suggests that during childhood and adolescence there is significant development of the networks related to specific cognitive functions such as the visuospatial working memory used in object-permanence tasks. These networks are argued (Klingberg, 2006) to consist not only of cortical areas but also of the white-matter tracts connecting them, and for visuospatial working memory this network could consist of the superior frontal and intraparietal cortex.

Working memory: maturation or training?

The evidence presented previously would suggest a maturational view of the development of working memory and success in object-permanence tasks. However, Johnson and de Haan (2010) have argued that such a view may need to be amended to account for evidence that shows how working-memory capacity can be improved when individuals are specially trained. For example, adults were trained over a period of five weeks on a task that involved working memory. They developed an increased working-memory capacity and also showed an increased level of brain activity in the frontoparietal region (Olesen et al, 2004). The development in both capacity and activation suggests that the influence of skill learning and the interaction between experience and brain development needs to be considered rather than simply accepting that it is all about maturation.

An interactive specialisation view

An interactive specialisation view, where learning from the environment and brain development drive cognitive and further brain development, for example increased and decreased neuronal networks associated with experience of manipulating numbers (Battista et al, 2018), could also be argued to be supported when considering evidence examining the neural basis of working memory in human infants. Kaufman, Csibra and Johnson (2003, 2005) found high-frequency EEG activation in right temporal regions in six-month-old infants during a test phase where the infants kept information in their working memory between the disappearance and reappearance of objects. A broad range of brain regions have been found to be activated in infants in tasks where they are required to switch to working-memory tasks, whereas by four years of age only the frontal regions are activated during working-memory tasks (Bell and Wolfe, 2007). It would seem that working-memory regions are spread across different regions of the brain at birth and specialise with age and experience into the frontoparietal network (Kaldy and Sigala, 2004), including early-age-related increases between five and ten months in EEG power during working-memory tasks in medial frontal, central, temporal, medial parietal, lateral parietal and occipital electrode sites (Cuevas and Bell, 2011), with increased lateralisation of verbal and spatial working memory during adolescence (Marek and Dosenbach, 2018). 'EEG power' here refers to a measurement of the excitability of groups of neurons. More excitement equates with more development.

Thus, neuroscientific evidence has led us to rethink Piaget's ideas about object permanence. It could be argued that success on such Piagetian tasks is about the development of specific regions in the brain and increases in working memory capacity, as well as an increasing ability to inhibit responses.

Sensory processing and cognition

Do infants have cognition?

There is an ongoing philosophical debate about what it means to claim that infants have cognition at all (Goswami, 2008; Meltzoff et al, 2009). For example, Haith and Benson (1998) have suggested that lingering sensory information about an object, rather than a conceptual representation, could account for infant reactions to hidden objects. Perceptual information such as novelty, familiarity and discrepant images may mean that children and infants look longer on the basis of sensory rather than conceptual information. Indeed, work with monkeys based on single-cell recordings shows that the same neurons are active when an object is present as when it is absent, indicating a possible neural mechanism for degraded sensory information (Haith and Benson, 1998). Yet some research (e.g., Barsalou et al, 2003) has shown that mental representations are widely distributed in the brain, and neuronal activity for relevant sensory information is present when a cognitive representation is activated.

New methods have cast doubts on Piaget's rather strict interpretation of his object-permanence studies. Neuroscientific evidence has shown that infants develop a different set of capacities that enable them to perform successfully on traditional A not B tasks. Studies that show events that they were not expecting (that is, experimental violation of expectation paradigms) can be taken to demonstrate that infants have lingering sensory information, rather than wholly formed concepts when an object is hidden (occluded). Piaget's notion that object permanence does not fully develop until 18 months of life is clearly incorrect. However, his claim that sensorimotor learning enables the infant to explore their world remains supported. Piaget argued that sensorimotor responses were the basis of learning because what starts as sensorimotor behaviour soon becomes thought. However, cognition seems to be embedded, as we can see that mental representation is widely distributed, indicating that sensorimotor experiences are part of cognition.

Into adolescence

Adolescence marks multiple significant changes in cognitive processing compared with childhood cognitive processing and for structural development in the brain. There is sustained development in the prefrontal cortex and parietal lobes, and researchers have investigated how these changes may influence cognition supported by the prefrontal lobes. Griffin (2017) explains that cortical development changes primarily from a focus on proliferating neurons to developing and reinforcing connections within the network. Cognitive processing becomes more connected, integrated and efficient with more distributed functioning, while ranging connections increase to connect distal parts of the brain. With maturation therefore comes greater processing capacity and efficiency for a range for cognitive abilities. Continuing brain plasticity can also result in cognitive creativity and openness to new ideas and solutions. There are also abilities that follow different developmental pathways and do not develop as quickly as others across this lengthy developmental period. We shall examine some gains and pauses in cognitive development in adolescence in this section.

Executive function

There are great gains and changes in executive control processes during adolescence. As Blakemore and Choudhury (2006) report, a key focus on how changing brain structures, primarily of the frontal cortex as revealed by fMRI studies, may impact on cognition during adolescence has focused on developments in **executive function**. Executive function refers to the ability to control, regulate and coordinate our thoughts and attendant behaviour (Diamond, 2013). There are many abilities that influence cognitive control, such as working memory, decision making and impulse control, which can contribute to our ability to filter attention to relevant stimuli, remember planned actions and control impulses to perform a desired function.

Increase in abstract reasoning

One key marker of the transition of cognition from late childhood to adolescence (generally 12 to 18 years) is the increase in abstract reasoning. Adolescents learn to reason such that they can manipulate ideas in more sophisticated ways without the need to refer to visible concrete entities (Dumontheil, 2014). Although Piaget's theory of formal operational thought has been criticised for not being universally displayed in adult cognition (Keating, 1980), the idea that the general shift in ability to reason about information through abstraction is more likely in adolescence than mid- or late childhood stands.

One key marker of the transition of cognition to adolescence is the increase in abstract reasoning

From a systems neuroscience perspective on cognition, where brain development and complex interactions across areas and processes are studied in relation to cognitive outcomes, as Blakemore and Choudhury summarised (2006), different facets of executive function have slightly different developmental pathways in relation to activity in the frontal cortex, where myelination and pruning processes differentially influence aspects of cognitive ability. For example, gains in processing speed and working memory (Luna et al, 2004; Luciana et al, 2005), along with linear developments in selective attention and problem solving, have been found between the ages of 11 and 17 years (Anderson et al, 2001). Other abilities such as planning and coordinating strategic behaviour (Shallice, 1982) are already well established by this time.

Cognitive complexity and control theory

Cognitive complexity and control (CCC) theory (Zelazo and Frye, 1997) argues that age-related changes to the executive function of the brain are related to both the complexity and the number of rules that children and adolescents can manage to process when solving problems, and this in turn is dependent on their ability to reflect the basis of these rules. Extensive study of children's cognitive flexibility has shown that children between three and four years of age have similar trouble to adults with frontal-lobe damage when trying to apply different rules to the process of card sorting. A study by Zelazo and colleagues (2003) used nine experiments to test the ability of children to follow an increasingly complex set of rules when problem solving. In the first experiment children were asked to sort cards with pictures of things, such as a rabbit, a boat, a bus, or a coat by colour – that is, put the red ones in one pile and the blue ones in another. In another experiment they were asked to sort the cards according to more complex rules: if it can walk put it here, if it can be worn put it there (Figure 3.4). The revised CCC model suggested by Zelazo and colleagues gives more detail on how and where children will have difficulty in applying rules and also takes into account factors such as intentionality.

An emerging ability between the ages of 4 and 12 years is the ability to suppress information and actions, as shown by behavioural reaction-time tasks and accuracy of response rates (e.g., Diamond, 1991; Diamond et al, 1994).

Figure 3.4: Example of rule-based card sorting-stimuli

Developmental neuroscience has provided many insights into how the developing brain enables such metacognitive abilities.

Executive command and the frontal cortex

Imaging children's frontal lobe activity using fMRI scanners when they are engaged in tests of executive-function tasks has allowed scientists to study the brain processes involved. A study by Bunge and colleagues (2002) of children aged eight to 12 and adolescents involved them undertaking a single test of executive control while lying in an fMRI scanner. The test combined what is known as the **Eriksen flanker task** (Eriksen and Eriksen, 1974) with a **go/no-go paradigm**. In the Eriksen flanker task participants are asked to press either a right arrow or a left arrow key in response to a left or right arrow shown on a screen. As well as the arrow showing which key they should press, the screen also displays lots of other similar symbols, known as 'flankers'. These might be arrows pointing in the same direction as the arrow they are trying to follow or arrows showing contradictory commands. The addition of the go/no-go paradigm means that on some occasions the screen instructions will require them to not press any of the keys. In other words, they have to be able to suppress their normal response, that is, show that they have executive control over how they behave.

The brain scans showed that there is activity in the left ventrolateral prefrontal area of the brain in tests of interference suppression, which is where participants are asked to concentrate on pressing the correct key and ignore all the distracting or flanking information. Scans of the children showed that they used the left ventrolateral prefrontal area, whereas adults used the right ventrolateral prefrontal area of their brain during such tasks. The team then selected just those children whose performance was on a par with that of the adults. These children, when engaged in response-inhibition tasks (such as the go/no-go task), did not show any activity in the right ventrolateral areas. So what does this mean? Ston and colleagues (2002) used event-related fMRI imaging to understand which parts of the brain are active as children's inhibitory behaviour develops. Their study compared ten adults with ten children who had a mean age of 8.7 years. They used the same go/no-go paradigm as the study described previously, but this time they used five Pokémon characters that would have been familiar to the children. When the children saw any of the characters except for Meowth on a computer screen, they needed to press a button to 'catch' the character. When they saw Meowth, they should not press any button. The researchers varied the number of go trials that preceded no-go trials, having one, three or five go trials before each no-go trial. The expectation was that the more go trials that occurred before a no-go trial, the more difficult it would be for the children to inhibit their go responses on the no-go trial.

The same brain areas in children and adults showed activation during response-inhibition phases, that is, when they were required to not press any button in response to seeing a picture of Meowth. However, the amount of brain activity as measured by a magnetic resonance signal was higher in children. Areas were activated on both sides of the brain in the ventrolateral prefrontal cortex, the right dorsolateral prefrontal cortex and the right parietal lobe. The ventral prefrontal cortex activation was highest in adults and correlated with the number of preceding go trials (that is, the number of times they were required to press a button before needing to not press), whereas the activity was high for children regardless of the number of preceding go trials. This experiment supports the view that it is much harder for children to inhibit their responses than it is for adults. It also supports the idea that children's cognition is more susceptible to interference than is that of adults.

Decision-making strategies

Alongside these developments in connectivity and neurotransmission, maturation of the prefrontal cortex affords an increase in cognitive capacity, abstract reasoning skills and the ability to tolerate more ambiguity (Paulsen et al, 2011; Griffin, 2017). Decision-making strategies tend to improve across the period of adolescence overall (Paulsen et al, 2011). Yurgelun-Todd (2007) reviewed evidence to suggest a linear increase from childhood to adulthood, indicating that cognitive development during adolescence marks progressively increased efficiency of cognitive control and affective modulation. Yurgelun-Todd (2007) showed indicators of maturation via increased prefrontal activity (Rubia et al, 2006) and reduced action in less engaged regions (Durston, 2005). However, there is also a wealth of evidence that certain cognitive changes, for example gains in decision making, are not linear across the period and may follow a U-shaped trajectory for some. For example, Defoe and colleagues (2015) conducted a systematic meta-analysis and found that decision-making gains could follow a U-shaped curve, where they slow down mid-adolescence and then improve towards adulthood.

Changes in goal-directed behaviour

Changes in managing goal-directed behaviour emerge across adolescence. A key component of cognition is the ability to inhibit competing thoughts and actions to focus and act on goal-directed actions, often in the presence of a motiving reward (Casey et al, 2005). These skills increase throughout childhood and adolescence (Pascual-Leone, 1970; Keating and Bobbitt, 1978). There is debate about how these changes progress. Some argue they are potentially due to increased processing efficiency and speed (Bjorklund, 1987; Casey, Getz and Galvan, 2008). Others argue that they are due to developments in inhibitory processes regulating goal-directed action and cognitive suppression (Harnishfeger and Bjorklund, 1993). As Casey, Getz and Galvan (2008) have summarised, immature cognition can be seen as a susceptibility to interference from competing sources that must be suppressed (e.g., Munakata and Yerys, 2001). Goal-directed behaviour may therefore require impulse control or the delay of gratification for optimal outcomes.

Risk taking

Variation also exists in the progression of capacities argued to underpin more or less optimal decision making. So-called risky decisions are made more often in adolescence relative to characteristic childhood and adult decision making (Griffin, 2017). Impulse control and risk-tasking decision processes are underpinned by neurobiological systems with different operating characteristics and different developmental pathways (Casey, Jones and Hare, 2008; Griffin, 2017). Casey, Jones and Hare's (2008) review of the literature showed that impulsivity decreases significantly across childhood and adolescence in a fairly linear way related to prolonged development of the prefrontal cortex (Casey et al, 2005; Galvan et al, 2007).

Risk taking is less linear in progression. It is associated with subcortical systems involved in appraising incentives and affective data (Griffin, 2017). For example, raised activation in the accumbens and amygdala located in subcortical regions has been found when people are engaged in making risky decisions related to emotion processing (Ernst et al, 2005). Moreover, this activation is heightened in adolescent compared with child and adult populations (Ernst et al, 2005; Galvan et al, 2007).

Such findings suggest distinct neurobiological developmental pathways for impulse control and risky decisions. Whereas the limbic subcortical systems seem to be developed by adolescence, control systems necessary for overriding inappropriate choices and actions in favour of goal-directed ones show a prolonged and linear course into young adulthood (Casey, Getz and Galvan 2008).

Luciana et al (2018) are conducting a large-scale, ten-year longitudinal study to examine many facets of why and how adolescents engage in risky decisions. They are assessing a dual systems theory that proposes a tension between increasing cognitive control capacities and the emergence of strong incentive strivings which may be so strong that control mechanisms cannot be used consistently enough to regulate them, steering action towards the pursuit of rewards (Steinberg, 2005; Casey, Jones and Hare, 2008; Luciana and Collins, 2012).

The development of the frontal cortex allows children and adolescents to develop greater control over their cognitive processing. The ability to use metacognition – to think about and adjust how they are thinking about a particular task – gives children far more control and versatility. Brain studies show that functions depend on the maturation of frontal areas of the brain. Maturation of this area also allows for greater complexity of functioning and the ability to override stimuli that are interfering with a task – in other words, it allows for greater concentration and increased efficiency. The gradual development of the frontal area of the brain allows for greater sensitivity to environmental factors. This area develops in response to the experiences of the child. Unnecessary and underused cortical connections can be pruned out, and learning can drive the growth and strengthening of neural connectivity. There is much more to be learned about the timescale of these developments, as well as understanding the extent to which genetic factors and environmental influences are mutually dependent.

Summary

- Children's thinking can be seen as qualitatively different from the formal operations and abstract logical reasoning that adolescents and adults tend to exhibit.

- Research into the development of processes related to executive function, such as abilities to inhibit distracting information and reason abstractly, processes underlying risky decisions as well as experimental challenges to stage-like theories of development, have given us a more accurate and broader understanding of the ways in which cognitive development can be driven.

- Neuroscientific approaches have given us detailed information about the development and roles of cortical regions that enable changes in types of thought that facilitate higher mental functions.

Test your knowledge
1. What is object permanence?
2. What is the A not B error?
3. What stages of cognitive development did Piaget propose?
4. What are two key challenges to Piaget's theory of cognitive development?
5. What does the interactive specialisation view of cognition propose?
6. What is the theory of cognitive complexity and control?
7. What is executive function?
8. What roles do the ventrolateral prefrontal areas have in executive function?
9. What decision-making strategies increase in adolescence?
10. What types of risky decisions can adolescents make?

Discussion questions
1. Why do you think infants reach for an object in a place where they have seen it before even though they have seen that the object has been moved?
2. How can the ability to suppress information benefit children and adolescents?
3. What do you think causes risky decision making in adolescence?

Our answers

1. Piagetian theory says that this tendency could be because infants are in a stage of solipsism where they may not yet appreciate that the physical world exists beyond their grasp. However, different kinds of experiments have shown that infants' seeing rather than needing to reach for the moved object show gaze patterns, indicating that they know the object has been moved. This suggests that motor coordination may account for some A not B responses rather than a lack of awareness of object permanence or because they are solipsistic.

2. Gains in executive function allow children and adolescents to perform better on a range of tasks where an immediate and familiar response may no longer be helpful. For example, supressing information can allow for time to select different cues to respond correctly when rules may change, such as during a maths test where a plus is then swapped for a minus. The ability to suppress a response can also help with impulse control. For example, where once a child may have reached for someone else's toy, realising it is not theirs, they may then change their behaviour and reach for their own toy.

3. On the one hand, adolescents experience increased decision-making abilities and executive cognitive control during this developmental time. On the other hand, compared with child and adult populations, there is heightened activation of emotion processing areas associated with incentive and reward which can influence assessments of risk and potentially drive decision making towards riskier choices during adolescence.

Further reading

Blakemore, S.-J. (2019) *Inventing Ourselves: The Secret Life of the Teenage Brain*, London: Black Swan.

Blakemore, S. and Choudhury, S. (2006) 'Development of the adolescent brain: Implications for executive function and social cognition', *Journal of Child Psychology and Psychiatry*, 47(3–4): 296–312.

Casey, B.J., Jones, R.M. and Hare, T.A. (2008) 'The adolescent brain', *Annals of the New York Academy of Sciences*, 1124: 111–126.

Eslinger, P.J., Flaherty-Craig, C.V. and Bentonb, A.L. (2004) 'Developmental outcomes after early prefrontal cortex damage', *Brain and Cognition*, 55: 84–103.

Goswami, U. (2019) *Cognitive Development and Cognitive Neuroscience: The Learning Brain* (2nd edn), London: Routledge.

Griffin, A. (2017) 'Adolescent neurological development and implications for health and well-being', *Healthcare* (Basel, Switzerland), 5(4): 62.

On our website

You can find lots more material on our website at https://policy.bristoluniversitypress. co.uk/child-development-and-the-brain/companion-website

4

Health and the developing brain

This chapter:

- considers the effects of diet on the developing brain;

- presents a clear account of what is needed to grow healthy brains;

- examines the effects of poor diet on the adolescent brain;

- evaluates the effects of drugs on brain development including nicotine, alcohol and illicit drugs such as marijuana and cocaine;

- considers the effects of alcohol and marijuana use on the developing brains of teenagers.

Introduction

This chapter covers a broad range of issues around the relationship between what we put into the bodies of developing infants, children and young people and consequent brain development. We begin with food and diet and provide evidence to show that poor diet and poverty can have a devastating effect on brain development. We consider the problem in many parts of the world of simply getting enough to eat and look at the role of protein and fatty acids in building a healthy brain. In the second half of the chapter, we move away from food and look at the consequences of other substances such as drugs, cigarettes and alcohol on brain development. We evaluate the effect of these on the developing foetus and on the brains of teenagers.

Food and brain development

> The baby's brain is built in the womb

Pregnant mothers and young babies need a healthy diet if they are both to thrive during the early developmental stages (Figure 4.1). The World Health Organization (WHO) recommends that pregnant women eat a diet that 'contains adequate energy, protein, vitamins and minerals, obtained through the consumption of a variety of foods, including green and orange vegetables, meat, fish, beans, nuts, whole grains and fruit' (WHO, 2016, p 3). Likewise, a healthy and well-balanced diet is essential for the brains of young infants to develop and function properly. First and foremost, pregnant mothers and young babies need enough protein. They also need a diet that contains fatty acids as well as iodine, zinc, choline and B-vitamins. This needs to have enough food, and the right diet applies particularly to the early period of brain development. The baby's brain is built in the womb. What the mother eats, drinks or otherwise ingests during pregnancy can have consequences for the brain development of the foetus. In the majority world (what we still sometimes call third-world countries), as well as in some areas of the minority world (i.e., the developed West), there may be problems around not having enough food. This can have dire consequences for both the mother and the baby.

Figure 4.1: Pregnant mothers and young babies need a healthy diet to thrive

Source: Shutterstock, Photo ID 175250939

Problems with getting enough food

One of the sad facts about the world in the 21st century is that there are still many areas where people are living in abject poverty. Data from the World Bank shows that the percentage of the world's population that must live on less than $1.90 per day has fallen dramatically in the last 35 years, from 42.1% in 1981 to 9.9% in 2015 (World Bank, 2019). Despite this massive decline there are still far too many people living at this terrible level of poverty. For example, the numbers of those living in absolute poverty in sub-Saharan Africa continues to rise. The World Bank forecasts that by 2030, 90% of the world's poorest will live in this region (Wadhwa, 2019).

The World Poverty Clock puts the percentage of the world's population living in extreme poverty at over 593 million. Other countries with high levels of extreme poverty include Angola, Chad, Democratic Republic of the Congo, Madagascar, Niger, Nigeria and South Africa (World Poverty Clock, 2018). Other sources indicate that the situation is even worse. For example, according to the United Nations, 734 million people live on less than $1.90 a day, based on 2011 prices and wages (United Nations, nd). Poverty at this level has a huge impact on the infant mortality rate. In sub-Saharan Africa, for example, one in 36 children dies in the first month of life. This compares with one in 333 in developed countries (Ouattara, 2018). But it is also likely to have a huge impact on the brain development of the children who survive.

Getting enough protein

Both animal and human studies show that nutrition plays an important role in brain development at all stages, from the formation of the neural plate through to apoptosis, the pre-programmed pruning of unused neurons. As we saw in Chapter 2, the creation of neurons begins about seven weeks after conception and continues through to birth and in some areas of the brain even beyond this.[1] According to Nyaradi and colleagues (2013), experiments on rats have shown that malnutrition affects almost all aspects of brain development including the number of neurons produced, synaptogenesis, myelination and neurotransmission. One of the few ethical ways of studying this in humans is to conduct post-mortems of children who have died through malnutrition. These studies are usually, perhaps thankfully, on a small scale. Benítez-Bribiesca and colleagues (1999) carried out such a piece of research, comparing the brains of 13 malnourished children with those of seven babies who died of other causes. They found that the brains of the malnourished children had fewer neurons and fewer and shorter dendritic spines on the dendrites.

Malnutrition, whether *in utero* or after birth, can have a permanent effect on the brain of the growing baby. Dewey and Begum (2011), for example, looked at the effects of stunting, that is, children whose height is greatly restricted.[2] Stunted growth is usually the result of an inadequate supply of nutrients to the brain. The process also causes both cognitive delay and permanent cognitive deficiencies. There have been quite a few studies showing the long-term impact of malnutrition, producing, for example, a smaller visual cortex, as well as its effects on the development of the cerebellum and neuronal growth (for an overview of this see Yan et al, 2018).

Fatty acids

Fatty acids are also seen as critical for foetal brain development. Fatty acids also play a key role in postnatal development. Long-chain polyunsaturated fatty acids (LC-PUFA), particularly docosahexaenoic acid (DHA) and arachidonic acid (AA), facilitate the growth of neurons and promote signal transmission in the brain. They are also seen as playing an important role in gene expression.

A pregnant woman needs to store fairly large amounts of fat during pregnancy, particularly between week ten and week 30, for both herself and her foetus (King, 2000). Fatty acids are seen as critical for the development of the brain (Nyaradi et al, 2013). A lack of fatty acids can cause reduced neuronal growth, leading to cognitive impairment. According to Prado and Dewey (2014) they are seen as essential at many different levels of brain development. The growth of new neurons requires lots of phospholipid molecules to help build the cell membrane, and these require fatty acids. Both AA and DHA are needed for the building and maturation of the synapses, and fatty acids are a key component of the myelin sheath which coats white matter as the nervous system develops.

Similarly, studies which explore the use of both DHA and AA supplements show that such interventions can be effective in boosting cognitive functioning (for a fuller account of this see Prado and Dewey, 2014).

Iron

Iron deficiency in the diet is a problem in many parts of the world. According to the WHO (2008), iron deficiency affects 1.62 billion people, that is, 24.8% of the world population. Among pregnant women the figure is about 38%, which accounts for 32.4 million women worldwide.

There is a lot of evidence that iron deficiency and anaemia have a negative effect on the developing brain. Iron is needed for several enzyme systems to function. This includes the production of dopamine, the process of myelination and the regulation of brain growth (Nyaradi et al, 2013). Animal studies have also shown that it can lead to a decrease in the size of the hippocampus with likely consequences for learning and development. There is evidence that diets that are poor in iron lead to poorer cognitive skills, reduced language skills, lower levels of attention and also impact on motor skills (Tamura et al, 2002).

You would imagine that if iron deficiency is the problem, then iron supplements to the diet would be the solution! The evidence for this is not strong. Two reviews of trials have both shown that there is not convincing evidence that iron deficiency treatments improve cognitive development in very young children (Sachdev et al, 2005; Wang et al, 2013). There is better evidence that children aged six and over who are anaemic do benefit from iron supplements. A meta-analysis by Falkingham et al (2010) showed that iron supplements improved attention and concentration and improved IQ scores by 2.5 points in children aged six and over who were anaemic.

Problems with relative poverty and brain development

It is clear from both animal and human studies that extreme poverty has a huge impact on the developing brain. However, even in more developed countries, where the extremes of poverty seen in parts of Asia and sub-Saharan Africa are generally not found, what we might term relative poverty has been shown to have a serious effect on brain development. In the United States there are about 15 million children (21%) who live in families whose income is below the

> Children living in poverty have smaller white matter and cortical grey matter and smaller hippocampi and amygdalae

federal poverty threshold (National Center for Children in Poverty, 2019). In the United Kingdom, the Children's Society (2018) estimates that four million children, that is, about a third of the child population, live in poverty.[3] A recent study in the United Sates (Luby et al, 2013) showed that children living in poverty had smaller white matter and cortical grey matter as well as having smaller hippocampi and amygdalae. Another American study (Hair et al, 2015) concluded that children from low-income families scored up to seven points lower on standardised tests, which they associated with the late maturation of the frontal and temporal lobes.

As well as neuronal development, other processes can also be affected by poor diet. For example, a 1993 post-mortem study of ten three- to four-month-old infants who died from pneumonia showed a substantial difference in the growth of their dendritic trees between the five who had been malnourished and the five who had received an adequate diet (Cordero et al, 1993). The poorer children had a less developed span of dendritic connections than the non-poor children.

Problems with getting the right sort of food

A more common problem in the minority world is eating the wrong sort of food or eating too much food. A UK study of obesity in pregnant mothers showed that increased body mass index in expectant mothers brought with it a range of health risks such as gestational diabetes mellitus and proteinuric pre-eclampsia (Sebire et al, 2001).

Obesity and brain development

The UK Government reports that around 25% of children are not at a healthy weight when they begin school, and this rises to one in three by the time they leave primary school (Office for Health Improvement and Disparities, 2022). In the United States the picture is similar, with the Centers for Disease Control and Prevention (CDC) reporting that obesity is now at 13.9% for two- to five-year-olds, rising to 18.4% in the six to eleven age range and even higher, 20.6%, in 12- to 19-year-olds (CDC, 2019b).

The problems of obesity in children seem highly concerning in terms of general health. But what about brain development and functioning? A meta-analysis of studies from 1976 to 2013 by the University of California (Liang et al, 2014) found mixed results. They found a strong and consistent correlation between obesity and problems with executive functioning, attention, visuospatial skills and motor skills but not such a strong correlation with general cognitive functioning, learning and memory, and academic achievement. However, remember this is correlation *not* causality.

BOX: The difference between correlation and causality

If two sets of numbers correlate it means that as one of them changes in size the other one also changes. It doesn't mean that one change is caused by the other. Let us give an example. In Bognor Regis, a town in West Sussex in the United Kingdom, there is a correlation between foot size and intellectual capacity. Those with bigger feet are more intellectually capable than those with small feet. How come, you might well ask? The answer is simple. Very roughly, about 11% of the population are under the age of nine (iLiveHere, 2019). These children are not yet physically fully grown, and neither their shoe size nor their intellectual capacity has yet reached maturity. Feet continue to grow until the mid-teens and intellectual capacity for many years beyond. Therefore, statistically, those with smaller feet – that is, the young children – will be intellectually less developed than those with larger feet, the adults. There is a correlation between the two numbers. **However, there is no causality**. Having small feet does not cause reduced intellectual capacity. There is no cause and effect. In science the difference between correlation and causality is a very important.

There have been several useful studies to help us understand the brain regions involved in obesity in children and adolescents. A recent small-scale study of 36 children (aged seven to ten years) showed that one area of the brain, the right inferior frontal gyrus, showed greater activity when children were shown pictures of large portion sizes (English et al, 2016). This area of the brain processes language and is thought to play a role in inhibition. The hypotheses of the authors, which they found were at least moderately supported by the evidence, was that brain areas that are linked to cognitive control would respond to both the amount of food presented and the energy density of that food.

Junk food consumption during adolescence

Adolescence in many Western societies is a time of considerable freedom. Many 18-year-olds move away from home either for work or for higher education. Many also begin to exercise freedom of choice over how they live and what they eat. A number of studies have looked at the quality of food consumed by adolescents (e.g. Bremer and Lustig, 2012; Lipsky et al, 2017).

The consensus is that energy-rich junk food that is cheaply and readily available has a particular appeal to this age group (Figure 4.2). Both animal and human studies (e.g., Adair, 2008; Friemel et al, 2010) have shown that adolescence is also a time of hyperphagia, that is, eating too much. As we saw in Chapter 2, reward-driven behaviour is common during adolescence. The part of the brain that is most often associated with this is the mesocorticolimbic dopamine reward centre, often just called the **mesocorticolimbic pathway**. It is made up of many dopamine-releasing neurons and links the ventral striatum of the basal ganglia in the forebrain to the ventral tegmental area in the midbrain. It is associated with the rewarding effect of eating as well as other pleasures, including, of course, those derived from sex and drug taking.

Figure 4.2: Junk food consumption often increases in adolescence

Source: Shutterstock, photo ID 705104968

> Adolescence is a period in life when eating energy-rich junk food has huge appeal

We will discuss risk taking during adolescence in more detail later. For now we simply note that the part of the brain that inhibits risk taking is still under development in the teenage years. There is some research to indicate that the overconsumption of food with high levels of both fat and sugar leads to long-term changes in both inhibition and cognition. These types of diets can also affect the hippocampus and so lead to poor memory functioning (for a fuller discussion around these issues see Reichelt and Rank, 2017).

BOX: Is breastfeeding better than bottle-feeding for brain development?

According to the UK National Health Service (NHS), 73% of mothers start breastfeeding their babies (NHS, 2017a). According to the CDC, the figure in the United States is higher, at 83.2% (2019a). The WHO puts the figure at 40% globally (WHO, 2017). According to these organisations, the benefits are many. Breastmilk is safe; it is served at the right temperature; it contains all the vital nutrients and vitamins; it reduces the risk of diarrhoea and sudden infant death syndrome (SIDS) as well as childhood leukaemia and obesity. But what does it do for the brain? A systematic analysis and meta-analysis has shown that breastfeeding produces adults with 3.44 higher IQ points and claims that this link is causal (Horta et al, 2015). A 2018 review came to similar conclusions and claimed that breastfeeding contributed to advantages in terms of both human capital and an increased earning ability.

A study of preterm babies concluded:

> Predominant breast milk feeding in the first 28 days of life was associated with a greater deep nuclear grey matter volume at term equivalent age and better IQ, academic achievement, working memory, and motor function at 7 years of age. (Belfort et al, 2016, p 133)

BOX: What about vegan and vegetarian diets?

According to the Vegan Society, the number of those following a vegan diet quadrupled in the United Kingdom in the period 2014–2018. This was fuelled by several factors including health and climate change concerns. There is evidence that plant-based diets reduce the risk of several serious illnesses including coronary heart disease, high blood pressure, type 2 diabetes and cancer (McEvoy et al, 2012; Ekmekcioglu et al, 2018). There has been some popular concern that such diets might impact on brain development. For example, an article in the UK *Metro* on 29 August 2019 carried the headline: 'Vegan diets "risk lowering intake of nutrient critical for unborn babies' brains" ' (Hartley-Parkinson, 2019). As is often the case, the truth is more complicated and much more nuanced. In some parts of the world vegetarianism is a diet of necessity rather than one of choice. In these countries, as we have seen, such diets may well lack the micronutrients and the protein necessary for the healthy development of the baby and good brain development. In more prosperous countries where veganism or vegetarianism is a lifestyle choice, it is more about the quality of the diet rather than the absence of meat or animal products. What is required is both an awareness of the nutritional needs of the developing child and the capacity to fulfil those needs. A recent study on the effects of veganism and vegetarianism on mothers and babies concludes:

> Vegetarians and vegans are at risk of nutritional deficiencies, but if the adequate intake of nutrients is upheld, pregnancy outcomes are similar to those reported in the omnivorous population. (Sebastiani et al, 2019, p 20)

BOX: A very quick guide to intoxicating substances

Alcohol (AKA booze, bevvy) comes in many different forms, colours, tastes and strengths. An alcoholic drink contains ethanol and is produced by fermentation. It is a depressant, often reducing inhibition in lower doses, while drinking more can result in problems in balance, slurred speech and ultimately unconsciousness.

Cigarettes (AKA smokes, rollies, ciggies, baccy) contain tobacco, which is made from plants in the Nicotiana genus. It is highly addictive. Many smokers believe that smoking is relaxing, although, in fact, nicotine is a stimulant.

Marijuana (AKA cannabis, weed, skunk, pot, hash, grass, ganga, dope) is usually eaten, smoked or vaped. It comes from the Cannabis plant and is a psychoactive drug. The effects vary considerably both from person to person and from the exact chemical blend of the drug. Effects include feeling relaxed, happy, giggly, sleepy and hallucinatory. Stronger versions of the drug can also increase paranoia, confusion and anxiety.

Cocaine (AKA Charlie, blow, coke, crack) is a powerful stimulant that is either snorted in powder form (coke) or smoked in the form of small rocks (crack).

Pregnancy: the effect of drugs, medicines and other substances

Smoking cigarettes when pregnant

Smoking while pregnant has long been known to harm the developing foetus (Figure 4.3). A review article (Ekblad et al, 2015) points to the fact that a surprisingly high percentage of women (5–26%) in the United States and Europe continue to smoke during pregnancy despite pretty much universal recognition

Figure 4.3: Smoking during pregnancy is known to harm the developing foetus

Source: Shutterstock, Photo ID 386102302

that this will have a negative effect on the health of the foetus, especially on brain development. Single women, younger women and those who have a low socio-economic status are at particularly high risk (Ekblad et al, 2013). It has been known for some time that the presence of nicotine in the bloodstream raises levels of carbon dioxide and so decreases the amount of oxygen available to the foetus (Cole et al, 1972). Exposure to cigarette smoke, including passive smoking, has been associated with lower birth weight, premature birth and SIDS (Thompson et al, 2009). There is substantial evidence to show that foetal head size is lower among infants exposed to prenatal smoking (e.g., Jaddoe et al, 2007; Himes et al, 2013). Two studies have indicated that foetal brain volume is affected by mothers smoking particularly during the later stages of pregnancy (Roza et al, 2007; Anblagan et al, 2013). There is also growing evidence that epigenetic changes during pregnancy can also arise through smoking (e.g., Knopik et al, 2012), although these mechanisms are not yet fully understood.

Smoking during pregnancy has many adverse effects on the growing foetus. Ekblad and colleagues (2015) conclude that these effects can continue into adulthood and can even affect subsequent generations. One of the significant ways in which we can improve the health of young babies is to help pregnant mothers through the incredibly difficult process of stopping or reducing smoking.

Drinking alcohol when pregnant

There is a huge amount of evidence to suggest that mothers consuming alcohol while pregnant can have negative consequences for the developing foetus. However,

Figure 4.4: Drinking alcohol during pregnancy can affect the longer-term development of the infant

Source: Shutterstock, Photo ID 1911287698

many women continue to consume alcohol during pregnancy. A recent meta-analysis found that 9.8% of women from 50 countries worldwide consumed some alcohol while pregnant (Popova et al, 2017). The five countries with the highest consumption were Belarus, Denmark, Ireland, Russia and the United Kingdom. The lowest were Kuwait, Oman, Qatar, United Arab Emirates and Saudi Arabia.

Most studies assert that drinking alcohol at any point during pregnancy can affect the longer-term development of the infant (Figure 4.4). It has been linked with difficulties in learning, intellectual functioning, attention deficits, problems with motor development and hyperactivity (Thompson et al, 2009). A recent meta-analysis concluded that even moderate amounts of prenatal alcohol consumption can affect later child behaviour in terms of social engagement and behaviour (Flak et al, 2014).

When alcohol is consumed by the mother, it can pass into the bloodstream of the developing embryo. At its most severe it can cause what is called foetal alcohol syndrome, which causes permanent damage to the CNS (Jones and Smith, 1973). A recent study showed that prolonged exposure to alcohol *in utero* often leads to less brain plasticity during later development (Lebel et al, 2012).

It must be added that there are dissenting voices to this strict embargo on drinking when pregnant. For example, a study at UCL concluded that '[c]hildren born to mothers who drank up to 1–2 drinks per week or per occasion during pregnancy were not at increased risk of clinically relevant behavioural difficulties or cognitive deficits compared with children of abstinent mothers' (Kelly et al, 2009, p 129). And law professor Colin Gavaghan accuses the UK Department of Health and the British Medical Association of 'medical paternalism' (Gavaghan, 2009, p 300) in insisting on a precautionary approach to alcohol consumption when pregnant. A recent Swedish study (Comasco et al, 2018) poses a set of questions that remain unanswered and calls for a large-scale research project to provide the answers. Among the questions it poses are whether low to moderate alcohol consumption affects neuropsychological, cognitive and psychosomatic development; how gene expression relates to this; and what part other environmental factors play in increasing or lessening the impact of alcohol consumption. These are all excellent questions. However, given that it is the life of a child that is being discussed, it seems wise to err on the side of caution until full and definitive answers are provided by medical science.

In the United Kingdom the advice from the Department of Health is unambiguous. It tells women:

> If you are pregnant or planning a pregnancy, the safest approach is not to drink alcohol at all, to keep risks to your baby to a minimum.

And that

> Drinking in pregnancy can lead to long-term harm to the baby, with the more you drink the greater the risk. (Alcohol Policy Team, Department of Health, 2016, p 32).

Likewise, in the United States the CDC says:

> There is no known safe amount of alcohol use during pregnancy or while trying to get pregnant. There is also no safe time during pregnancy to drink. All types of alcohol are equally harmful, including all wines and beer. (CDC, 2018)

Smoking marijuana when pregnant

> Taking cannabis can have a detrimental effect on the brain of the growing foetus

A study in the United States has shown that the use of marijuana among pregnant women increased by over 60% during the period 2002–2014 (Figure 4.5). Women in the 18–25 age range are the most likely users, with 7.5% of them taking the drug (Brown et al, 2017). One of the reasons for this increase might be the effect of marijuana on nausea. THC (delta-9-tetrahydrocannabinol), one of the active ingredients in cannabis, has a potent, if limited, suppressant effect on feelings of nausea (e.g., Parker et al, 2011). However, there is some evidence that taking cannabis can have a detrimental effect on the brain of the growing foetus.

A recent review article (Wu et al, 2011) showed that it can impair executive functions such as impulse control; impair visual memory; and have a negative effect on school-age children's attention spans. Jutras-Aswad and colleagues (2009)

Figure 4.5: Cannabis use in pregnancy can have a damaging effect on infant brain development.

Source: Shutterstock, photo ID 1047100399

have shown that THC affects the endocannabinoid system, which in turn has a direct bearing on how neurons communicate with each other and affects the production and migration of neurons in the early stages of brain development. The American College of Obstetricians and Gynecologists recently examined evidence which showed that prenatal exposure to cannabis lowered scores on tests of visual problem solving, visual-motor coordination and visual analysis. It was also shown to increase the likelihood of such children themselves taking marijuana by the time they are 14 (American College of Obstetricians and Gynecologists, 2017).

Taking cocaine when pregnant

A study in the 1980s showing the adverse effects of cocaine use during pregnancy (Chasnoff et al, 1985) led to an overreaction to the idea of using this drug during pregnancy, particularly in the United States. For a time, such children were labelled 'crack babies' and were written off as suffering from irreversible neurological damage. Most notorious, perhaps, was the case of a woman in Tennessee, who was shown to have taken cocaine, being jailed for using a 'deadly weapon' against her unborn child (reported in Thompson et al, 2009, p 303). Attitudes changed, however, and later studies were less condemning (see, e.g., Zuckerman et al, 2002). A recent meta-analysis (Gouin et al, 2011) of studies of antenatal cocaine exposure and pregnancy outcome published between 1966 and July 2009 has shown that exposing the foetus to cocaine is associated with a range of issues including preterm birth and low birth weight. Another review

(Meyer and Zhang, 2009) has shown that many studies have demonstrated that using cocaine during pregnancy has an adverse effect on the developing cardiovascular system. Animal studies conducted by McCarthy and colleagues (2014) indicate changes in executive functioning and show that responses to fear and trauma could be greater when there has been prenatal exposure to cocaine.

Taking prescribed medication when pregnant

There have been substantial increases in the numbers of women taking antidepressant medication while pregnant. In the United States, a study showed that 6% of women were prescribed selective serotonin reuptake inhibitor (SSRI) medication when pregnant (Andrade et al, 2016). In the United Kingdom the figure is slightly lower at 3.6–3.8% of women taking SSRIs during pregnancy (Charlton et al, 2015).

Link with autism spectrum disorders

There are some studies which show an increased risk for autism spectrum disorders (ASD). However, this remains controversial. Andalib and colleagues (2017) have suggested there is an increased risk of ASD, whereas a Chinese meta-analysis has concluded that there was not a significant association between ASD and antidepressant use (Zhou et al, 2018). These differences can be partly explained by different methodologies, particularly in how the studies were analysed. In a critical review Sujan and colleagues (2019) suggest that the studies need to look at individual drugs, for example, citalopram, paroxetine and fluoxetine, all of which will have different effects. There might also be differences in the levels of depression being treated and the timing of the medication – whether it is taken, for example, in the first or third trimester. Sujan and colleagues conclude that taking SSRIs 'is unlikely to substantially increase the risk ASD and ADHD [attention–deficit/hyperactivity disorder]' (2019, p 371). The other consideration is whether there are other forms of support available other than SSRI medication.

Other issues around SSRIs and pregnancy

Campagne (2019) provides a broader meta-analysis of the issues around taking SSRIs when pregnant. He finds that there are a wide range of problems, including **poor neonatal adaption (PNA)**, in between 20% and 77% of infants of women taking SSRIs. PNA is usually shown in symptoms such as mild sleep disturbance but can also, although rarely, include convulsions. He also reports on studies which show changes in the brain white matter in neonates whose mothers had taken SSRIs in the first or second trimester and other studies indicating a greater likelihood of miscarriage in mothers who took SSRIs in the first trimester. Conversely, he reports on a Dutch study showing that untreated depression in the mother can lead to lower body and head growth in the developing foetus. This latter study shows the difficult dilemmas around the issue of antidepressants and pregnancy.

The use of medication to treat depressed pregnant women is a difficult medical and ethical area. Depression in mothers, and other mental health issues, can affect the health of the growing foetus, while the taking of medication also represents a danger. It is important also to consider the psychological effects of withdrawal from antidepressant drugs. Campagne's (2019) conclusion is that such drugs should only be prescribed once the alternatives have been exhausted; he also stresses the need for long-term studies that will help us reach a consensus. There is a broad spectrum of alternatives to medication, including transcranial magnetic stimulation (see Felipe and Ferrão, 2016), yoga (see Battle et al, 2015), aerobic exercise (see El-Rafie et al, 2016) and psychotherapy (see Genovez et al, 2018).

Alcohol, marijuana and the teenage brain

There has been much consternation in the press regarding teenage drinking as well as regular moral panics regarding drug use.

'Teenage Drinking has Doubled' UK *Daily Mail* (Marsh, 2019).

'British teenage girls are among the heaviest drinkers in Europe – and have overtaken boys' UK *Daily Telegraph* (Quadri and Matthews, 2018).

'Now nine in ten teens at drug clinics are being treated for marijuana use' UK *Daily Mail* (Adams and Beckford, 2018).

Alcohol and teenage brain development

There is good news and bad news. The good news is that in many countries it looks as though alcohol consumption among teenagers is falling. A report from the American Academy of Pediatrics shows that binge drinking has fallen by over 50% in the 13–17-year age range (Ryan and Kokotailo, 2019). In Europe the trend is downwards, particularly in countries that have previously had high levels of youth drinking such as the United Kingdom and the Nordic countries (Inchley et al, 2018). The bad news is that, according to the WHO, levels are still dangerously high. Drinking large amounts of alcohol is still common across Europe. One in four boys and a fifth of all girls report that they had been drunk more than two times by the age of 15 (Inchley et al, 2018).

In a systematic review of how drinking alcohol affects the teenage brain, Feldstein Ewing and colleagues (2014) found that drinking at a young age affects development in terms of both brain

> Drinking alcohol when young affects brain development particularly in the frontal areas of the brain

volume and its connectivity. This is especially true of important frontal areas of the brain that are used for executive control such as the middle frontal gyrus, superior frontal gyrus and left frontal cortex. These executive control areas are important in relation to teenagers being able to decide when and where (and how much) they will drink. Alcohol also affects reward systems in the brain, particularly the dopamine pathways. This can lead to teenagers feeling they want or need alcohol rather than simply liking it. The review also showed that adolescent girls are particularly vulnerable to the effects of alcohol on brain development, probably because of the different ages at which male and female brains mature.

Marijuana and teenage brain development

In terms of drug taking, marijuana remains the most popular drug among adults and teenagers. In many countries such as Canada, Uruguay and South Africa recreational use has been legalised. In the United States, as of January 2023, while many states have legalised the medical use of marijuana, it remains illegal under federal law. In the United Kingdom it remains illegal except for very particular medical uses such as severe epilepsy or multiple sclerosis, when it can be prescribed by a specialist doctor. In the United States about one in 16 17–18-year-olds admit to taking it regularly (National Institute on Drug Abuse, 2019). In the United Kingdom in 2016, 24% of children aged 11–15 reported that they had taken drugs, an increase from 15% in 2014. Some 8% reported taking marijuana, which is down considerably from the 13% reported in 2001. The difference is probably due to increases in consumption of nitrous oxide and psychoactive drugs (Stats Team, NHS Digital, 2018).

There are several factors that make studying the effect of cannabis on the teenage brain difficult. The first factor involves how early children start using the drug. The second is related to how much and how regularly they take it. The third is the need to separate out those who use this drug alone and those who also drink alcohol. Lastly, there are now many different ways of ingesting the drug including smoking, vaping and eating.

The marijuana and alcohol issue is best illustrated by looking at two studies. In 2014, Gilman and colleagues (2014) compared 20 18–25-year-olds who smoked marijuana regularly with 20 who did not. They found evidence of changes to grey matter density and volume as well as changes to both the nucleus accumbens and amygdala. A year later, Weiland and colleagues (2015) published a similar study of 16 male and 13 female marijuana users matched with a similar number of non-marijuana users. This study found 'no evidence of differences in volumes of the accumbens, amygdala, hippocampus, or cerebellum between daily versus nonusers, in adults or adolescents' (Weiland et al, 2015, p 1509). The Weiland study can be distinguished from the Gilman study in two ways. Firstly, the Weiland study matched for alcohol consumption. Secondly, the study also focused on those who were involved in the criminal justice system but not in jail and tried to overcome the problem of matching those who take risks by taking illegal drugs with those who are averse to such risks.

This is not to say that marijuana does not have any effect on the brain. It clearly has a short-term effect on both memory and the capacity to learn as well as affecting attention, concentration and abstract reasoning (Crane et al, 2013). Persistent use of cannabis also seems to have a negative effect on cognition. A New Zealand longitudinal study (Gonzalez and Swanson, 2012) followed 1,037 people born in the period 1972–1973 from birth

> Persistent and heavy use of marijuana in the teenage years leads to problems with cognitive decline and executive control

to age 38 years. The study showed that persistent cannabis use over a period of 20 years caused what the authors call 'neuropsychological decline'; that is, persistent cannabis users scored six points lower on IQ tests than those who did not take cannabis. The study also showed a greater decline in those who began taking it during adolescence. This is reflected in other studies. Fontes and colleagues (2011) looked at 104 chronic cannabis users (mostly men), 49 of whom started using around age 15, and compared this with both non-users and late-onset users. They found cognitive impairment in the early-onset users but not in those who started cannabis use later. This has been affirmed by a recent meta-analysis of both human and animal studies (Gorey et al, 2019) which found that heavy and persistent cannabis use in the early teenage years led to cognitive decline as well as problems with executive control, sustaining attention and working memory. These problems were not evident in those who only took cannabis once or twice a week.

Summary

- Pregnant mothers and young infants need a healthy and well-balanced diet that contains enough protein, fatty acids, iodine, zinc, choline and B-vitamins to facilitate proper brain development.

- While the numbers of those living in absolute poverty have fallen, there are still many areas of the world where people live in awful poverty. This has a terrible effect on infant mortality and on the brain development of the infants who survive.

- In the United States and the United Kingdom there are still many families living in relative poverty. Children from these families have been shown to have less white matter and cortical grey matter and smaller hippocampi and amygdalae.

- In the United Kingdom and the United States the number of obese children is growing. There is a correlation between obesity and problems with executive functioning, attention, visuospatial skills and motor skills.

- Correlation is not the same as causation.

- Adolescence is a time when hyperphagia is common. This might be driven by the availability of cheap, energy-rich food and by reward-driven behaviours associated with the mesocorticolimbic pathway.

- Smoking cigarettes when pregnant has many adverse effects on the growing foetus including the risk of lower brain volume.

- Most studies assert that drinking alcohol when pregnant has an adverse effect on the baby's brain development, although there is a need for much more research.

- Taking cannabis and cocaine when pregnant has also been shown to have an adverse effect on infant brain development.

- Taking antidepressant medication while pregnant remains a difficult area, particularly in trying to balance the mother's mental health with the risks to the growing foetus.

- Drinking alcohol as a teenager can damage frontal areas of the brain associated with executive control.

- While moderate cannabis use in the teenage years has not been found to have a long-term effect on brain development, heavy and persistent use leads to problems with cognitive decline and executive control.

Test your knowledge
1. How does not getting enough food affect foetal and infant brain development?
2. What are the effects of relative poverty on the brain development of children?
3. How does breastfeeding affect the brain development of young infants?
4. How would you explain the different risk levels for pregnant mothers between alcohol consumption and smoking cigarettes?
5. Should pregnant mothers who are feeling depressed continue taking SSRI antidepressant medication?
6. Is there a correlation between taking SSRI medication and autism? Is there evidence of causation?
7. Should pregnant mothers who experience nausea take cannabis as a remedy?
8. Is cocaine a dangerous substance for pregnant mothers?
9. What are the dangers of drinking alcohol when you are a teenager?
10. How would you advise a group of 14–18-year-olds on the problems of marijuana use?

Discussion questions

1. Does poverty impact on brain development?
2. Why do women continue to drink alcohol/smoke cigarettes/take drugs when pregnant when the research evidence suggests that these activities will harm their babies?
3. Does smoking marijuana affect the development of the teenage brain?

Our answers

1. The easy answer to this is, yes it does! Both absolute poverty and relative poverty affect the health of pregnant women, infants and young children. We hope we have given enough evidence in the chapter to argue that poverty has a physical and biological impact on brain development. In a later chapter we also look at the impact of trauma on development. We hardly need add that as well as the physical effects of deprivation, there are also many psychological effects, many traumas, that are also directly linked to being a child in an impoverished family.
2. That's just such a hard question! Firstly, the question ignores the fact that many of us lead difficult and stressful lives and often use drugs, alcohol or cigarettes as a means of trying to manage the stress of living. Secondly, these substances are all in one way or another addictive. Stopping doing them is often incredibly difficult. Thirdly, becoming pregnant can be joyful, but it can also be very stressful. In times of managing increased stress, we might use these substances even if we know that they are harmful. Fourthly, none of us lead our lives in isolation. We are all part of one or even many social groups and those groups will have different attitudes and values, some of which might overlap with government advice and some of which might not. One of the many lessons we have learned from COVID-19 is that scientific advice is open to interpretation and that many people distrust such advice or suspect that it might have an ulterior motive.
3. This remains a hugely controversial question and one that is likely to exercise the minds of many politicians as countries decide whether or not to go down the route of legalisation! The big question is whether it has long-term effects. On the balance of the evidence, we would say it probably does. It's very difficult to give a definitive answer, of course. It depends on how much is smoked, how young the teenager is when they start to smoke it and whether or not it is consumed in combination with other substances such as alcohol. Critical here is the question of whether THC has a long-term effect on the hippocampus. Research evidence, as we have seen in the chapter, is mixed. Long-term studies such as the current ABCD study (see https://abcdstudy.org/) in the United States will, we hope, allow neuroscientists to better answer this question.

Notes

[1] It would be highly unethical to conduct experiments about food deprivation on human populations: an experiment which starved pregnant mothers for the benefits of science is

unlikely to get ethical approval. Sadly, the same ethics do not apply to animal experiments, and hence most of the published evidence for the effects of malnutrition come from animal studies.

2   According to Golden (2009), a child is considered stunted if their height is more than two standard deviations below the mean height for that population based on WHO standards.

3   In the United Kingdom a child is considered to be living in poverty when their family has an income that is below 60% of the UK average. In the United States the federal poverty threshold is defined in terms of the number of people living in a household. A family of four, for example, living on an annual income of less than $25,750 is said to be living in poverty.

Further reading

Campagne, D.M. (2019) 'Antidepressant use in pregnancy: Are we closer to consensus?', *Archives of Women's Mental Health*, 22(2): 189–197.

Gorey, C., Kuhns, L., Smaragdi, E., Kroon, E. and Cousijn, J. (2019) 'Age-related differences in the impact of cannabis use on the brain and cognition: A systematic review', *European Archives of Psychiatry and Clinical Neuroscience*, 269(1): 37–58.

Nyaradi, A., Li, J., Hickling, S., Foster, J. and Oddy, W.H. (2013) 'The role of nutrition in children's neurocognitive development, from pregnancy through childhood', *Frontiers in Human Neuroscience*, 7: 97.

Reichelt, A.C. and Rank, M.M. (2017) 'The impact of junk foods on the adolescent brain', *Birth Defects Research*, 109(20): 1649–1658.

Stallen, M. (2017) 'Poverty and the developing brain', *Behavioral Scientist*, 25 September, Available from: https://behavioralscientist.org/can-neurosci entists-help-us-understand-fight-effects-childhood-poverty/ [Accessed 6 September 2021].

On our website

You can find lots more material on our website at https://policy. bristoluniversitypress.co.uk/child-development-and-the-brain/companion-website

This includes:

How to grow a good brain: https://policy.bristoluniversitypress.co.uk/child-development-and-the-brain/companion-website/grow-a-good-brain

Nine key people in our understanding of brain development: https://policy. bristoluniversitypress.co.uk/child-development-and-the-brain/companion-website/nine-key-people

5

Emotional and social development

This chapter:

- considers the debate between a natural emergent view of emotional development and the view that emotions are culturally constructed;

- evaluates the contributions of neuroscience to this debate;

- explores the beginnings of social development in infancy and childhood;

- evaluates the current neuroscience research on social development;

- considers the neuroscience of emotional and social development in adolescence.

Introduction: emotional development during infancy

The urgent bawl of a newborn baby would suggest that there is a capacity for emotional expression from the get-go, even if the range is somewhat limited. Yet we cannot be sure that what we are seeing is the expression of a discrete emotion such as anger or sadness or rather something more basic and undifferentiated that cannot be understood as a specific emotional expression.

Are emotions developed or constructed: two paradigms

There are two distinct paradigms. There are those who see emotions are 'natural', arising from distinct neural pathways in the brain that are present at birth. This paradigm seeks to understand which emotions are present at birth and which develop during the early years of life. This is sometimes referred to as a **locationist** model as it seeks to locate emotions in discrete areas of the brain.

The second paradigm is proposed by the constructionist school. In this approach emotions are seen as 'mental events that are constructed of more basic psychological processes' (Lindquist, 2013, p 356). Emotional experiences are created in the mind, are not located in specific brain areas and are dependent on language for their construction.

The natural, developmental paradigm

Philosophers from Descartes onwards have suggested that we have a set of what are usually labelled basic emotions or **primary emotions**. They are primary in two ways:

- they are seen in some way as hardwired into the body rather than learned;
- our further emotional responses grow from these as we develop.

Exactly what we might include in the category of primary emotions (Figure 5.1) varies between theorists; however, they usually include emotions such as joy, fear, anger, distress, sadness, interest and disgust. **Secondary emotions** are those that are more complex and, in most theories, are not seen as developing until about the second year of life. These include feelings such as pride, jealousy, shame, guilt and empathy.

There is no single theoretical account of how emotions develop, but rather a series of complimentary theories which differ in how they describe emotions, how such emotions have evolved and how they develop in infancy. Most of the research in this area depends on observation of how emotions are expressed in the face, in the body and through sound. The two main variables here are the two V's – volume and valence: how loud is

> We can distinguish between primary emotions such as joy, fear and anger and secondary emotions such as jealousy and guilt

Figure 5.1: Primary emotions in infancy

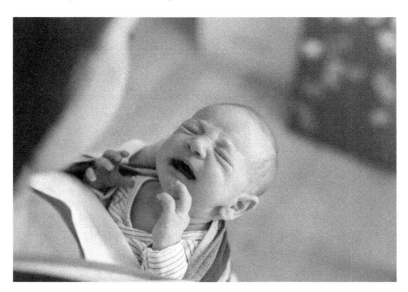

Source: Shutterstock, photo ID 496255705

the sound or how big is the expression; and where does it sit on the pleasure/displeasure spectrum? As well as observing and perhaps even measuring these variables, we must also take into account cultural differences in how emotions are expressed. The most obvious cultural difference is around whether young males, from a very early age, are permitted to express emotions at all, let alone show distress.

We review here three of these natural developmental theories: Izard's theory of discrete emotions; the work of Campos and Barrett, which presents a functionalist view of emotional development; and Sroufe's theories of basic emotion.

Carroll Izard's discrete emotions theory

Carroll Izard (2007), in his development of the discrete emotions theory, distinguishes between basic emotions and emotional schemas. Izard considers interest, joy/happiness, sadness, anger, disgust and fear as truly 'basic' emotions (Figure 5.2). He argues that the neural substrates for the expression of some of these emotions, such as interest and joy, are already in place at birth, while the others develop in the first two years of life.

For Izard, basic emotions have five characteristics.

1. They involve movement of the body emerging early in life and having within these movements the capacity for expressive behaviour.
2. They appear in response to a stimulus rather than relying on complex appraisal, that is, they are not thought through.

Figure 5.2: Basic emotions include joy, anger and sadness

Source: Shutterstock, photo ID 345101900

3. They are unique and innate and depend on a set of neural pathways that Izard suggests 'derives primarily from subcortical neural systems in the upper brain stem' (2007, p 263). They cannot be taught: you cannot teach a child to be happy or sad, Izard says.
4. The fourth and fifth characteristics work together: they have unique regulatory processes and …
5. … they have the power to motivate, influencing both thought and action.

They are regulatory and motivational in that basic emotions increase or dampen activity: interest will sustain and prolong an experience; fear will have the opposite effect, producing a desire to turn away from or stop an activity.

Izard distinguishes these basic innate emotions from emotional schemas. These are learned behaviours that build upon the basic emotions to provide more complex, more long-lasting adaptations to the environment. The development of language is seen as central to the development of such schemas, although Izard also argues that 'rudimentary emotion schemas' (2007, p 266) are formed in early infancy as babies make connections between their natural, inbuilt emotions, such as pleasure and interest, and the human face.

The Campos and Barrett functionalist views of emotional development

Much like Izard's account, a functionalist view (Campos and Barrett, 1984) sees the development of emotions as a natural process but focuses on the relational purpose of the emotion. It examines what the baby is seeking to change, maintain or stop happening in the environment around them. Developmentally it assumes that babies do not have the ability to consciously process emotions but nonetheless are able to show these feelings to the world around them. If the baby is angry, then this shows that they want to change something that is harming their well-being; happiness is a signal to continue or even improve what is happening; fear is about needing to stop an experience. In the early months of life infants have little capacity to process the effect their feeling might have on their environment. Yet these emotions are very effective. For example, we referred earlier to the cry of the newborn baby. It is an almost unbearable sound and, as such, it is a highly effective means of communication that demands attention. Over time, of course, the infant develops an awareness of these emotions and an awareness of the impact of them on the world around them. A baby's smile, for example, can have a huge impact on the behaviour of the parents. It works to draw attention to the baby and to improve the quality of the interactions. The more the baby smiles, the better the outcome.

Sroufe's theory of emotional development

Sroufe's (1997) model of emotional development suggests three innate mechanisms: fear, joy and anger. These three develop together alongside other physical and cognitive changes, becoming more environmentally interactive as the infant becomes more capable of reacting to and controlling the world around them. For example, at three months an infant will smile undiscerningly at parents and strangers. By four months they begin to direct their smile predominantly at their caregivers and will be much warier of strangers. By nine months this wariness develops further and becomes what Sroufe calls 'stranger distress'. The capacity to remember what has happened in the past leads the infant to develop alongside this a capacity for anticipation. Thus, a game of peek-a-boo has elements of both remembering what happened last time the game was played and an anticipation of what is to come, combining both cognition and emotion. As Bruner (1983) shows, the game also becomes more sophisticated as language develops; this, together with a growing sense of self, leads to the development of more sophisticated emotional responses such as shame and embarrassment.

We will consider the ways in which brain imaging confirms or denies these approaches later. For now let us just say that there are areas of overlap and areas of disagreement between these theories. Izard suggests five 'basic emotions', while for Sroufe there are only three. All these theories suggest an innate capacity that is present at birth and which develops relationally as the baby begins to react to the world around them. They vary, however, in their assessment of how organised and how differentiated this emotional capacity is during the very early period of life.

The constructionist model of emotions

Constructivist theories of emotions (e.g., Barrett, 2006; Lindquist, 2013) seem at one level to run against common sense. Our perception of our feelings as adults is that they arise from somewhere within us and that as we grow up we develop a level of 'emotional literacy' and so become able to provide a linguistic label and say 'I am sad' or 'I am happy'. Constructivist theories argue instead that emotions such as fear, disgust and anger need to be seen as psychological compounds arising from more basic elements such as our auditory and visual sensations. Kirsten Lindquist, a leading proponent of these theories, explains it using a cooking metaphor:

> Just as gastronomic delights such as croissants, brioche, tarts, cookies, sauces, and puddings emerge from the combination of basic ingredients (flour, water, salt, etc.), we hypothesize that emotions such as anger, disgust, fear, happiness, and sadness emerge from the combination of more basic 'psychological ingredients.' (Lindquist, 2013, p 360)

The two core ingredients are **core affect** and **conceptualisation**. The core affect is firstly the sensation that arises from our body – the heart that beats faster, the palms that sweat, the adrenaline in the pit of the stomach – and secondly the exteroceptive sensations that we receive via our senses – sound, taste, smell and so forth. Conceptualisation is the process by which we make meaning from these internal stimuli – the crack of a floorboard as we lie in bed at night (fear), the light touch of a hand on our cheek (pleasure). As such it makes no sense to talk about the development of these emotions. They are learned. They are put together conceptually by means of language. There is evidence, for example, that different cultures with different languages and different customs separate out their emotions in ways that are dissimilar to those in the West (see, e.g., Gendron et al, 2014).

The neuroscience of emotional development in infancy

A key question here is whether neuroscience can help us decide which of these very different approaches is right. Is there evidence that we are born with a part of our brain that contains the neural correlates of sadness and fear, or are these parts of a more basic level of affect, part of what we might call the experience of consciousness?

Two meta-analyses in the early 2000s (Phan et al, 2002; Murphy et al, 2003) both concluded that neuroimaging studies only partially support a theory of basic emotions. The 2003 study found, for example, some specialisation in areas of the brain for fear (the amygdala) and disgust (the insula and globus pallidus) but other emotions were distributed widely around the brain.

A 2010 meta-analysis came to a very different conclusion. Vytal and Hamann (2010) used a quantitative method called **activation likelihood estimation** to assess the relationships between brain regions and basic emotions. They concluded that each basic emotion can be associated with patterns of activity across particular regions of the brain. So, for example,

- fear was associated with increased activation in the amygdala and insula;
- happiness was linked with the rostral anterior cingulate cortex and right superior temporal gyrus;
- sadness activated the middle frontal gyrus and the head caudate/subgenual anterior cingulate cortex.

They concluded that 'all five basic emotion states were associated with consistent and discriminable patterns of neural activation' (Vytal and Hamann, 2010, p 2879).

Lindquist and colleagues (2012) provide a huge amount of data to support their view that we construct our emotions and that this construction does not rely on specific and discrete networks in the brain. Their meta-analysis of brain research failed to find any evidence to support a locationist model. It also questioned the assumptions behind the model, suggesting, for example, that the disgust felt when watching a surgical operation is very different (and involves different brain regions) from the disgust felt when watching someone eat revolting foods. They conclude that areas of the brain that are identified as having a role in emotional processing are also involved in processing other perceptual and cognitive activities. The amygdala, for example, is often identified as the locus of fear in the brain as well as being seen as playing a key role in anxiety. In contrast, the constructionist view is that the amygdala is involved in signalling uncertainty, that is, when the brain is struggling to predict what the sensations it is receiving might mean and what should be done about them. Of course, events that induce fear fit into that category, but for Lindquist the activity of the amygdala is not specific to fear. It is also active when it receives novel stimuli, uncertain stimuli and unusual stimuli.

So, has neuroscience sorted out the spat between the locationist/natural paradigm of emotion and the constructionist paradigm? As yet it hasn't, but it has provided more evidence for each side of the debate. It's fair to say that at the current state of play, the constructionists are in the lead. It is proving hard to find evidence for the location of specific emotions and harder still to prove a developmental pathway to go with the locations that have been suggested. We will leave the last words on this, for now at least, to the constructionist team:

> [W]e found that the bulk of the empirical evidence is more consistent with the hypothesis that emotions emerge from the interplay of more basic psychological operations. We hypothesize that these operations and their corresponding neural networks influence and constrain one another to produce a variety of brain states that correspond to a variety of emotional state. (Lindquist et al, 2012, p 28)

Social development

The social brain

Blakemore defines the social brain as:

> … the complex network of areas that enable us to recognize others and evaluate their mental states (intentions, desires and beliefs), feelings, enduring dispositions and actions. (2008, p 267)

The social brain enables us to interact with others by recognising that they act and feel in ways that are similar to the way we do. Being social involves discrete activities such as how we speak, how we look at each other, how we dress, how we move as well as our capacity to hold others in mind and the extent to which we have the ability to **mentalise** (sometimes referred to as **Theory of Mind**), that is, our ability to recognise that both we and other people have desires, beliefs, emotions and knowledge. Our social ability involves several regions of the brain including the anterior cingulate, the medial prefrontal cortex, the inferior frontal gyrus, the superior temporal sulcus, the anterior insula and the amygdala.

Infant social development

Humans are social creatures and human babies enter this social world at birth. Newborn babies are already familiar with their mother's voice. We also know they are drawn towards faces and will engage with them and imitate behaviour. Meltzoff and Moore have shown that newborn babies will imitate a limited range of facial expressions (1983) and that by 12–21 days they can imitate a range of gestures such as finger movement and tongue protrusion (1995). By eight weeks they are making direct eye-to-eye contact and beginning to engage in overt social behaviours (Stern, 2000).

In terms of peer interaction, it used to be believed that infants had very limited social capacity and even that they were unaware of each other until they were at least six years old. More recent studies (Rubin et al, 1999) have shown that infants become increasingly aware of each other's presence and, given the opportunity, will take a growing interest in each other's activities.

Development of mentalising in infants

As we have seen, babies' social awareness develops very quickly in that they are able to read faces and distinguish facial expressions by the age of nine months. However, it takes some time for them to develop the skill of mentalising. By 18 months they are better able to recognise that other people might have different views from their own. They can show, for example, an understanding that someone might like a particular food that they themselves do not enjoy. This is often called 'the broccoli test', as Alison Gopnik and colleagues (Repacholi and Gopnik, 1997) showed that 18-month-old children understood that an adult might love broccoli even though they themselves did not like it.

Development of the smile in infancy

There are many functions that develop in relation to the infant's immediate environment. Smiling, for example, grows in relation to feedback from caregivers (Figure 5.3). Aksan and Kochanska (2004) describe the social smile of the seven-month-old infant that develops in relation to encouragement from caregivers. Infants are tuned into the voices, sights and smells of those around them. Another study of 26 infant–mother pairs (Minagawa-Kawai et al, 2009) showed that infants responded to their mothers' smiles, which produced increased neural activity in the anterior **orbitofrontal cortex**.

Sensitivity to the voice in infancy

We are just starting to learn how different parts of the brain are stimulated by these experiences. For example, a small-scale study by Blasi and colleagues (2011)

Figure 5.3: Development of the smile in infancy

Source: Shutterstock, photo ID 154217945

of 21 infants aged three to seven months showed a sensitivity to the human voice, particularly to sad intonations of the voice. In this study sad vocalisations changed activity in several brain regions, particularly the orbitofrontal cortex and the insula. These and several other studies are starting to show the significance of the orbitofrontal region of the brain in the development of social interactions.

The neuroscience of infant social development

The use of fNIRS has allowed scientists to examine the brain of the young infant and begin to map the areas that respond to the infant's awareness of their social world. In an experiment by Farroni and colleagues (2013) a small group of newborn babies watched a video showing a female actor making eye, mouth and hand movements. They were able to measure activity in the right and left posterior temporal cortex. These responses increased during the first few days of life. A similar experiment with a slightly larger group of five-month-old infants (Lloyd-Fox et al, 2009) showed that there was increased activity in the superior temporal sulcus, an area that has been shown in adults to be important in social interactions. These findings, the authors assert, provide evidence for the hypothesis that even young infants have an area of their temporal cortex that specialises in processing social encounters (Figure 5.4). A later study (Lloyd-Fox et al, 2017) of Gambian children aged from four months to two years measuring both auditory and visual social stimuli supported this idea. It compared the Gambian data with

Figure 5.4: The brain develops in response to social interaction

Source: Shutterstock photo ID 463995221

similar studies of children in the United Kingdom and found that in both cohorts the same areas of the brain responded to social stimuli. These areas are regions in the posterior superior temporal, anterior temporal and inferior frontal cortex.

These studies show that infants have a growing capacity for social interaction that is facilitated by particular areas of the cerebral cortex, particularly in the frontal and temporal cortices. This is an area where non-invasive imaging provided by fNIRS allows researchers to examine the brains of babies and infants in real time without sedation.

Development of face recognition

Adults have an astonishing ability to distinguish one face from another, often based on a quick glance. There has been considerable disagreement over how this capacity develops. It used to be thought that face perception and recognition evolved slowly, through experience, during infancy and did not reach maturity until adolescence. However, methodological advances from the 1990s onwards have begun to show genetic influences on the infant face-recognition system and that face-discrimination abilities are even present in newborns. This suggests that these abilities might have an innate element, with the role of experience being responsible for narrowing the range of different types of faces infants can discriminate between, which in turn enables infants to discriminate between the precise facial features of the different types (for a fuller account see McKone et al, 2009). It is now thought that this ability matures quite quickly, with something approaching an adult capacity being achieved by the age of five (McKone et al, 2012).

Face recognition in infancy

Infants prefer adult faces within the first weeks of postnatal life. Imitation of adults' facial expressions has been repeatedly observed in newborns (e.g., Reissland, 1988). Indeed, preferences for faces and face-like patterns occur hours after birth (Johnson et al, 1991) when infants are arguably discriminating between individuals and bonding with carers (e.g., Quinn and Slater, 2003). They recognise and prefer the face of their mother (Quinn and Slater, 2003) and can identify her face in the first week of life (Pascalis et al, 1995). However, critics suggest that this identification relies on discriminative ability based on general head shape and hair rather than the configuration of facial features, and there is more evidence that suggests that face processing in cortical regions emerges in the first two months of life (for a full review see Johnson, 2005).

The fusiform face area

The cortical regions responsible for face processing in adults are relatively well understood. The **fusiform gyrus**, lateral occipital area and **superior temporal sulcus** have been demonstrated as potentially face-specific processing areas in the recognition or detection of faces (McKone et al, 2009). The **fusiform face area** (FFA) has been found to activate more when faces rather than other complex stimuli, such as hands or horses, are being perceived (Kanwisher et al, 1997). Johnson and de Haan (2010) observe that faces rather than other kinds of complex objects seem to produce more FFA activation, and distribution of processing across the ventral cortex for facial stimuli differs from that for other objects, in that the activity is more focal and less influenced by attentional mechanisms. Most recent studies have shown the existence of an FFA in children at the youngest ages that were tested (McKone et al, 2012).

Adults have a face-sensitive event-related potential (ERP) that has been called the N170. You may recall from Chapter 1 that this is measured using electroencephalography, which measures electrical activity in the brain. The N170 is a negative electrical current that occurs in the temporal and occipital areas in response to human faces. This has been found to be present, albeit with a slightly longer latency (time delay) than in adults, in infants from three months and, with age, to become increasingly attuned to upright adult faces (e.g., de Haan, Johnson and Halit, 2007).

In adult studies, those who are right-handed have more accurate face recognition after seeing the face in their left visual field than in the right. The FFA is also usually larger in the left hemisphere than the right; likewise, the N170 is also strongest in the right hemisphere. These traits have also been identified in studies of children, occurring at all the ages that have been studied.

Elinor McKone and colleagues (2012) provide a compelling meta-analysis of studies from the previous few decades. They argue that we are born with an innate face-processing facility that is improved by experience during childhood and then fine-tuned in adolescence and adulthood. One interesting effect seems to be a narrowing of ability after childhood, much like the loss of linguistic abilities identified in research into language development. For example, our ability to recognise faces of people from other 'races' is now known to decline with age. There seems to be a critical development window here; if we see faces of adults and children of other 'races' before we are 12, we develop the capacity to distinguish between individuals from those backgrounds: otherwise, it is lost (McKone et al, 2019). What seems even more astonishing is that the latest research shows that face selectivity in the lateral fusiform gyrus develops in the same way in those who have been blind from birth – developing in response to touch rather than vision (Murty et al, 2020).

Developmental prosopagnosia

One key piece of evidence for the existence of an FFA is a condition called prosopagnosia or face blindness. Sometimes this occurs after the FFA has been damaged, but it can also occur without such damage and is then seen as a developmental condition. The ability to recognise faces is quite varied within the population. Some of us are brilliant at it and others struggle. Those with developmental prosopagnosia have never been able to recognise faces and so might not even realise that they lack this ability. It is thought to be genetic and so runs in families.

It was once thought to be quite rare, but research by Bradley C. Duchaine has led him to conclude that it may affect one in 50 of us (see, e.g., Duchaine and Nakayama, 2006). You can test yourself and get involved in research into this topic by visiting www.faceblind.org.

Social development in childhood

There is a sparsity of research into the development of the social brain during childhood with one exception: the development of mentalising. Here there is considerable evidence of developmental changes during childhood.

Development of mentalising in childhood

The development of language is often well under way by the age of two. This allows children to begin telling us about their state of mind. By the age of three they have what Henry Wellman (2017) describes as a belief–desire psychology, that is, they can relate what they observe someone doing to the understanding they have of their desires and beliefs. Peter Fonagy and colleagues (2018) suggest that this development is dependent on complex processes associated with attachment. They dispute that there is a natural process of maturation or that the capacity for reflection is innate. Instead, they argue that this process is dependent on interactions with more mature minds. This links with ideas about attachment and the difficulties that adults who have experienced abusive or neglectful childhoods have in holding others in mind.

If the child has been able to develop a capacity to mentalise, by the age of four or five they will be able to understand that someone might hold a belief that is false. The most well-known psychological test of this aspect of mentalising is the Sally–Anne task devised by Baron-Cohen and colleagues (1985). In this task the child is presented with a scenario involving two dolls, Sally and Anne. The scene takes place in a room with a box and a basket. Sally has a marble which she puts in the basket. When Sally is out of the room Anne takes the marble from the basket and puts it in a box. The child is asked: where will Sally look for the marble when she returns to the room? Three-year-olds tend to do badly on the test; they are unable to understand that Sally does not know the marble has been moved. They say she will look in the box as they know this is where the marble has been moved. Once they get a bit older, they can understand that Sally has a false belief and will look in the basket.

There is an important developmental question here: why are most children not able to complete this task successfully until they are aged four and over? It might have to do with language development, or it could be about the inability to inhibit a response. Experiments that have measured where children look rather than what they say have suggested that even infants as young as 15 months can represent false beliefs (see Onishi and Baillargeon, 2005).

Brain development and mentalising in childhood

The parts of the brain that both adults and children use in mentalising are reasonably consistent across many studies, leading to these areas being described as a **mentalising network**. This network includes the medial prefrontal cortex (MPFC), parts of the precuneus, the posterior superior temporal sulcus (pSTS), the temporo-parietal junction (TPJ) as well as areas in the amygdala. Other areas of the brain have also been found to be more activated in mentalising tasks including the cerebellum, the dorsal premotor area and the fusiform gyri (Ohnishi et al, 2004). The MPFC plays an important role as, according to Frith and Frith (2003), this is the area of the brain that allows us to discriminate between our own experiences and those of other people and recognise that these are thoughts or feelings happening inside the mind, as opposed to something happening out there in the real world. There is also evidence of a developmental path. The TPJ becomes increasingly responsive to information related to mental states between the ages of five and seven (Gweon et al, 2012).

Emotional and social development in adolescence

There are huge changes that take place physically, cognitively, emotionally and socially in adolescence. In this section we look at the emotional and social changes that occur and how these are influenced by the social world of adolescence. Adolescence is a time when there are many changes on the social level. Friendships can become intense, and this is also the period when many of us experience romantic love, sexual intimacy for the first time, and quite possibly feelings of jealousy and rejection.

Developmental studies show that the way adolescents experience themselves emotionally is significantly different when compared with how they experienced themselves as children in terms of both valence and intensity (Larson et al, 2002). Several studies have shown that teenage boys and girls can quickly change their mood in response to events in their lives, showing a greater responsiveness to these events than we see in adults. There may also be considerable emotional volatility: such mood changes often are comparatively short-lived (Guyer et al, 2016). Increases in the intensity of emotions and the frequency of such feelings can be particularly apparent in the social world of adolescence.

Adolescence may well also be the period when emotional problems start to become apparent, with increases in reported incidences of depression, eating disorders and suicide (see, e.g., Kessler et al, 2007).

The social world of adolescence

Friendships during our adolescent years are of more importance to us than at any other period in our lives (Blakemore, 2019). Peer influence is also likely to be very strong. At this age, how we are seen and judged by our peers is of vital importance. This need for peer approval can have an impact on decision making and risk taking (Blakemore, 2019).

Risk taking in adolescence

One of the areas that has been of particular interest to those that study the teenage brain has been the observed tendency of adolescents to engage in risky behaviour. This might be in the form, for example, of drug taking, excessive use of alcohol or experimental sex. A 2017 by Laurence Steinberg and colleagues (2018) of 5,404 individuals aged between ten and 30 from 11 countries around the world found that risk taking, while it may differ in form, is common in adolescents around the world.

There is a growing body of evidence to support what is known as a **dual systems approach** (Steinberg, 2010). In simple terms this suggests that in adolescence there is an imbalance between the motivational areas of the brain which produce desire and impulsive behaviour and those areas which manage and control these feelings (Hwang et al, 2016). While some executive control is in place by the time we reach adolescence, what develops during this period are the connections to other parts of the brain. In a battle between reward-driven behaviour (I want that and I want it now) and reason (maybe it would be better to wait and think this through), it is more likely that the impulsive behaviour will win!

Figure 5.5: Friendships in adolescence are more important than at any other time in our lives

Source: Shutterstock, photo ID 2221389777

Blakemore describes this as a 'developmental mismatch' (2018, p 135): the parts of the brain that are associated with reward and motivation mature earlier than the parts that allow us to control this behaviour. The limbic system, the part of the brain most associated with emotions and behaviour, is mature before the teenage years begin. In contrast, the frontal cortex, which is associated with executive control, does not fully connect up with other areas of the brain until later. Some evidence for this mismatch comes from the study by Mills and colleagues (2014) which shows that the amygdala reaches an adult volume by mid- to late adolescence whereas the frontal areas of the brain are still developing and continue to do so until we are in our late 20s.

We should not run away with the idea that the teenage years are all about taking risks and that there is no capacity for reason. Beatriz Luna (2017) suggests that there is this capacity but that it can, at times, be overridden by the desire for more immediate reward. We also need to recognise the importance of individual differences. Not all teenagers are risk takers. Several of the teenagers in the Mills study showed no mismatch between the maturity of the important subcortical brain regions and that of the prefrontal cortex.

Changes to the brain during adolescence

Adolescence is seen as a sensitive period for brain development. A sensitive period is when the capacity of the brain to make structural and functional changes in response to the environment is highly experience-expectant as opposed to being experience-dependent (Fuhrmann et al, 2015).

Studies have shown that elevated levels of gonadal hormones (including estradiol and progesterone from the ovaries, and testosterone from the testes) play an important role in brain development during adolescence (Schulz and Sisk, 2016). The effect of this hormonal surge depends on environmental factors, particularly peer influence. To put it simply, boys who have friends who behave badly are likely to behave in the same way themselves, whereas boys who have friends who are well behaved are more likely to react to hormonal changes by engaging in activities leading to increased social status and leadership. The pattern for girls is slightly different. A 2015 meta-analysis of animal studies (Schulz and Sisk, 2016) found a probable link between increased estradiol levels and an increase in depression and mood variation.

Research on the emotional life of the adolescent brain has focused on a small range of areas. These include areas of the prefrontal cortex (PFC), the amygdala, striatum, insula and anterior cingulate cortex (ACC). Changes such as increased emotionality and a tendency towards risk taking have been linked to the effect of gonadal hormones on neural activity in these brain regions. In a review of our current knowledge about the neurobiology of adolescence, Guyer and colleagues (2016) cite evidence to suggest that as well as changes in particular areas there are also significant changes in the connectivity between regions, particularly between subcortical areas and the prefrontal cortex.

Another important change in the adolescent brain is that the amount of grey matter (that is, neurons that are not sheathed in myelin) decreases considerably. Blakemore (2019) speculates that this may be due to synaptic pruning but, given that some cortical areas decrease in volume by up to 17%, this, she asserts, is not a sufficient explanation. Currently the resolution of the MRI process is not detailed enough to explain and understand this decrease in grey matter during the teenage years. There is some evidence that this cortical thinning is more likely to be genetically controlled rather than a response to environmental factors in the life of the teenager (Van Soelen et al, 2012).

Face processing in adolescence

Studies of our ability to process faces often sees it as combining two separate skills: a perceptual task – can we discriminate between different features and configurations of faces; and a memory task – can we learn and remember the faces we see? There is a modest consensus that in order to recognise a face we need to put it together. The **composite face illusion** experiment matches an identical top half of a face with a series of different bottom halves. Those who observe these pictures when they are aligned are slower and make more mistakes in a matching task than when viewing them unaligned (Rossion, 2013).

There are several studies that use the composite face illusion to show that this aspect of face processing gradually improves during childhood and that by adolescence it is at adult levels of competency (McKone et al, 2012). However, other aspects of face processing are slower to mature. There is some evidence (e.g., Carey et al, 1980) to show that face processing improves during childhood but then becomes worse at the beginning of adolescence before improving again as we move into later adolescence/adulthood. Other studies show a more linear improvement from childhood to adulthood (Song et al, 2015).

A 2016 study from the Institute of Cognitive Neuroscience, UCL, looked at face and memory perception in 661 participants (397 female; 264 male) that were divided into four age groups: younger adolescents, mid-adolescents, older adolescents and adults. The study used two tests: the Cambridge Face Perception test and the Face Same–Different test.

In the Cambridge test participants are presented with three views of the same face (front, left side, right side) and are then asked to pick out the face from a line-up of three faces. You can try out the test here: http://www.bbk.ac.uk/psychology/psychologyexperiments/experiments/facememorytest/.

The Face Same–Different test measures the participants' ability to recognise changes in gaze, identity or expression between different faces. Faces are said to be the same only if all three of the variables have not changed.

This study showed that our ability to process information from faces and to remember that information sufficiently to make comparisons with other faces is developed over time. The younger adolescents and the mid-adolescents were worse at the tasks than the older adolescents and the adults.

Impact of social media on the adolescent brain

An issue that seems to be the subject of recurring periods of moral panic (Cohen, 2002) revolves around whether increased use of the Internet in its numerous forms is having a damaging effect on the brains of children and teenagers. We are told, for example, that:

- 'Excessive internet use may cause parts of teenagers' brains to waste away', *Mail Online* (Harris, 2011);
- 'Internet addiction disrupts nerve wiring in teenagers' brain' (*Daily Mirror*, 2012);
- 'Teenagers who use their phones excessively are more likely to suffer from depression and anxiety', *Mail Online* (Pinkstone, 2017);
- 'Radiation from SMARTPHONES could cause memory loss in teenagers', *The Sun* (Dirnhuber, 2018).

What is the scientific evidence to affirm or dispute such claims?

To deal with the mental health claims first, an eight-year longitudinal study of 500 adolescents aged from eight to 13 taken from the Flourishing Families

Project found that 'there is no evidence that time spent using social media might influence an individual's mental health' (Coyne et al, 2020, p 8). Not all studies are quite this certain. An American review of the literature finds that there is still a lack of 'coherent empirical evidence' and that 'research showing causal effects of general digital technology use on well-being is scarce' (Dienlin and Johannes, 2020, p 139). Despite these caveats it still concludes that 'the current evidence suggests that typical digital technology use will not harm a typical adolescent' (p 139).

The second claim is that using social media causes neurological damage, either because addiction damages the wiring of the brain or because excessive use of mobile phones leads to damage by means of radiation. One of the worries is that radio frequency signals may damage the cells in our body, particularly those in our brains. A review of 300 previous human and animal studies published between 1990 and 2015 (Halgamuge et al, 2020) found that 45.3% of the studies showed potential effects whereas 54.7% did not. However, the cells that were significantly affected were those that were immature such as human spermatozoa and epithelial cells (these are found on the surface of the body such as in skin, blood vessels and the urinary tract). Most mature cells such as glial cells in the brain are only affected at a statistically insignificant level.

The evidence to support claims that the use of the Internet causes harm to adolescent brains seems slim to non-existent. The evidence that phone use leads to damage to the brain by radiation is similarly extremely slender.

The idea that adolescent behaviour might be affected by social media has somewhat more credibility. The dual systems approach, where there is an imbalance between the emotional processing systems and the cognitive control mechanisms, means that teenagers can be very vulnerable to peer influence. Several studies have shown that adolescents are more likely to like photographs on social media of both risky and neutral behaviours if the photos have had many other likes on social media platforms such as Instagram. In a study by Sherman and colleagues (2016) a group of 34 adolescents in the 13–18 age range exhibited such behaviour. fMRI scans showed greater activity in brain activity when viewing the photographs with more likes, particularly in areas associated with social cognition and social memory such as the precuneus, medial prefrontal cortex and hippocampus.

Conclusion

This chapter has explored many contentious issues. Emotional development in all its different guises is still unresearched when compared with areas such as cognitive development and visual development. The debate around whether we are born with a discrete emotional toolkit or whether we build one for ourselves from cruder elements remains unresolved. While neuroscience will eventually settle the argument, the capacity of neuroimaging to identify the development of emotions is still some way off. In other areas there is more certainty. Face processing, for example, is considerably less contentious, although there is still much to learn. Likewise, the work of Blakemore and colleagues has massively improved our knowledge of adolescent emotional and social development. One area where neuroscience can sometimes provide answers is in response to the moral panics around issues such as mobile phones and social media. It is hugely unlikely that radiation from phones damages brain development. New communication technology also seems unlikely to damage brain development. Peer influence during adolescence seems a very tangible issue – teenagers are very sensitive to the opinions of their peers. The mismatch between impulse and reasoning that has often seemed a feature of the adolescent years is supported by brain research that shows frontal executive control parts of the brain lag behind those areas that seek reward, risk and pleasure.

Summary

- The issue of which emotions develop and when they do so remains contentious. The majority view is that we are born with some emotional capacity and that this ability arises from specific regions in the brain.

- Secondary emotions, often referred to as self-conscious emotions, develop later in life.

- Babies develop social awareness very early, although the capacity to mentalise does not develop until a little later. The frontal and temporal areas of the cortex are thought to be important for social interaction.

- An area called the fusiform face area is thought to be important in facial recognition. There is some evidence that the capacity to recognise faces exists from birth. This capacity seems to develop during childhood and there is some evidence that it might briefly deteriorate in mid-adolescence.

- Adolescents are more likely to engage in risky behaviour, possibly as a result of hormonal changes to areas of the PFC and ACC.

- There is almost no evidence to support the view that social media damages the brains of adolescents. However, the idea that the behaviour of teenagers might be affected by their use of social media has more credibility.

Test your knowledge
1. What is the difference between primary and secondary emotions?
2. According to Carroll Izard, what are the five characteristics of basic emotions?
3. According to Campos and Barrett, what is the function of anger?

4. What are Alan Sroufe's three innate emotions?
5. According to constructionist theorists, what's the difference between core effect and conceptualisation?
6. How does smiling develop?
7. What's the name of the area of the brain responsible for face recognition?
8. What does the mentalising network do?
9. What's the supposed difference between the way boys and girls are affected by elevated levels of gonadal hormones?
10. How does social media affect the teenage brain?

Discussion questions
1. Does it matter whether we are born with a set of basic emotions or we develop them from more primitive building blocks?
2. Should we ban children and teenagers from using social media?
3. Are all adolescents risk takers simply because their brains have not developed sufficiently?

Our answers
1. Yes, it does. One of the key themes in the book has been that the brain is a very adaptable organ. If basic emotions are hardwired, then this could mean that this fundamental aspect of who we are is not fully under our control. If, for example, fear is a basic emotion that we are born with, then we might expect that we will all experience fear in the same way. Specifically, it would suggest that all babies feel fear in the same way. What about the relationship between fear and the complex emotional responses that are built up from this emotion such as wariness, anxiety and even phobias? If fear is pre-programmed, does it mean that we have less control over how these more complicated responses develop? The idea of basic emotions might mean that we have an automated set of responses that aid survival, but it might also mean that we are less able to control developmental processes.
2. This is a huge issue. At the time of writing, China has done just this with online gamers under the age of 18, restricting their access to just one hour per week. As we said earlier in the chapter, the research on the adverse effects of social media on brain development is highly unsubstantiated. In a post-COVID world there is growing research evidence that social media has helped all age groups feel less isolated and more socially connected. Jessica Hamilton and colleagues (2020), for example, provide guidance for parents and educators to help teens to manage social media during a pandemic. For further discussion we suggest a recent article by Hamilton and colleagues (2020).
3. No. This would be a gross misinterpretation of the research. The dual systems model suggests an imbalance between executive control and impulse which may make some teenagers more likely to take risks. In the Mills and colleagues (2014) study the authors are careful to avoid suggesting a link between

individual brain development and risk taking. Another aspect of this is that risk taking is often seen as a negative aspect of adolescence, which misses out on the narratives about teenagers who win, for example, international tennis tournaments or gain golds in the Olympic Games.

Further reading

Blakemore, S.-J. (2019) *Inventing Ourselves: The Secret Life of the Teenage Brain*, London: Black Swan.

The Blakemore lab, Available from: https://sites.google.com/site/blakemorelab.

Buss, K.A. et al (2019) 'Theories of emotional development: Where have we been and where are we now?', in K.A. Buss, V. LoBue and P.-E. Koraly (eds) *Handbook of Emotional Development*, Cham: Springer Nature, pp 7–25.

Dahl, R. et al (2017) 'The adolescent brain: A second window of opportunity', Available from: https://www.unicef.org/guatemala/media/381/file/The%20Adolescent%20brain.pdf.

McKone, E. et al (2012) 'A critical review of the development of face recognition: Experience is less important than previously believed', *Cognitive Neuropsychology*, 29(1–2): 174–212.

On our website

You can find lots more material on our website at https://policy.bristoluniversitypress.co.uk/child-development-and-the-brain/companion-website

6

Attachment and trauma

This chapter:

- gives a critical account of attachment theory;
- considers what neuroscience tells us about attachment;
- considers how damaging childhood experiences can affect brain development;
- explores the impact of severe emotional trauma on brain development.

Introduction

We begin this chapter with a critical account of attachment theory and then consider how neuroscientific knowledge is furthering, or in some cases limiting, our understanding of these theories. We briefly explore the relationship between attachment and childhood adversity and consider the question: does one lead to the other? We then explore what we know about the effect of poor and potentially damaging childhood experiences and consider the brain research in this area. We look at the areas of the brain that have been most fully researched: predominantly the amygdala, the hippocampus, the prefrontal cortex and the hypothalamic-pituitary-adrenal (HPA) axis. Lastly, we look at the work that has taken place to investigate the plight of Romanian orphans, victims of the ill-fated Ceauşescu regime of the period 1965–1989.

Attachment theory

The concept of attachment was developed in the 1950s by several researchers, although it is usually credited primarily to the psychologist and psychoanalyst John Bowlby (1969, 1973, 1980). The work of Bowlby, alongside his colleague Mary Ainsworth (Ainsworth et al, 1974, 1978) in the United Kingdom and Harry Harlow in the United States, fundamentally and irrevocably changed our understanding of the relationship between infants and parents. Bowlby presented evidence from studies of both humans and animals to demonstrate his theory, including Konrad Lorenz's (2002) work on imprinting and Harry Harlow's work with Rhesus monkeys (Harlow and Zimmerman, 1959). This latter work showed, for example, that young monkeys separated from their mothers will prefer to cling to a cloth-covered wire doll rather than a bare wire doll, even if it is the bare wire doll that provides them with milk.

Since its inception in the 1950s attachment theory has experienced variable levels of popularity. Its initial acceptance was blunted by many criticisms from feminist writers and others, but as Barbara Tizard (2009) shows, Bowlby changed his position quite radically during his working career. Attachment theory has more recently re-established a position as the dominant explanation for early emotional development, boosted by many populist accounts of affirmations from neuroscience. However, it is not without its detractors (e.g., Bruer, 1999), who point to the lack of empirical evidence to support many of the claims made by attachment theory.

Bowlby defines attachment behaviour as 'seeking and maintaining proximity to another individual' (Bowlby, 1969, p 241). For Bowlby, the attachment that develops between children and parent figures is an innate way of behaving that is firstly about proximity. It is a system he saw as slow to develop and one that varies a great deal during the first year or so. However, by the age of two, when the child has become more mobile, it is activated if the mother leaves the child or if the child experiences anything frightening. After the age of three, according to Bowlby, these behaviours usually become less easily triggered and the child can tolerate being separated from the mother. Bowlby was writing without the knowledge that brain scans have given us regarding the workings of the infant brain. For him the infant 'only slowly becomes aware of his/her mother and only after he/she has become mobile does he/she seek her company' (Bowlby, 1969, p 245).

The 'strange situation'

Mary Ainsworth and colleagues (1978) developed a means of categorising attachment styles in an experiment called the 'strange situation'. This experiment takes about 20 minutes and involves eight episodes involving a child aged 12–18 months, a mother and a stranger. It begins with mother and infant playing in a room and then in a succession of choreographed scenarios the infant is twice left in the sole charge of the stranger and in each case reunited with the mother. These episodes are observed. The behaviour of the infant when left with the stranger and then when reunited with the mother is evaluated.

The experiment attempts to observe differences in the quality of the attachment relationship between the mother and the infant. Mothers who are sensitive to the needs of their children and consistent in how they respond are said to have established a secure attachment with their child. About 60–65% of American infants were observed to have a secure style of attachment. Such infants are only slightly upset when their mother leaves them in the care of a stranger and show affection when the mother returns. This contrasts with infants who show either an insecure avoidant or an insecure resistant style of attachment. Insecure avoidant infants avoid close proximity with the mother and fail to cry or to be overtly upset when she leaves the room. When the mother returns, these young children actively avoid contact with her. About 20% of American children were classified in this way. The remaining 15% were classified as insecure resistant. These infants react strongly to separation. When the mother returns, they seek reunion and comfort, but they may also show anger or passivity. They do not settle easily and tend to cry in a way that is inconsolable. Later work by Main and Solomon (1990) showed a fourth classification which they called insecure-disorganised. These children behave unusually in the 'strange situation'. They may, for example, freeze completely or start rocking and may stay in this confused state even when the mother returns.

Attachment styles

Mary Ainsworth and colleagues (1978), by means of her 'strange situation', identified several attachment styles which are essentially broad categories of behaviour.

Secure attachment. In this style the infant can treat the mother as a safe base, sometimes called a 'safe haven', from where the infant can explore the world. In the experiment the baby will explore the room and from time to time check that the mother is still present. When the mother leaves the room, the infant becomes distressed but is easily comforted when the mother returns.

Insecure/resistant attachment. In this style the infant is more clingy and reluctant to leave the mother. Consequently, play and exploration are much restricted. The infant is very upset when the mother leaves the room and more difficult to comfort when the mother returns.

Insecure/avoidant attachment. The infant is observably less connected to the mother and will appear aloof, even turning away when the mother tries to make contact. The child does not explore as much as the secure infant, nor do they react as much to either the mother's absence or her return.

A fourth category of attachment has been added by Ainsworth's colleague Main (Main and Solomon, 1990).

Disorganised/disorientated attachment. As the name suggests, infants in this category behave in a way that is often confusing and contradictory. They may seek comfort from the mother but then not seem to want it. They may appear calm for a while but then either freeze or become disorientated.

Criticisms of attachment theory

What we learn from studies of the 'strange situation' in other countries is that ideas about parenting are not seamlessly transferable across cultures. A study (Grossman et al, 1985) of maternal behaviour in Germany concluded that the 'strange situation' did not accurately measure attachment behaviours in other cultures, finding that German mothers encourage more independence than American mothers. John Bruer (1999) describes studies in both northern Germany and Japan where the percentages of secure versus insecure infants are very different from those in the United States. Gillies and colleagues (2017) report on studies in Indonesia, Israeli kibbutzim and Chile where again the patterns of attachment are very different.

BOX: The myth of the first three years

The idea that infants go through a period of rapid synapse formation that ends at around three years of age has become accepted by many who study early childhood (e.g. Johnson and de Haan, 2010). It is seen as a 'sensitive period', meaning that it can be easily damaged by poor parenting and likewise can be enhanced by what are often termed 'enriched environments'.

John Bruer (1999) is a strong critic of this mainstream view. He argues that much of the rapid synaptic growth we see in infants is driven by genetics rather than environment. Moreover, the skills and learning that we as humans prize so dearly continue to have the potential to expand long after the initial period of rapid synaptogenesis. Bruer points out that there is no simple relationship between synaptic growth and human development. He argues that even for those areas of development for which there may be a window of opportunity such as vision and language, the view that this is a one-off, use it or lose it chance is far too simple. Language development, for example, continues well beyond the early years, and even vision develops in a complex way, with different critical times for visual acuity, stereopsis and binocular vision. The idea that cultural and social skills also have critical periods for development is a step too far and one which lacks any reliable evidence. It is, for Bruer, simply a **neuromyth**. A consequence of this is that parents are encouraged to provide enriched stimulation for children from a very young age, with very limited evidence that such environments are needed or are even of much benefit. An enriched environment 'neither initiates early synapse formation nor influences when or at what level synaptic densities peak' (Bruer, 1999, p 99).

Other writers have pointed out that the emphasis on the first three years of brain development is problematic in many other ways. Gillies and colleagues write that accounts such as Sue Gerhardt's *Why Love Matters* present us with an alarming, fragile version of the infant brain: 'One wrong move and attachment becomes disorganised, with potentially terrible consequences ...' (2017, p 53). Not only is this picture of neural development misleading, but it also puts unbearable pressure on parents. A more reassuring message to parents from developmental neuroscience is that babies only need what paediatrician and psychotherapist Winnicott (1964) wisely referred to as 'good enough' parenting: they need love and care and attention, but they do not need, and almost certainly do not benefit from, superhuman dollops of anxious devotion. As Winnicott also says, any attempt to provide everything an infant needs is likely to be damaging rather than helpful.

The extent to which attachment patterns, once established in early childhood, remain fixed throughout life is another area of contention. Early studies (e.g., Sroufe, 1979; Main and Cassidy, 1988) suggested that they remained remarkably stable over time, but later studies (e.g., Vondra et al, 2001) questioned these findings, suggesting that attachment patterns were much more volatile and dependent on a range of factors such as poverty, difficult life events and problems with social support.

Studies of the brain and attachment

The first issue to address here is the quantity of the evidence. Given that attachment theory has established a hegemony over other competing theories, it is surprising to find that there have been very few studies which seek to establish a human neurobiological correlation with attachment styles.

> It has proved difficult to identify biomarkers for attachment styles

We would go as far as to say that it has proved difficult to identify specific biomarkers for different attachment styles. Perlini and colleagues (2019) have found only 11 brain-based studies of attachment, all of them involving adults rather than children. Most of these had a small number of participants, with only recent studies having more than 35. The results were also variable such that it has proved difficult to establish significant overlap. There are also some striking differences between the sexes, with one study, for example, showing that for men with an avoidant attachment style grey matter volume in the right middle occipital gyrus decreases, while for women with an avoidant attachment style the grey matter in this area increases (Zhang et al, 2018).

Recent studies have indicated a correlation between attachment style and the amygdala (Schneider-Hassloff et al, 2015, 2016), while other studies have confirmed the idea that the hippocampus is activated in attachment situations (Quirin et al, 2009; Von Der Heide et al, 2014). Even so, work that attempts to establish a neural correlation to attachment has been sparse; there has been far more work that looks at the effect of neglect, abuse and trauma in childhood on brain development.

BOX: Allan Schore and the neurobiology of attachment

American clinical psychologist Allan Schore has developed an interdisciplinary model of emotional development and regulation which takes account of findings in fields such as developmental psychology, neurobiology, evolutionary biology, neurochemistry, neuroanatomy and psychoendocrinology (see, e.g., Schore, 1994, 2003a). His work has had, and continues to have, a strong influence on how several fields, particularly counselling and psychotherapy, view the emotional development of the brain.

Schore presents evidence that emotions originate from subcortical areas of the brain, particularly the amygdala, whereas control of these emotions occurs within the cortex, particularly within the **orbitofrontal cortex**. His hypothesis is that while large parts of the subcortical brain are already connected when the baby is born, the higher parts of the brain develop after birth and so are highly dependent on what is happening in the baby's immediate environment. His central thesis is that what happens in the relationship between the young infant and the primary caregiver has a direct influence on the way in which the brain develops and that this in turn has long-term effects on the social and emotional development of the child. He has argued extensively and consistently (e.g., Schore, 1994, 2003a, 2012) that a healthy and positive relationship between mother and child is central to good emotional development. Like Bowlby, he argues that the kind of attachment relationship we have with our primary carer will determine the ways in which we are able to regulate how we feel and how we express those feelings. Schore's work is an attempt to provide neuroscientific evidence to support and develop psychological theories of attachment.

Schore considers that the development of the frontal cortex is experience-dependent and that the pattern of the relationship between mother and infant is critical in determining how this structure will mature and develop. Early events will have a huge significance for emotional development, particularly the relationship with the mother, which 'acts as a template, as it permanently moulds the individual's capacities to enter into all later emotional relationships' (Schore, 1994, p 3).

Schore argues that the right hemisphere of the brain develops earlier than the left hemisphere. He also presents evidence that this right hemisphere mediates many emotional functions within the infant's brain (Schore, 2000). He identifies connections between the right amygdala and the right orbitofrontal cortex. He maintains that as the infant begins to develop, the orbitofrontal cortex develops connections with both the limbic regions in the subcortex and other parts of the brain that deal with vision, sound, smell and bodily sensations. The orbitofrontal cortex in a baby who has a good and functional attachment relationship with their primary carer will slowly begin to develop the capacity to control and regulate emotions.

In Schore's model there is a great deal of non-verbal communication between mother and infant in early infancy. This is of central importance in both the development of emotions and the regulation of affect. In early infancy the mother and baby who are working well together will often spend a lot of time gazing into each other's eyes. This is often referred to as mutually sustained gaze and it has an important role to play in development. There is a lot of communication which happens in these often very tender moments. The infant is able to tell the mother when they are content and happy, and the mother is able to show the baby that she too is in a state of contentment. There is an intense communication loop which takes place between the mother and infant in which each tells the other that they are enjoying this close, mutually enhancing relationship.

In Schore's work the emotional synchrony between the attentive mother and the young infant is of particular importance during the first two years of life. Here there are moments of intense connection between mother and baby. These are followed by periods of mutual disengagement to allow the infant to recover and not be overwhelmed by the intensity of the feelings that are aroused. In these periods of being together there is what can be seen as an emotional dance in which there are 'mutually attuned synchronised interactions' (Schore, 2003b, p 30). The emotional intensity of this engagement is followed by disengagement when the mother intuitively knows that it is time to step back and allow the infant space to enjoy her presence in a less intensive manner.

Critical analysis

This area of the neurobiology of attachment remains controversial. Despite the acceptance of these ideas in many counselling and psychotherapy texts (e.g., Howard, 2017; Wilson, 2017), many of Schore's claims are not accepted by those working in cognitive neuroscience. The idea that there is a hemispherical division and that the right brain is dominant in the processing of emotion is seen by many as a neuromyth (e.g., Goswami, 2006; Lindell and Kidd, 2011; Pasquinelli, 2012; Tokuhama-Espinosa, 2018). The idea that the right brain develops first in infancy is also contentious and questions need to be asked about the sufficiency of neuroimaging studies which support this premise.

Schore's account gives an idealised version of what needs to happen between mother and child for emotional self-regulation to develop. Many children do not enjoy extended periods of blissful, mutual loving as part of their interaction with their carers. The way in which this lack of responsive and sensitive care affects brain development is still not understood. Even though Schore presents evidence from a broad range of studies to support his ideas, we need to remember that emotional regulation and development is still a much under-researched area and many of these ideas still need much more extensive investigation.

The development of the orbitofrontal cortex, for example, is not understood, and there is much that we yet need to learn about the subcortical brain and the way in which it communicates with the cerebral cortex. Attachment theory is, in essence, an empiricist theory, evidenced largely by observation. It sees the role of the caregiver, often the mother, as paramount. As such the approach does not take much account of biological predispositions and largely ignores the complex interplay between genetic encoding and the environment.

Abuse and neglect in childhood

Introduction

While there may be few direct studies of attachment and the impact of less functional attachment styles on brain development, there have been many studies that consider the impact of abuse and neglect. Before considering these studies and what they tell us about brain development, we are going to look at the extent of the problem and consider the different ways in which abuse is described in the literature.

Extent of abuse and neglect

> The number of children being abused across the world is both staggering and saddening

The number of children being abused across the world is both staggering and deeply saddening. A recent systematic review found that over a billion children worldwide experienced some sort of violence against them in the preceding year; that is, over half of all children in the world have been subject to some form of violence (Hillis et al, 2016). The NSPCC (2019) in the United Kingdom points out that we simply do not know how many children are being abused as it often goes unrecorded and unreported. With these limitations noted, the Office for National Statistics conducted a survey of adults (aged 16–59) in 2015–2016 asking whether they had experienced abuse as a child. Of these, 9% had experienced psychological abuse, 7% physical abuse, 7% sexual assault and 8% had witnessed domestic violence or abuse in the home (Flatley, 2016). In the United States, the Children's Bureau of the US Department of Health and Human Services reported that in 2017 an estimated 1,720 children died from abuse and neglect (Administration for Children and Families, 2019). It also estimated that in the United States in 2017 there were 674,000 victims of child abuse and neglect. Nationally the victim rate is 9.1 per 1,000 children. If the NSPCC warning is considered, these figures are likely to be underestimates.

prison

neglect alcohol

sexual abuse

violence

mental health

physical abuse

divorce drug

What we mean by abuse

Abuse is a very broad term that includes physical, emotional, sexual and verbal abuse. There are also different ways in which abuse is understood and categorised. We can look, for example, at what happened to the child, when it happened, how often it occurred or who perpetuated the abuse. We also need to think about the effects of this abuse and how it is understood. Ways of explaining and classifying the effects of abuse can be very different, as we will show.

Post-traumatic stress disorder

Post-traumatic stress disorder (PTSD) is a defined disorder categorised in the *Diagnostic and Statistical Manual of Mental Disorders* (DSM V) (American Psychiatric Association, 2013). This is the controversial classification of mental disorders used in the medical world that for some has an almost biblical status, while for others it represents everything that is wrong with the medical model of mental 'illness' (e.g., Johnstone and Boyle, 2018; Watson, 2019). DSM V includes specific criteria for diagnosing PTSD in children aged under six and acknowledges that the loss of a parent can be experienced as traumatic for young children as well as for adolescents. The criteria for PTSD in children and adolescents include such things as irritability, angry outbursts and reckless behaviour. The symptoms of PTSD include reliving the event, often through nightmares and flashbacks, feeling isolated, feeling irritable and having difficulty sleeping. Alongside PTSD we also find the term PTSS, meaning post-traumatic stress symptoms, to denote the occurrence of the symptoms of PTSD which, for whatever reason, have not been formally diagnosed as PTSD.

There is also complex PTSD, which is not yet included in the DSM. This is a diagnosis for children and adults who have repeatedly experienced trauma. It includes children who have been repeatedly abused over a long period of time, particularly by a parent. The symptoms of complex PTSD include difficulty in controlling emotions, frequent feelings of shame, poor concentration as well as often physical symptoms including headaches, chest pains and stomach aches (NHS, 2017b).

Adverse childhood experiences

Another way of understanding and analysing childhood abuse has been formulated through a long-term study carried out jointly between Kaiser Permanente and the CDC (for more details see CDC, 2019c). The study recruited over 17,000 volunteers in southern California between 1995 and 1997. The study divides adverse childhood experiences (ACEs) into three categories: abuse, neglect and household challenges. These are then further subdivided. Abuse is divided into emotional, physical and sexual. Neglect has two categories: emotional neglect and physical neglect. Household challenges include the mother being treated violently, someone in the house drinking excessively or taking drugs, someone being mentally ill or imprisoned, and divorce or separation.

Problems with the ACE model

The ACE model has been criticised on two broad fronts. The first is methodological and the second is in terms of application. Methodologically it has been criticised (Walsh et al, 2019) for ignoring socio-economic positioning. It does not take

> ACEs do not account for social and structural problems but tend to blame individuals and families

account of poverty, the poor social structure that people are often forced to live within or the political systems that are responsible for such poverty. This means that individual families often get the blame for situations that they are powerless to change. It also means that attempts to improve the situation are directed at individuals when, in fact, structural, societal changes are needed to ameliorate the problems.

The second issue focuses on how ACE studies are used on the Internet. The original questions asked in the ACE study have been popularised in several Internet-based 'quizzes' which supposedly produce an ACE score. They ask, for example, whether as a child you were sworn at or humiliated; whether you were physically hurt; whether your parents were separated or divorced. However, we need to be careful how we use and interpret ACE scores. They take little account of the intensity and frequency of adversity, nor do they account for gender differences or the age at which the adversity occurs. The original study aimed to reveal a statistical pattern across populations but was not designed to be used as a diagnostic tool at the level of the individual. Such tools are a distorting attempt to measure complex patterns of events in the lives of individuals, and the scores obtained from such endeavours are of little value in relation to the original studies.

Links between poverty and abuse

It is surprising to report that there are no substantive international studies of the relationship between poverty and abuse. Leroy Pelton produced an updated report in 2015 focusing on the United States. His original 1994 report concluded that there is 'overwhelming evidence that poverty and low income are strongly related to child abuse and neglect' (Pelton, 2015, p 31).

In the United Kingdom the case for an association has been put forward compellingly by Paul Bywaters and his team for the Joseph Rowntree Foundation (Bywaters et al, 2016). This report considered the extent to which poverty increases the likelihood of child abuse and neglect (CAN) and whether CAN itself is predictive of poverty. The report noted that over the previous 25 years, between one in four and one in three families were living in poverty – that is, had a household income less than 60% of the median – in the United Kingdom. However, successive UK governments have failed to collect data on the links between such poverty and CAN. This situation remains the same at the time writing, with no signs that such a study will be undertaken despite rising inequalities, inflation and the ever-growing cost of gas and oil. The report states:

> There is a strong association between families' socio-economic circumstances and the chances that their children will experience CAN. Evidence of this association is found repeatedly across developed countries, types of abuse, definitions, measures and research

approaches, and in different child protection systems. This conclusion can be drawn despite the major limitations in the evidence from the UK. (Bywaters et al, 2016, p 3)

The lack of detailed and systematic research seems even more wilfully negligent given the growing understanding we have of how abuse and neglect impact upon brain development.

The neuroscience of abuse and neglect

Many claims have been made about the contribution that brain imaging studies can make to the study of abuse and neglect.

Amygdala

The amygdala is understood to play a central role in the evaluation of threat and the processing of fearful emotions. Animal studies have shown that adverse experiences such as extended maternal separation have a negative effect on the development of several brain regions including the amygdala (Lupien et al, 2009). Until recently there was little human evidence of changes to the amygdala following adverse experiences in childhood (Woon and Hedges, 2008). In the last 20 years, however, there have been several studies of the human amygdala and the way it reacts to abuse.

Recent human studies have provided some evidence that there is a neurobiological effect, although the findings can at best be described as preliminary and show very mixed results.

One study (Tottenham et al, 2010) of 38 previously institutionalised (PI) children with a mean age of 8.3 years showed evidence of amygdala enlargement when compared with a control group. This group also showed a reduced capacity for emotional regulation and high levels of anxiety. The study found that the longer the period spent in institutions, the higher the amygdala volume. In contrast, a 2019 study (Van Tieghem et al, 2018) showed that by the time PI children reach adolescence they have a reduced amygdala volume when compared with children who have not been institutionalised. They comment, however, that studies of younger PI children show increased amygdala size. A meta-analysis from 2017 (Calem et al, 2017) shows the same kind of trend. It found no evidence of increased amygdala size in PI adults. A 2017 meta-analysis of 20 studies involving 1,733 participants (Hein and Monk, 2017) showed that childhood maltreatment produced increased bilateral (that is, involving both left and right amygdala) activation in response to the presentation of emotional faces.

Analysis

The term PI presents some problems as a category. The children in such studies have often been institutionalised in several different countries. Institutions vary considerably across the world and the experiences of children in such institutions also vary enormously. In the study by Tottenham and colleagues (2010), for example, eight of the children were PI in Eastern Europe and 30 in Asia, but exactly where and in what conditions is not stated. This lack of definition as to what PI really means and the experiences that such children might have had in these institutions means it is impossible to make meaningful comparisons and also impossible to make links between such experiences and amygdala volume.

There is another problem in measuring the effect of early childhood abuse and neglect on the brains of older adolescents and adults. By the time such children reach adolescence they would have had many other and very varied experiences and it is very difficult to take all these into account when analysing the data. It might be that later positive experience compensates for early adversity. There have been quite a few studies that have shown that social support for maltreated children decreases their risk of developing depression in later life (Kaufman, 1991), decreases their risk of later developing PTSD (Fletcher et al, 2017) and can modify the reactions of brain circuits involved (Wymbs et al, 2020).

Hippocampus

The hippocampi are in the medial temporal region of the brain and are part of the limbic system. They play a key role in learning in terms of both processing new memories and retrieving existing ones.

Animal research (Arbel et al, 1994) has shown that the stress hormone corticosterone, if it is secreted at high levels in response to environmental changes such as stress, can damage cells in the hippocampus. The research is not directly transferable to humans as a different, if related, stress hormone, cortisol, is the main hormonal response to stress in humans.

The hippocampus is thought to be particularly susceptible to abusive experience. It contains large numbers of **glucocorticoid receptors** and so is vulnerable to excessive levels of these hormones including the most important human glucocorticoid, cortisol.

Studies of the relationship between stressful experiences and hippocampal reductions in human children, adolescents and adults have been very mixed. McCrory and colleagues (2011) report that ten structural MRI studies into children and adolescents have failed to detect a pattern of reduced hippocampal volume in those who have experienced PTSD. In contrast, McCrory and colleagues also show that almost all studies of adults who were maltreated as children have reported a reduced hippocampal volume. More recent studies seem to reinforce these findings. A 2017 meta-analysis (Nelson and Tumpap, 2017) of 37 studies found that PTSD led to a reduced volume in both hippocampi in adults. A 2020 (Joshi et al, 2020) study showed that reduced hippocampus activity in adults with PTSD had a very negative effect on memory recall as well as other functions. There are also quite a few studies that show a difference between genders, with males showing a greater reduction in hippocampal volume than females.

Two studies by Victor Carrion and his team showed different results from those of the McCrory studies (Carrion et al, 2009; Carrion and Wong, 2012). The first was a study of six boys and nine girls aged eight to 14 years who had experienced trauma and who had a severity score of equal to or greater than 12 on the PTSD Reaction Index.[1] This was a longitudinal study. The group was tested to establish a baseline and then tested again 12 to 18 months later. The researchers found that in children with a history of trauma both the severity of the PTSD and the levels of cortisol allowed them to predict reductions in hippocampal volume.

The second study (Carrion et al, 2009) looked at 16 young people aged 10–17 of mixed ethnicity who had a history of PTSS and matched them against 11 youths with no history of trauma. All the youths undertook a memory retrieval task while undergoing fMRI scanning. In the part of the test where they were asked to remember a set of words with which they had previously been presented, the 16 PTSS test subjects showed a reduced activation of the right hippocampus when compared with the control group.

Analysis

We have included Carrion's work here as it seems to buck the trend found in other research. Pretty much all the studies of the effects of trauma on the hippocampus show a reduced volume in adults who have experienced childhood trauma but no appreciable effect during childhood and adolescence. This is much the same as we found in studies of the effect of trauma on the amygdala.

McCrory et al (2011) report two possible explanations for this difference between adults and children. The neurotoxicity hypothesis (see Sapolsky et al, 1990) suggests that years of abuse and prolonged exposure to high levels of cortisone cause dendrite damage and cell death in the hippocampus, while the vulnerability hypothesis (see Gilbertson et al, 2002) argues that the smaller hippocampi of those who experience PTSD is the predisposing factor. In other words, the latter claims that it is because these children had smaller hippocampi in the first place that they were vulnerable to a traumatic response to stress.

> Almost all studies of adults who were abused as children show a reduced hippocampus

Carrion's studies are of small groups of children and we need to see if these results can be replicated. The problem remains that measuring an effect in adulthood might show a correlation between child abuse and brain volume in the hippocampus, but it does not establish causality. This is particularly problematic here as it is impossible to establish all the events that might have occurred in an individual's life between the traumatic experiences in childhood and their life as an adult.

The prefrontal cortex

The prefrontal cortex (PFC) plays an important role in executive function, that is, managing, controlling and sometimes inhibiting responses from other parts of the brain. It is also significant in managing working memory and our ability to engage in abstract thought. There have been many psychological studies that demonstrate that childhood trauma affects these processes. Some of these studies have looked specifically at children (e.g., DePrince et al, 2009; Cowell et al, 2015) while others have considered the effect of abuse on adult populations (e.g., Gould et al, 2012).

> Traumatised children often have problems with both attention and intrusive thoughts

Children who have experienced trauma often have difficulties in maintaining their attention and might suffer from intrusive thoughts, flashbacks and nightmares. Such behaviours are understood to rely on pathways in the PFC. Changes to brain structure in the frontal areas were also found in an inhibition–response test. A study by Carrion and Wong (2012) involved nine girls and seven boys with a mean age of 13.7 years, all of whom had a history of early life trauma. They were matched against 14 'healthy' children. In the test the children were presented with a succession of letters and were asked to press a button in response to every letter except for the letter X. The task requires several different types of thinking including decision making, response inhibition and response monitoring. An fMRI scan was used to study the brain activity of the children as they carried out the task. Both groups of children performed much the same in the tests. However, the brain scan showed clear differences in how they used their brains. The healthy children used their middle frontal gyrus much more than the traumatised children. This part of the brain is usually used in response-inhibition tasks. They also found that the abused children showed greater activity in the medial frontal and anterior cingulate gyri during the task. Abused children were using different parts of their brain to achieve the same result in a test that measured their ability to stop themselves pressing a button when presented with a rogue letter. In other words, the study indicated that childhood trauma affects brain activity. Other studies have also shown that similar disruptions to brain functioning persist into adulthood (Semple et al, 2000).

Traumatised children are also often found to have both smaller brain volumes and frontal areas which show less symmetry than those of children without trauma. The PFC is a highly connected part of the human brain. It is known to be essential for many higher-level functions. The fact that childhood trauma changes how it functions is not surprising, given the evidence from psychological studies that such trauma often affects both behaviour and thinking in adolescents and adults.

BOX: The Perry image of childhood neglect

In 2002 the short-lived publication *Mind and Brain* published an article by Bruce Perry entitled 'Childhood experience and the expression of genetic potential: What childhood neglect tells us about nature and nurture'.[2] It included the image in Figure 6.1.

It has since become an almost iconic image, appearing on the front of UK Government reports (Allen, 2011a, 2011b), in a range of UK newspapers (e.g., Palmer, 2017; Downey, 2018) and in a mass of other publications and websites far too numerous to mention. A Google Image search in June 2020 produced an astonishing 3,110,000,000 reported hits!

It looks compelling. On the left is the CT scan of a 'normal child' while on the right is an image showing a child 'suffering from severe sensory-deprivation neglect' (Perry, 2002, p 93). Yet when we start to critique the image in terms of where it comes from and what it shows, then it begins to unravel.

There have been several attempts to find more information about the children involved in the study, particularly the child with the shrivelled brain. There have also been many questions asked about the image and what it means.

The 2002 Perry paper describes 122 children who had been referred to his child trauma academy in Houston. Perry says that the histories of the children were taken from a number of sources including child protection workers, the family and police, but he does not give us any of that background information. We know nothing about age, gender, length of time spent in abusive environments, specifics of the sort of abuse they may have encountered, or whether there was also physical neglect or other health issues. In fact, we know almost nothing about the children except that Perry himself divides them into four groups: global neglect, global neglect with prenatal drug exposure, chaotic neglect and chaotic neglect with prenatal drug exposure. Global neglect is only vaguely defined as 'when a history of relative sensory deprivation in more than one domain was obtained (e.g., minimal exposure to language, touch and social interactions)' (2002, p 92). This is contrasted with chaotic neglect, which Perry sees as more common and based on a history that is 'consistent with physical, emotional, social or cognitive neglect' (2002, p 92).

Forty-three of the children had MRI or CT scans, not specifically for Perry's study but 'as part of a medical or neurological evaluation' (Perry and Pollard, 1997, p 2). Of those who were scanned, 11 of the children classified as having global neglect showed abnormal brain scans, and Perry notes that '[t]he majority of the readings were "enlarged ventricles" or "cortical atrophy"' (Perry and Pollard, 1997, p 2). One of the primary differences that

Figure 6.1: The Perry image of childhood neglect

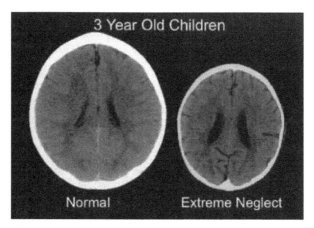

Source: Perry (2002)

Perry identifies is **frontal-occipital circumference**, a measure of head size. As the image suggests, the head size of these children is significantly smaller than that of the 'normal' children. Head size is a very crude measure and tells us nothing about the brain in terms of structure, neural density, neural connections or the areas of the brain that in other studies are reactive to trauma.

Hilary Rose and Steven Rose wrote to Perry to obtain more information about the study and the images. His reply is not particularly helpful. He told them that the initial observations had not been published. Significantly, though, he did admit that the only conclusion to be drawn from the study was that 'severe neglect impacts brain development' (quoted in Rose and Rose, 2016, p 78). More recently Perry has commented on Twitter that he would prefer that the image not be used. He said, '[t]he image is related to severe, total global neglect which is a much less common situation than "trauma in childhood" ' (Perry, 2019). This does not provide any real clarification.

The questions raised by the image have been identified by a number of authors. Gillies and colleagues, for example, ask:

> What was the level of sensory deprivation and lack of interaction that the child involved was subject to? Was it the effect of malnutrition, massive birth trauma, or a genetic or physiological condition? Given that 'normal' children don't have identical brains, what was the range of measurements involved for the children in the study and why wasn't the 'extreme neglect' image compared with a smaller 'normal' scan? (Gillies et al, 2017, p 10)

These are all important questions, and without the answers to them the image is meaningless. Context is all. The images may appear shocking, but without knowing why, for example, one image is smaller than the other, we can make no sense of them. Of most significance is that no other studies have produced similar images. As we explore elsewhere, most studies of trauma and neglect show few, if any, effects on brain structure during childhood. Yet, of course, we know from many studies that childhood trauma has a massive negative impact on the lives of children and adults across the world.

The hypothalamic–pituitary–adrenocortical (HPA) axis

The hypothalamic–pituitary–adrenocortical (HPA) axis (Figure 6.2) is understood to be one of the mechanisms through which the body controls its response to stress, although it also supports aspects of growth and development (Figure 6.2). It is also responsible for the maintenance of a daily rhythm, often referred to in the literature as a diurnal rhythm.

The stress response

Typically, in difficult situations the HPA system will produce a series of hormonal changes that focus the body's attention on functions that are necessary for survival. In doing so, some other functions having to do with growth and repair are put on hold.

There are three key organs involved in the HPA stress response:

The **hypothalamus** lies in the centre of the brain, just beneath the thalamus, and plays a major role in regulating aspects of the body such as temperature, hunger and thirst.

The **pituitary gland** is quite small, about the size of a pea, and sticks out from the bottom of the hypothalamus. It produces a number of hormones that regulate the internal environment of the body.

The two **adrenal glands** sit just above the kidneys and produce hormones in response to stress.

When the body becomes psychologically stressed, these three organs work together to register and react to this stress. The hypothalamus increases production of corticotropin-releasing hormone (CRH) and arginine vasopressin (AVP). These communicate with the pituitary gland, which in response produces adrenocorticotropic hormone (ACTH) (we can think of hormones as being chemical messengers that travel via our blood to different organs in the body). This hormone in turn stimulates the adrenal glands to produce the stress hormone cortisol, which tells the rest of the body that it needs to focus its energies and deal with the stress. Once the situation causing the stress reaction has stopped, a number of feedback loops in the adrenal glands and several brain regions, including the hypothalamus and the frontal cortex, act to shut down the HPA axis and get the body back to a state of normality.

Figure 6.2: The HPA axis

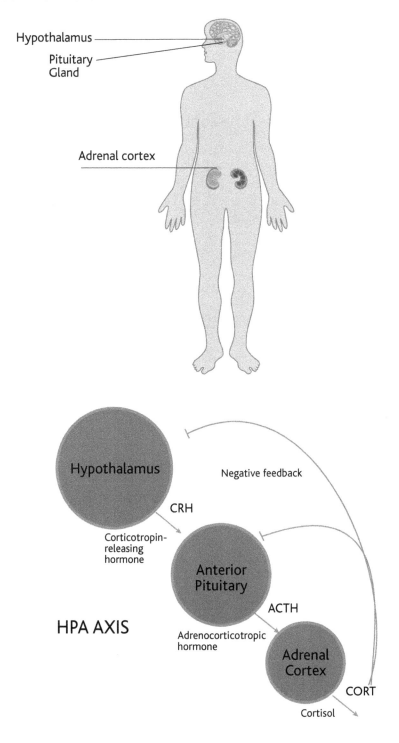

The role of cortisol

From some accounts of the role of cortisol you would imagine it to be a toxic poison that we should avoid at all costs. In fact, healthy adults, and infants after the first few months, have a daily rhythm of cortisol production. Cortisol is a steroid hormone that has many different functions in the body. For example, it stimulates the production of glucose; it helps prevent inflammation; it helps with memory formation; and, most relevant to our discussion here, it reacts to stress and trauma by increasing the level of glucose in the bloodstream and dampening down other functions in the body that might get in the way of fight/flight/freeze reactions.

As well as its role in reacting to stress, the HPA axis also regulates the daily (diurnal) production of cortisol. In fact, the stress response really sits on top of the daily rhythm. In adults, cortisol levels increase before waking. There is then usually a peak after about 30 minutes of being awake. This increased production is often measured as the cortisol awakening response (CAR). After this, cortisol levels fall quite rapidly until mid-morning, which is followed by a slower rate of decline, with levels near zero by midnight. The diurnal rhythm of cortisol is produced in pulses which are controlled by the **suprachiasmic nucleus**, a region in the hypothalamus.

Circadian cortisol levels in children

At birth babies do not have a circadian (that is, a 24-hour) rhythm. There is considerable disagreement about exactly when the circadian rhythm appears, with some studies suggesting it begins to appear after only a few weeks (e.g., Santiago et al, 1996) and others arguing that it may not appear until nine months (e.g., Kiess et al, 1995). It seems there might be considerable differences between children, although these big differences in research findings can also be explained to some extent by different methodologies. What seems more certain is that an adult pattern of cortisol production does not fully establish itself until children are old enough to not need a daytime sleep, which might not be until the age of four to five.

Cortisol and stress

Cortisol is often described as a stress hormone, so it might be assumed that there is a straightforward relationship between the experience of stress and increases in levels of cortisol often evidenced by visible displays of unhappiness (Figure 6.3). This is not always the case. Some studies have even shown cortisol levels decreasing in situations that might be

> The relationship between cortisol and stress is not as straightforward as is often supposed

Figure 6.3: Crying baby

Source: Shutterstock Photo 340818158

assumed to be stressful for children. For example, Gunnar and Donzella (2002) describe how novel events, such as a car trip to visit the lab where they would meet new people, produced lower cortisol levels in children aged nine months. Similar studies with children at other ages have not produced this effect. Apart from being slightly puzzling, these studies show that we need to be careful in the conclusions we draw about the relationship between stress and cortisol. For a start we are measuring only one part of a complex chemical dance and we are a long way from fully understanding everything that is happening. The studies also demonstrate the importance of obtaining a baseline measure of what cortisol levels are usually like for individual infants within their home environment

It's important to note that quite a lot of the current knowledge about the HPA axis comes from studies on animals, particularly rats and monkeys. Several studies (e.g., Caldji et al, 1998) have shown that licking and grooming of young rats by their mothers has a measurable effect in lowering CRH. Rats that have been given the appropriate maternal care seem to be more resilient when placed under stress, often showing a decreased HPA response to fearful situations and a quicker recovery rate (Kiess et al, 1995). There have also been some rather ghastly experiments with monkeys showing that raising them in socially deprived conditions produces very fearful monkeys (for a review see Sanchez et al, 2001). Two points are significant here. Firstly, while the behaviour of the monkeys has clearly been modified by experience, the measurable responses in terms of the HPA axis are much less consistent. Secondly, we cannot seamlessly translate animal experiments to human experience. For example, monkeys and rats have differences in the way their HPA axes are organised and regulated. Moreover, animals that are caged and experimented upon are likely to produce very different responses to stress than humans who are not subject to such restricted lives.

Two recent meta-analyses give us a growing picture of how cortisol affects stress responses. The first (Bernard et al, 2017) looked at the way stress in childhood affects the diurnal cortisol pattern. The second (Bunea et al, 2017) considered the effects of early life adversity on the salivary cortisol response to stress. Between the two they give a reasonably clear picture of what is currently known about the relationship between childhood adversity and adult HPA responses.

The analysis by Bernard and colleagues (2017) considered 37 published articles covering 27 studies. It showed a very mixed picture in terms of daily cortisol rhythm. Some studies had shown that child maltreatment had resulted in hypocortisolism, that is, an underproduction of cortisol; others had reported hypercortisolism, or an increased production of cortisol; while still others had shown no response at all. They write, '[t]here was no overall effect of maltreatment on wake-up cortisol, the CAR or the diurnal slope' (Bernard et al, 2017, p 62). However, that is not quite the whole picture. There was a difference between those who self-reported their maltreatment and those who had been identified and reported by means of an outside agency such as a child welfare service. These latter individuals show a pattern of low morning cortisol. Bernard et al (2017) suggest that a pattern of repeated and pervasive neglect/abuse may lead to a reduction in morning cortisol production. They warn, though, that while this is an identifiable pattern in the data, we need to be cautious about inferring a simple cause and effect relationship. We cannot say that maltreatment/abuse causes low morning cortisol production. There is a need to take account of many other factors such as family poverty and chaotic home life, bearing in mind that daily routines such as changing or irregular sleep patterns can also have a significant effect on diurnal cortisol rhythms.

Bunea and colleagues (2017) evaluated 29 articles published up to 2017 involving 4,592 participants aged from eight to 62. The types of early life adversity considered in this study were defined widely to include all forms of abuse plus other factors such as witnessing parental violence, separation from parents and death in the family. The study agreed with the prevailing view that the salivary cortisol response in adults is blunted by adversity that occurs early in life.

> The cortisol response to stress in adults is blunted by adversity that occurs early in life

The blunted levels were more evident in the peak and recovery phases of the stress response and were not apparent in the daily cortisol rhythm. The effect was highest in those who had experienced maltreatment and lower in those who had lived through other forms of childhood adversity. It also showed that this blunting of the cortisol response is noticeable in adults but only has a small effect on children.

We need to be careful how we interpret this finding. The evidence is overwhelming: abuse damages children in many ways including how they behave, how they feel about themselves and how they interact with others. Research from all around the world shows that children suffer massive and long-term effects from abusive childhood relationships (e.g., Stirling et al, 2008; Al Odhayani et al, 2013; NSPCC, 2020).

However, measuring the cortisol response, for the moment at least, does not give us a biological measure of the damage that abuse inflicts on children. The finding that we can measure this response in adults but not in children and adolescents also fits with our discussion about the neuroimaging of the amygdala and other brain regions, all of which show that we can see quantifiable changes in adult brains but that these are not measurable in children.

Childcare and the HPA axis

The issue of childcare for children under the age of three years is one that has been much debated both within the media and in more academic circles (e.g., Biddulph, 2006; James, 2011). Several studies have shown increased levels of cortisol in children in childcare compared with children who remain at home. For example, Watamura and colleagues (2003) conducted a study of 20 infants with a mean average age of 10.8 months and 35 toddlers with a mean age of 29.7 months. The study compared mid-morning levels of cortisol to those measured midway through the afternoon. It showed that when children are in childcare cortisol levels rise during the day, and that this rise grows larger during the period from infancy to toddlerhood. It seems to decline as children start school. This pattern does not happen on days when children are not in childcare but remain at home. The authors tentatively ascribe this pattern to the stresses associated with peer play. Children who struggled to find ways of playing with other children showed higher increases than those who engaged more easily in group play (e.g., Dettling et al, 2000; Sims et al, 2006).

The pattern that children who attend preschool care settings show either a flat or a rising level of cortisol throughout the day on days they attend care but a more normal declining pattern on days they stay at home has now been established by many independent studies (e.g., Geoffroy et al, 2006; Watamura et al, 2010). This may be affected by the quality of the childcare. A number of studies have found that cortisol levels rise in settings with poor quality care and fall in those with higher-quality programmes (e.g., Dettling et al, 2000; Sims et al, 2006). Another factor might be the number of hours spent in childcare settings. A recent study suggests that part-time childcare is better than full-time (Lumian et al, 2016).

It is much more difficult to establish the longer-term effects of childcare; indeed, this topic has been rarely studied and there is clearly a need for some long-term work in this area.

Romanian infants: studies of severe neglect

Our understanding of how the brain reacts to adversity is based on many studies of children who have experienced terrible neglect and abuse. One such group of children were those who were born in Romania in the 1960s and sent to state-run institutions.

In October 1966 Romanian Communist leader Nicolae Ceaușescu (Figure 6.4) issued Decree 770 (Figure 6.4). This aimed to increase the working population of the country by means of a 'natalist' policy banning contraception and abortion. High levels of poverty and other social and economic problems led to over 65,000 children being put into state-run nurseries. Many were institutionalised during their first year of life and experienced very poor and frequently abusive care, often being left in their cots for over 20 hours each day (Chugani et al, 2001). In 1989 Ceaușescu was overthrown and the terrible conditions of many of these institutionalised children were uncovered. Nathan Fox was one of the academics who investigated the Romanian orphanages. In an interview for the

Figure 6.4: The official portrait of Nicolae Ceaușescu, 1965

Source: CPA Media Pte Ltd/Alamy Stock Photo

American Psychology Association he described his incredulity on first visiting one of these nurseries:

> The most remarkable thing about the infant room was how quiet it was, probably because the infants had learned that their cries were not responded to. (Weir, 2014, np)

The Bucharest Early Intervention Project began with a feasibility study in late 2000 and is a joint collaboration between Tulane University, University of Maryland and Boston Children's Hospital. It looked at 136 children who were abandoned at birth and placed in six institutions in Romania. At the start of the study, the children were aged from six to 31 months and had all spent at least half their lives in an institution. The study followed these children for four and a half years. Sixty-nine of the children were randomly assigned to foster families and 67 remained in institutions. These two groups were compared with a third group of 72 children who had never been institutionalised. The children were assessed using a wide range of measures including attachment, emotional reactivity and caregiver–child interaction, as well as EEG measures of brain activity.

We concentrate here on just a few of the findings from this study, focusing on those that are relevant to the emotional development of the brain. The study found that quality of care was directly related to whether or not children had an attachment disorder (Nelson et al, 2007). Marshall and Fox (2004) used EEGs to look at differences between children who had been institutionalised and those who had not. They found differences in a number of bandwidths and in a number of different brain regions between the two groups. For example, the institutionalised group of children had reduced brain power in the 6–9 Hz and 10–18 Hz ranges in the frontal and temporal regions of the brain. The authors suggest that the differences they found might be the 'electrophysiological signature of deviations in brain development common to a variety of disorders or contexts' (Marshall and Fox, 2004, p 1334).

Conclusion

In this chapter we have explored ideas about the way in which young children relate to their carers, particularly as described by attachment theory. We have seen that while the theory remains dominant across the social sciences, there is not as yet enough strong supporting evidence from brain imaging to support all its assertions. In contrast, we have seen that biological studies of abuse and neglect show that adults who were poorly treated in childhood show changes to a number of brain structures including the frontal cortex, the amygdala and the hippocampus. We have also seen that such adults are likely to have changes to the way their HPA axis reacts to stressful situations. We have noted, though, that these biological changes have mostly not been measured in children, although we stress that this does not indicate that children are not deeply affected by such experiences.

Summary

- Attachment theory was developed in the 1950s and remains today the dominant theory of how children learn to relate emotionally to others.

- Imaging studies only provide a small amount of evidence to substantiate this social theory.

- Imaging studies show us that childhood abuse and neglect have a significant impact on the brains of adults, particularly in the PFC, the amygdala and the hippocampus.

- The HPA axis has a dual role in managing a daily cortisol rhythm and providing an instant and overriding response to stress.

- Measures of adults who were neglected and abused as children show a blunted cortisol response to stress, although the daily cortisol rhythm seems less impacted.

Test your knowledge
1. What are the main features of attachment theory?
2. Describe the 'strange situation' experiment. What does it purport to measure?
3. In the 'strange situation', how does a securely attached infant behave when reunited with the mother?
4. What are the main criticisms of attachment theory?
5. Why might imaging studies of the amygdala and hippocampus not show significant changes to the brain structures in abused children?
6. Why should we be wary of individual ACE scores?
7. What are the main problems with the Perry brain images?
8. What's the role of the HPA axis in managing stress?
9. What do measures of cortisol tell us about the way children manage stress?
10. What lessons should we draw from the studies of Romanian infants?

Discussion questions
1. To what extent does your experience support the notion that emotional development is highly dependent on the sorts of social interactions the child has with parents and carers?
2. Can professional childcare ever be a sufficient replacement for the kind of sensitive and responsive parenting that some brain research sees as being ideal for young infants?

3. To what extent do studies of cortisol levels in young children serve as a warning about protecting children from unnecessary levels of stress?

Our answers

1. One of us (Rob) is a counsellor working with adults who often seek counselling to help them manage strong feelings that arise from close emotional relationships. This is his answer.

> My experience is that most of the problems my clients present have their roots in the relationships they had with parents and carers. Where this relationship was strong and caring with clear boundaries, then it becomes easier to have those sorts of relationships with others as an adult. Where there was neglect or abuse, then it becomes much more difficult to trust others and to be vulnerable in a mature relationship.

As we have seen, the brain science clearly shows that abuse does impact on brain development, although there are many variables here such as when the abuse happened and for how long it continued as well as more positive factors such as whether a period of abuse was followed by good levels of care and how that individual was able to make use of such care.

2. This is a much-debated topic. There are those who doubt that professional care can ever replace high-quality parenting. For many children, of course, professional care supplements (or even complements) the love and care they get from parental figures. For other children who experience abuse and neglect at home, good-quality professional care might be what provides their only experience of secure attachment.

3. It shows that trying to use just one biological measure to try to ascertain complex emotional outcomes is never going to give you a simple answer. It also demonstrates to limits of our knowledge and reminds us that brain science is still in its infancy.

Notes

1   The Post-Traumatic Stress Disorder Reaction Index for children and adolescents was developed for the DSM version IV and then revised for version V. It attempts to measure PTSD using four criteria including past exposure to a traumatic event and negative changes in cognition and mood.

2   In fact, the image had appeared in an earlier poster presentation (Perry and Pollard, 1997) at the Society for Neuroscience Annual Meeting, New Orleans, 1997.

Further reading

Gerhardt, S. (2014) *Why Love Matters: How Affection Shapes a Baby's Brain* (2nd edn), London: Routledge.

Keenan, T., Evans, S. and Crowley, K. (2016) *An Introduction to Child Development* (3rd edn), London: SAGE.

Nelson, C.A., Fox, N.A. and Zeanah, C.H. (2014) *Romania's Abandoned Children: Deprivation, Brain Development, and the Struggle for Recovery*, Cambridge, MA: Harvard University Press.

On our website
You can find lots more material on our website at https://policy. bristoluniversitypress.co.uk/child-development-and-the-brain/companion-website

This includes:

Eight ways to grow a good brain: https://policy.bristoluniversitypress.co.uk/child-development-and-the-brain/companion-website/grow-a-good-brain
Brain development in the news: https://policy.bristoluniversitypress.co.uk/child-development-and-the-brain/companion-website/brain-development-in-the-news

7

Language development

This chapter:

- explores theories of language development from Skinner, Bandura, Chomsky, Pinker and Bruner;

- considers how neuroscience has changed our understanding of language development in children and adolescents;

- examines the ways in which babies and young children learn language and shows how brain studies have extended this knowledge;

- shows how learning other languages extends our cognitive capacity;

- argues that children need a supportive environment where they hear and can respond to language in order to develop their linguistic capacity.

Introduction

Language is a uniquely human phenomenon. While other species can communicate with each other in all sorts of sophisticated ways, from the songs of humpback whales to the dances of bees, there is no other species that has developed language in the same way that humans have. Whenever we look at the communication of other species, we find that it has severe limitations that our own complex language system can overcome. For example, human language can express new ideas in ways which have never been said before. Our languages have words that, with a reasonable degree of consistency, retain their meanings across time. We can use language to reflect and record our experiences. Most importantly, our language has structure and grammar, which gives it an order and logic that is not contained in any animal communication. Our language is also something that is learned, something that depends on the language that is spoken by others around us. It is the way in which it is learned that has been the subject of a great deal of study and considerable disagreement.

In this chapter we argue that while language development is an innate human capacity, infants and children respond positively to an environment where they hear language spoken and have the opportunity to develop and practise these skills for themselves. As

> Children thrive in an environment where they hear and use lots of language

elsewhere in this book, we also argue that factors such as poverty, deprivation, neglect and abuse have a negative impact on all forms of development, focusing here on how these impact on language development.

We begin by taking an historical tour of the main theories around the development of language: the behaviourist ideas of Skinner and Bandura, the nativist theories of Chomsky and Pinker and the social interactionist ideas of Bruner.

We then explore some of the early ideas about where language is situated in the brain, particularly Wernicke's area and Broca's area. The question of where language is processed in the brain is still much debated. And we consider more recent ideas of this debate alongside the arguments for and against equipotentiality: whether the left side of the brain is particularly special in terms of language development. In the later parts of the chapter we look at the process of language development and consider how neuroscience is helping us understand this process more clearly.

Debates around language development

There is a long-standing debate concerning the apparent speed and effortless ease with which young children learn to understand and use language. Most four-year-old children have a vocabulary of at least 6,000 words (Bates et al, 2001). The processes by which they achieve this have long fascinated all sorts of people, including parents and caregivers as well as developmental psychologists and neuroscientists. Over the years there have been quite a few theories that have attempted to explain this process, but it is only now, as we are beginning to understand what happens inside the brain, that we are starting to appreciate the complexity of language development.

Empiricist theories

Parents tend not to correct their children's language

The most generally accepted explanations of language acquisition in the 1950s were those of the behaviourists, led by Burrhus Frederic Skinner (Skinner and Frederic, 1957), usually known just as B.F. Skinner.[1] This theory of learning was about reinforcement. The idea is very simple: as we learn to do something, we are rewarded for doing it correctly and that encourages us to carry on doing it more. When we do it incorrectly, then either this is just ignored or we get some sort of penalty and so we do it less. Applying this very simple principle to the learning of language seemed at the time a very good idea. Parents, the behaviourists argued, rewarded children when they spoke properly and corrected them when they didn't. Children were seen to learn from this and so they gradually learned to use language correctly, encouraged by the feedback they received from their elders and betters. The difficulty is, of course, that it just doesn't happen this way. Parents do not tend to correct their children when they make grammatical errors; they are more likely to be indulgent and accept the content of what is said rather than worrying about how it is said (Brown and Hanlon, 1970; Hirsh-Pasek et al, 1984).

More likely explanations of how language is acquired are offered by another theory which developed later in the 20th century. This is known as social learning theory and it was led by Albert Bandura (1969, 1977). The emphasis here was on learning through imitation. Children listen to and observe the speech of others and imitate how they do it. As we will see, research on the brain has shown that some aspects of this theory are correct. Imitation most certainly does play a part in language acquisition (Bates et al, 1982; Leonard et al, 1983). However, how it happens is slightly more complicated than Bandura's theories suggested. Furthermore, there are some pretty obvious problems with a theory that says it is all about copying what you hear. For example, the way in which young children speak is far more creative, as well as being often too grammatically incorrect to be based solely on imitation. For instance, when the child says 'I goed there', they are unlikely to be using something they have heard their parents say.

What is important about both these theories is that they emphasise that language development is not a passive process. It requires interaction – language is performed; it is not developed as a silent internal process. In Skinner's model infants are rewarded for their efforts; in Bandura's model imitation is dependent on hearing and responding to the sound of language in the environment surrounding the child.

Nativist theories

In response to these theories, which stressed the environmental aspects of language learning, another theory that developed in the 1950s and 1960s emphasised what happens inside the brain rather than in the world outside, although, as we shall see, this is not a process that can be divorced from the experience of hearing spoken language. Noam Chomsky (1957, 1968) proposed an internal structure that he called a language acquisition device (LAD). The LAD contains the universal rules of grammar and allows the child to develop a set of rules that govern their understanding and their use of language. A key feature of Chomsky's argument is that children do not hear enough correct speech around them to be able to use this as a model for their own language. This is known as the **poverty of stimulus** argument, and as we shall see, it has been severely challenged by evidence from neuroscientific studies, which have shown that most infants in fact hear an incredibly rich amount of speech and seem to have an inbuilt capacity to make the most of this.

All human societies use language

The nativist argument has been developed further, and in a slightly different direction, by Steven Pinker. In his book *The Language Instinct*, Pinker (1994) offers several arguments as to why language might be innate. The first of these is quite simply that language is ubiquitous: all human societies speak a language. Secondly, he describes the way in which pidgin languages, with rules and structures, can develop within the space of a generation from collections of individuals who initially find themselves working and living together and speaking many different languages. He also refers back to one of Chomsky's arguments regarding the limited amount of language children receive, upon which they base their own language performance. Children produce new forms of language that they have never heard before. This shows that they are learning not through imitation but through a creative process. Pinker argues that children can produce grammatically correct questions even though they have not heard these before or have heard them in the form of a statement, which they have the capacity to rearrange.

Again, we want to stress that in both the Chomsky model and that of Pinker, children need to hear language in order to develop a process that, while it might be innate, still requires stimulus. Even the poverty of stimulus argument does not suggest that language can develop on its own in a world where there is no linguistic stimulus.

Social interactionist theories

Another set of theories, which developed largely outside the world of neuroscience, are those that are called 'the social interactionist perspectives'. One key figure here is Jerome Bruner (1983), who cites George Miller in critiquing both the nativist and the empiricist theories of language acquisition:

> We now had two theories of language acquisition: one of them, empiricist associationism, was impossible; the other, nativism, was miraculous. (Bruner, 1983, p 34)

For Bruner, games provide children with a rich source of language

Bruner argues that infants are 'tuned to enter the world of human action' (Bruner, 1983, p 27). Even very young babies can tune in to both the human voice and the human face. Alongside this there are environmental factors such as, for example, the huge amount of social activity that takes place between carers and infants in the first few years of life. Rather than a LAD, Bruner proposes a language acquisition support system (LASS). This term, and the resulting acronym, is clearly intended to be an amusing parody of Chomsky but has proved to be a very useful and influential proposition. Bruner writes that there is much that happens between the primary carer and the child that is both routine and repetitive and that is accompanied by (or even created by) language. What is more, the communication that takes place goes two ways, as the young infant falls into the pattern that is established by the carer's communication. Games, Bruner says, are a rich source of language, and in *Child's Talk* (1983) he provides a detailed analysis of peekaboo games between two mothers and their young sons. These games develop in sophisticated ways, and through these the children gain knowledge of both language and the social rules, such as turn taking, that are of great importance in human interaction.

It is worth noting that all these theories have a degree of legitimacy. Strict, Skinner-like reinforcement might not be how most children acquire language, but reward by encouragement and intimacy play a major role. Certainly, imitation plays a very important role in the development of language. Likewise, as we will explore later, there do seem to be some innate structures in the brain that greatly assist the learning of a language. Lastly, and perhaps most importantly, we are gaining more and more evidence that interaction and stimulation are absolutely vital in the development of language. In the next section we look at the idea that there are some structures within the brain that help young children learn language quickly.

The brain and language

Early experiments

In the 1860s Paul Broca (1861) carried out a post-mortem on a patient who for many years had been able to say only one nonsense word. Whenever he tried to speak, he could say only 'tan, tan, tan, tan, tan, tan ...'. When Broca examined the man's brain, he found that the part of the brain known as the left inferior frontal gyrus was damaged. Broca also studied quite a few other right-handed people with speech defects, who often also had weaknesses in their right arms and/or right legs. He concluded that one area that is important in the production of speech is the left inferior frontal lobe. This part of the brain is now known as Broca's area.

Another 19th-century physician, Carl Wernicke (1977), worked in Germany with patients who had difficulty in understanding spoken language. These patients had all had strokes. They all had a wider vocabulary than Broca's patient but nonetheless tended to speak nonsensical words and sentences. Wernicke performed a post-mortem on one patient and discovered that he had damage to the posterior region of the superior temporal gyrus. This part of the brain is now called Wernicke's area (Figure 7.1). He suggested that damage to this part of the brain affects our ability to understand language and that it is the part of the brain where related memories are stored.

Both Wernicke and Broca were working with fully developed adults. Their studies indicated that damage to particular parts of the left hemisphere of the brain led to difficulties with language. Late 19th- and early 20th-century research

Figure 7.1: Language areas in the brain

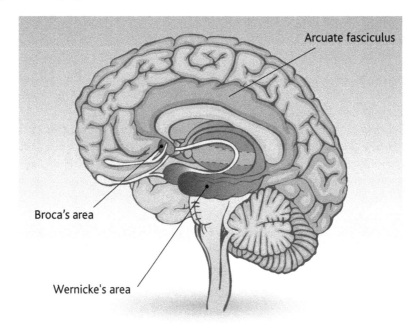

that looked at children with left-hemisphere damage came to a very different conclusion. Most of these early studies showed that children who suffered early left-hemisphere damage did not suffer from language difficulties. Even children who had large parts of their left hemisphere removed to control epileptic seizures almost always went on to develop normal speech abilities.

Brain structure and language development

> There are many areas of the brain involved in language processing

It is now understood that this classical account of the significance of these two areas in the left hemisphere is far too simplistic to explain the complexity of language processing. Many other parts of both the subcortical brain and areas in the cortex are involved in language processing. These areas include the anterior superior temporal lobe, the middle temporal gyrus (MTG), the temporo-parietal junction, the basal ganglia as well as areas in the right hemisphere of the brain. We also know that learning more than one language affects how and where language is processed in the brain. We look at bilingualism later in the chapter.

There is still evidence for a preference for the left temporal processing of language. Even in newborn babies we can see that the left hemisphere of the brain is more active in listening to speech than the right (Molfese and Molfese, 1979, 1980; Minagawa-Kawai et al, 2011). There is some evidence

(Merzenich et al, 2002) to suggest that this part of the brain has a slightly different structure to other parts of the cortex, which allows for the incredibly rapid processing needed when speaking and listening. In the 1970s researchers in the United States discovered that by the 29th week of gestation a part of the brain known as the left planum temporale, which is more or less at the centre of Wernicke's area, is significantly larger than the corresponding area in the right part of the brain (Wada et al, 1975). What is also becoming clear is that there are lots of different regions of the brain that are activated during both speaking and listening. Even newborn babies use quite a number of different areas to process language that are spread beyond those areas of the temporal cortex that we traditionally associate with language (Dehaene-Lambertz et al, 2002). These areas include the left planum temporale, the superior temporal gyrus, the superior temporal sulcus, as well as the inferior, middle and posterior temporal cortex.

Is the left temporal region special?

While research with children who have suffered from brain damage has continued to support the idea that the left hemisphere is usually the region where we process language, it has also generated a great deal of debate about whether there is anything special about this region of the brain that lends itself to the processing of language, or whether other areas of the brain also have the potential to be used for language. The debate can be expressed quite succinctly: are parts of the left hemisphere of the brain pre-programmed for language, or does the brain have what is called **equipotentiality**, that is, do both hemispheres have the potential to process language? There are, of course, parallels between this and the ongoing debate between developmental psychologists on whether language is an innate function of the brain or a product of the environment. If it can be proved that parts of the left hemisphere are 'naturally' adapted to deal with language, then this adds to the argument that we might have an innate language organ, much like Chomsky's LAD. If this is not the case, then it is more likely that we do not have any innate specialised organ and that our brains simply adapt to the environment.

What role does infant brain plasticity play in language development?

As we saw earlier, children's brains have a greater degree of plasticity than the brains of adults. In both adults and children, when there is damage to one part of the brain other parts can take over some of the functions that the damaged parts would normally do. In children, however, this capacity is greater. For example, when there is damage to the left-hemisphere language areas, young children can use other areas of the brain to process language. There are currently two debates around this issue of language and plasticity in children who are brain damaged. The first debate is about the levels of recovery that are possible when language-specific parts of the brain are damaged. The second debate is about which parts of the brain take over the functions that the damaged areas would normally have done.

In the 1960s Eric Lenneberg (1967) argued that when young children suffered damage to the left hemisphere it had little effect on their ability to develop language. Later studies provided quite a lot of evidence to oppose this view (Dennis and Whitaker, 1976; Vargha-Khadem et al, 1994). Studies since then (Stiles et al, 2002) have shown that while there is evidence of language difficulties in children who have suffered left-hemisphere injuries, significant levels of recovery are possible and most of these children have language abilities that fall within the normal range. Exactly which abilities recover, and the timescale over which they do so, remains a matter of some debate. For example, research by Reilly and colleagues (1998) argues that brain plasticity allows for most of the children who suffer focal damage to develop reasonably good, although often delayed, language skills. This delay is likely to reoccur at significant stages of development, and such children are likely to be less proficient in language than children who have not had left temporal damage.

The debate over which parts of the brain take over the functions when there is damage in the left hemisphere is also one that is unresolved. There has been a battle between those who argue for equipotentiality and those who argue for what is called irreversible determinism – that is, that the left side of the brain is uniquely equipped to deal with language and any damage to this area, particularly in children aged one and older, will cause language problems. Efforts have been made towards a resolution. For example, there is the 'emergent view' (Bates et al, 2001), which sees the differences between the left and right hemispheres as being of significance early in life but argues that they disappear as the child grows. By far the greatest number of studies in this area has been carried out by the San Diego Center for Research in Language, which was led, until her untimely death in 2003, by Professor Elizabeth Bates.

BOX: The forbidden experiment

One of the key debates in the study of language development can be characterised as the nature versus nurture debate. One way in which we could establish whether it is the internal structures within the brain that drive the acquisition of language or input from the environment would be to carry out what is sometimes called the forbidden experiment. If we could lock successive generations of children away from all contact with other human beings, so that they never heard any language at all, we would be able to see whether they developed some form of language. If they did, then this would show us that language is innate, that there is something in the brain that all by itself forces us to communicate using a structured language. If, after three or four generations, the children remained mute, then we would know that it is the environment that plays an important part. Of course, such an experiment would be unspeakably cruel and to undertake such work with human beings is unthinkable. However, there is one group of scientists who are managing to do something quite similar.

The work of Fehér and colleagues (2009) at the City College of New York Laboratory of Animal Behavior provides one partial answer to the problem of nature versus nurture by undertaking an experiment similar to the one described previously but using birds rather than humans. The distinctive song of the male zebra finch is used to attract suitable female mates. In Fehér and colleagues' experiment the males are raised in isolated cages and therefore cannot hear the song of other birds. The first generations of male birds raised in this way sing a very reduced and limited song and consequently find it difficult to attract female finches for mating. However, subsequent generations raised with access to only this limited model of singing gradually accumulate alterations, which over three or four generations evolve towards the wild variation of the song. There are always difficulties in applying the results of experiments on other species to human development. Even so, this looks as though it provides some evidence for an inbuilt capacity for language that is independent of experience.

Despite such experiments, it seems certain that for human babies, social interaction is an essential part of language development. The human capacity for mutual joint attention and the highly sophisticated levels of social interaction that exist between the primary carer and the young child would seem to be an integral part of language development.

Neuroscientific research has confirmed some aspects of what we already knew about the way in which young infants develop language, but it has also come up with a few surprises. Perhaps the most important finding from neuroscience is something that simply reinforces what we knew all along: that experience plays a hugely significant role in the development of speech and language. The more unexpected finding is that a huge amount of language acquisition occurs at a very early age. Although children do not start to say recognisable words until somewhere between ten and 15 months, we have known for some time that they are able to recognise words much earlier than this. Since the 1970s neuroscience has been telling us that even very young babies are able to process the sounds of speech and make complex decisions about the structure of the language they are hearing.

Is there a critical period for language development?

Further evidence for the significance of experience in developing language comes from studies of children who have been deprived of language during their early years. In some cases, this was due to almost unbelievable levels of abuse and neglect; other examples include deaf children who simply did not hear any language and did not get any input in terms of sign language either.

The most well known of the cases of deprivation is that of Genie. Genie was born in April 1957. She was discovered in November 1970 when she was 13 years and 7 months old. She was immediately sent to hospital to treat her extreme malnutrition and neglect. She was not toilet trained, had difficulty swallowing food and could not speak, cry or, indeed, make any sounds at all. From the age of 20 months she had been confined to a single room, was chained to a potty and punished if she made any noise. It seems likely that even before 20 months she heard little, if any, language (Curtiss et al, 1974).

Physically, cognitively and emotionally she showed remarkable development while in hospital. She gained weight and her non-verbal cognitive capacity grew from that of a 15-month-old child when she was discovered to that of a three-and-a-half-year-old in a period of six months. She was also able to develop relationships. In July 1971 she was well enough to be released from care to live with a foster family.

Early reports suggested that when she was found she had little capacity to understand language and was not able to produce any. In care she was able to develop a vocabulary, but her speech lacked questions, lacked demonstratives (statements such as 'This is an apple' or 'Take me to the shops') and had no participles (the, a, an). In an update on her linguistic development Curtiss and colleagues (1975) reported that her language production and comprehension was still problematic. In terms of comprehension and syntax she struggled to distinguish the differences in meaning between 'the girl pulled the boy' and 'the boy pulled the girl'. Her speech production was much more limited than her comprehension.

> Experience is essential for the development of language skills

Another source of understanding on this question comes from studies of children with a hearing impairment who are born to non-deaf parents. Such children may not receive sufficient language input for several years before they are fitted with a hearing device. Many studies on such children were caried out by Naama Friedmann and colleagues (e.g., Friedmann and Haddad-Hanna, 2014). These studies show that children who are given a hearing device before the age of eight months develop a normal syntax whereas children who do not hear language properly for the first year experience severe problems with syntax. For example, children who have not been able to hear for the first months of their life will struggle with producing and understanding relative clauses such as 'This is the girl that the grandma drew' (Friedmann and Rusou, 2015, p 29).

The evidence suggests both that experience of language is essential if it is to develop properly and that there is a critical age for language development. Children who, for whatever reason, do not hear sufficient language during the early years of their lives will not become as skilled at using language as other children. While some of these problems can be overcome, the critical area is that of syntax. Children who do not hear language during early infancy are likely to have problems with understanding the language spoken by others and will struggle to produce grammatically correct, syntactically appropriate language themselves.

Figure 7.2: Three phonemes in D / O / G

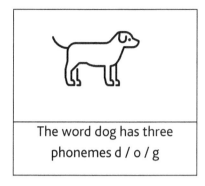

The word dog has three
phonemes d / o / g

The process by which children learn language

Phonemes

Language learning does not begin with the learning of words. It starts when young babies hear the sounds of adult speech in their immediate environment. When we, as adults, listen to speech we appear to hear whole words that we are

> A phoneme is the smallest unit of language

usually able to understand and give meaning to. In fact, what we are doing is recognising the difference between the individual phonemes that make up the words in our language. If I say the phrase 'good morning', then what I'm doing is using a whole sequence of sounds. There are three separate sounds in the word 'good' and four sounds in the word 'morning'. Each of these separate sounds is known as a phoneme. A phoneme is the smallest unit of sound that is used in a language. The word 'dog', for example, has three phonemes: /d/ /o/ /g/ (Figure 7.2), whereas the word 'caterpillar' has eight. If we look at the words 'cat' and 'cot' we can see that the words sound the same except for the middle phoneme. It is the /a/ sound or the /o/ sound that makes a difference to the way in which we understand what the word means.

The world's languages use two types of phonemes: consonant phonemes and vowel phonemes. If we take all the languages in the world, there are about 600 different consonant phonemic sounds and about 200 vowel sounds. The human brain at birth is capable of distinguishing all these different sounds. This is perhaps no great surprise and, of course, supports the idea that our capacity for language is based upon an innate capacity to process such sounds. Language develops from our ability to make this range of sounds and to hear the differences between them. Individual languages, however, tend to use only a small number of these phonemes: English, for example, uses about 44.

It is quite important here to understand the idea of what a phoneme is and what the differences are between them. We would like you to experiment with the differences between just two consonants: /b/ as in the word 'bat' and /p/ as in the word 'pat'. One way of understanding the difference between the two sounds is to experience the amount of breath we use to produce each of them (Crystal, 2003). If you put your hand in front of your mouth and make alternative /b/ and /p/ sounds you will notice that one produces quite a lot of puff and the other does not! Notice also what is going on in your voice box. The /b/ phoneme is known as a voiced consonant, as producing it involves the vibration of the vocal cords. The /p/ phoneme is known as a voiceless consonant, as to produce the sound we do not need to vibrate our vocal cords.[2] Another difference is what is known as voice onset time, that is, the time between when the air starts passing through your mouth and when your vocal cords begin to vibrate. There is a much shorter gap between the breath coming out of your mouth and your vocal cords vibrating when you make the /b/ sound than when you make the /p/ sound.

Categorical speech perception

Our skill in recognising these different sounds is known as **categorical speech perception**. This rather lofty phrase simply means that we can categorise the language sounds we hear and we do this by regular practice (Figure 7.3). In this case it means that we can hear and recognise that they belong either to the /b/ category or the /p/ category. When we listen to the sounds created or when we speak these phonemes, we can hear that they are quite similar, but we know instantly the category to which they belong. It is really rather vital to be able to distinguish these sorts of sounds and, without conscious thought, to be able to place them into categories. Without the speed of this unconscious processing, using language would be a much slower and more ponderous affair.

How babies learn language

We must be able to learn the sounds that are used within a language before we are able to proceed to the next stages, which are, firstly, to understand the meaning of the sounds and, secondly, to be able to produce these sounds ourselves. This process is known as phonological development. It is a form of statistical learning.

The early work of Peter Eimas and colleagues (1971) found that even babies who were just one month old were able to make the distinction between the different phonemes they heard. Their research used a speech synthesiser to produce a range of sounds along a continuum between a voiced and a voiceless consonant. In one experiment the sound shifted from the /p/ sound to the /b/ sound. For us, as adults, there is a measurable point at which sounds

Figure 7.3: Father and child practise making early sounds

Source: Shutterstock Photo ID 1648010488

that are so highly similar to each other stop being perceived as a /b/ and start being perceived as a /p/. This is our categorical perception. The brain makes the decision as to whether what it is hearing is a /p/ or a /b/. Eimas and colleagues (1971) found that babies between one and four months old were able to make the same distinction.

> Even very young babies can distinguish between similar-sounding phonemes

Clearly, young babies are not able to tell us when they can hear the differences between these two sounds. This experiment used a technique that is often used when working with young babies. The infant is given a pacifier (a dummy) to suck on. The pacifier is wired up to a machine so that sucking on it produces speech sounds. These and other experiments have found that if the same sound is played again and again the infant begins to suck less. Similarly, if a new sound is played to the infant, the rate of sucking increases. In this way it is possible to determine whether the baby is able to make a distinction between different sounds. New sounds produce more sucking; sounds that have been heard lots of times, to which the baby has become habituated, produce less sucking. Eimas and colleagues found that the babies showed an increased rate of sucking when they heard the sound change from a voiced consonant such as /b/ to a voiceless consonant such as /p/. In other words, they showed that the babies had heard that the new sound came from a different phonetic category, thus showing that they had very similar categorical speech perception to adults. Even babies as young as one month old were able to show that they could make this distinction.

The perceptual magnet effect

> After six months our capacity to hear the sounds of all languages begins to disappear

While babies can distinguish between the sound of the /p/ and the /b/ and show that they can put these sounds into one of two categories, there is another aspect of the way in which we hear language sounds which suggests that we might filter some of what we hear. This is called the **perceptual magnet effect** (Kuhl, 1991). This effect suggests that when we listen to language there is something like a magnet at work, pulling our perception of a sound towards one of the categories of language that we already have stored within our brains. For example, sounds that are similar to, but not the same as, the /p/ phoneme will be heard as a /p/. It is like a slightly over-keen filing system that insists that everything must go into one of the files, even if it is a little bit different to all the other things that are already in there. It does not work, of course, when the sounds that are heard are sufficiently dissimilar from any known phoneme sound. There is a point at which the magnet stops having an effect. It also does not work when we are listening to the sounds in a language we do not understand.

This last point is rather important. We know that infants learn the phonemes used in their native language very quickly but that at the same time they also lose the ability to distinguish between phonemes that are used in other languages but not in their own.

The perceptual magnet effect, alongside categorical perception, acts like a filter, changing what we hear. And this filter works differently for children who are learning to speak different languages. After the age of about six months infants in, say, China or Russia who are learning to speak their native languages will apply a filter to the sounds in their language. Learning to categorise them, to sort the sounds in one language, means that infants also start to lose the ability to hear distinctions between sounds in other languages. Up to the age of about six months infants show sensitivity to sounds in all languages of the world. From about six months to 11 months this universality diminishes (Werker and Tees, 1984, 1984; Kuhl et al, 1992), so that by the end of the first year infants are sensitive only to the sounds of their own language. This means that as we get older we are simply unable to distinguish phonemes that are not part of our native language. The example most well known to native English speakers will be the difficulties that native Japanese speakers have with the /r/ and /l/ sounds in words such as 'rake' and 'lake'.

Teaching American children Mandarin

However, other work has shown that this loss of the ability to hear sounds in other languages can be modified in slightly older children. In a series of experiments with American children Patricia Kuhl and colleagues (2003) compared the experiences of a group of 32 nine-month-old children. The children were divided into two groups of 16 children. The first group was exposed to native Mandarin-Chinese speakers who conducted the sessions in this language. The second group, which acted as a control group, had the same materials presented in English. Both groups were given 12 sessions of 25 minutes each, during which they had stories read to them for ten minutes and then played with the adults, who used a prepared script to make sure that all the adults used the same words. The adults in both groups used motherese (infant-directed speech) to communicate with the children. Both groups of children were then tested using a head-turning technique. It was found that the group that had worked with the Mandarin-Chinese speakers could discriminate particular phonetic sounds that occur only in that language. Unsurprisingly, the children who had been exposed only to English did not react to these phonemes.

As part of the same experiment a further group of infants were exposed to the same materials, but this time, rather than the lessons being presented by live human beings, the children watched them on a television screen. They were shown high-quality DVD material with close-ups of the speakers' faces, which were filmed from the children's perspective. These children performed no better than those in the control group who had not been exposed to any Mandarin-Chinese. Learning the sounds that make up a language requires real human beings and real human interaction. Just watching it on television simply does not work.

There are some important lessons to be learned from this work. Firstly, of course, it reinforces the idea that language development requires experience. It also shows that young infants have an astonishing capacity to learn the sounds of other languages.

> Children learn by engaging in social activity

While there may be a decline in the ability of young infants after six months to discriminate between their native language and other languages, this work with slightly older children shows that this decline can be reversed. It also shows that if we ever want to be really fluent in a language, then the earlier we start, the better.

Work on the way in which we can discriminate the sound of our own language from the sounds of other languages is really important. We now know that if we are exposed to a second language before the end of the first year of life, then we will develop an ability to discriminate the sounds of phonemes that are unique to that language. Yet we also know that this plasticity has not completely disappeared. There have been experiments (Cheour et al, 2002) with older children, aged three to six years, that have shown that even quite short but intensive immersion in a non-native language can lead to the children being able to discriminate non-native speech sounds.

As Kuhl and colleagues (2003) discuss, this work tells us something about the way in which young infants learn. It also shows that learning is a hugely social activity. Being engaged with another human being means that there is a lot of interaction: the infant following the gaze of the adult; adult and child both looking at the same object; the adult giving that object a name and so establishing a link between language and objects. If young infants are to learn successfully, then they need to be stimulated by real, live human beings. Kuhl and colleagues also point out that the use of multiple talkers increased the variability of sounds that were heard by the infants. Their work also demonstrates the preference that children have for motherese.

Motherese

> Using a high-pitched, sing-song language for babies seems to be a cross-cultural activity

Talking to young children in a sing-song, simplified, slightly higher-pitched language seems to be a feature of almost all cultures. As we search for a more politically correct name for this phenomenon, we are also starting to understand more about it. Let us begin with the name. Over the years it seems to have been called by a variety of names, including parentese, infant-directed speech, baby-directed speech, caretaker speech, baby speech and baby talk, to name just a few. In fact, we seem to be less sure about what to call it than we are about what it is!

Experiments in the 1980s in which young infants were required to show preferences for the sounds of mothers talking either to other adults or to their young infants (Fernald, 1985) established some scientific basis for what had already been observed in the wider world. More recent studies have confirmed these early findings and have also helped us understand some of the ways in which motherese can benefit children as they begin to understand the rules of language. In another study, Patricia Kuhl and colleagues (1997) studied children and their responses to motherese in Russia, Sweden and the United States. In these countries the research found that mothers considerably exaggerated the sounds of the vowels that they spoke to the young children. The researchers suggest that this helps young children in several ways. Firstly, the exaggeration makes the difference between one vowel sound and another much clearer. Secondly, they describe this exaggeration as 'hyperarticulated' such that even adults see the sound as sounding more like a perfect example of what the vowel should sound like. This makes it easier for infants to fit these vowel sounds into the correct category. More recent research (Schachner and Hannon, 2011) has shown that infants as young as five months old use an adult's ability to use motherese as a means of selecting whether they wish to have a relationship with them. In an experiment, infants showed that they preferred to look at pictures of an adult whom they had previously heard using motherese, rather than a picture of an adult who had been using ordinary speech.

Multilingualism

There is a continuing debate in the United Kingdom about the place of language teaching in our schools. This might in some ways be a particularly UK-based problem. There are about 5,000 languages in the world and the vast majority of the world's population speak more than one of them. Multilingualism across the world is the norm rather than the exception (Schwieter, 2019).[3]

> There are huge advantages to learning more than one language

There is evidence to suggest that it might be very helpful for young children across the globe to experience more than one language at a very early age. The work of Kuhl and others has shown that there would seem to be considerable benefit to very young children in spending time hearing and engaging with speakers of other languages.

There have been many claims about the cognitive benefits of multilingualism. Foremost among these is the idea that those who speak more than one language have to make very quick decisions about which language they are listening to. This leads to improved executive functioning in the dorsolateral prefrontal cortex. Improved executive functioning allows us to make quick decisions as to whether to respond to a stimulus or ignore it. Various studies have suggested that this gives an advantage in all stages of life. These include a study of seven-month-old infants (Kovács and Mehler, 2009) and a study of two-year-old infants (Poulin-Dubois et al, 2011), to name but two. Kovács and Mehler (2009) showed that bilingual children are better able to adapt to rule changes than their monolingual contemporaries. They are, in other words, better able to change their behaviour according to what is happening in the environment. Similar conclusions can be drawn from the study by Poulin-Dubois and colleagues (2011), in which two-year-old bilinguals performed better on a modified version of the Stroop tasks involving coloured pictures of fruit. This again showed the bilingual children had an advantage in executive functioning over the monolingual children. A further surprising claim by a group of academics is that multilingualism protects us against cognitive decline as we grow older (Klein et al, 2016). The study looked at data from 93 countries on both multilingualism and the incidence of Alzheimer's disease. It found there to be some support for the idea that multilingualism protects against cognitive decline.

Multilingualism also helps other aspects of learning. This is particularly the case when learning another language. Those who already speak more than one language seem better able to learn a new language (Kaushanskaya and Marian, 2009; Bartolotti and Marian, 2012).

BOX: The FOXP2 debate

In 2001 there was much excitement about the FOXP2 gene, which was seen as being responsible for human language. The debate and the excitement have come and gone since then. The discovery of a family (given the pseudonym KE) who had a rare condition that affected the way they talked but caused them no other cognitive or language problems added to the excitement. The family were found to have a single-point mutation to their FOXP2 gene. Some ideas about the FOXP2 gene were even more overstated. In February 2013, for example, the idea appeared in the press that the gene might be the reason why women putatively talk more than men (*Telegraph*, 2013), which started to go viral on the Internet. The truth, such as we currently understand it, is far less exciting. The FOXP2 gene, like all genes, does not cause or encode any particular condition. It seems to be involved in some aspects of neural plasticity, as well as in the ways in which motor neurons are controlled, including the way in which we can vocalise and read.

Language development in later childhood and adolescence

Language development in later childhood

While the most obvious aspects of language development occur during the early stages of our lives, such development does not come to an abrupt halt at some point during childhood. Language continues to develop and change in later childhood and adolescence. Marilyn Nippold explores how linguistic capacity is developed through later childhood. She writes about syntactic developments such as when older children learn how to use the passive voice in their speech or to construct more complex sentences (Nippold, 2004). She also explores the ways in which language changes in adolescence (Nippold, 2000). Teenagers spend much more time communicating with their peers than with family members; syntactically, language, particularly written language, becomes more complex as education requires, for example, the capacity to engage in persuasive styles of writing as well as a greater complexity of form. There are also semantic changes to language, including understanding and using figurative language such as similes and metaphors.

Language and brain development in adolescence

As we have described elsewhere in this book, adolescence is a period in which we see significant changes to the structure of the brain. There is also a growing body of evidence to show how these changes affect our language development. Our capacity to listen gets faster as we develop. Our brains can process auditory signals faster when we are adults than we can in later childhood (Poulsen et al, 2009). A small study has suggested that we also develop greater motor control over how we articulate words as we move into adolescence (Walsh and Smith, 2002). White matter extends in several areas of the brain. Of interest here is the **arcuate fasciculus**, a group of axons that connect the Wernicke's and Broca's areas of the brain. Maturation of white matter in this area has been correlated with language performance in adolescence (Ashtari et al, cited in Mareschal et al, 2007). There are also changes to the white matter in the frontal lobes, which Mareschal and colleagues report is associated with developments in both behaviour and language.

Gender and language acquisition

> Recent studies have focused on the similarities between the brains of boys and girls

The idea that females are somehow better at language than males is one that seems to be rooted in our cultural heritage. Studies in the 1970s (e.g., Maccoby and Jacklin, 1978) added to the generally held view that girls performed better than boys on language-related tasks. A much-publicised study in 1995 (Shaywitz et al, 1995) purported to show that women use both hemispheres of their brain in language tasks whereas men only use the left hemisphere. The study was based on just 19 men and 19 women and later studies showed this to be entirely wrong (Sommer et al, 2004). More recent studies have focused on the similarities between the brains of boys and girls in terms of both structure and function. A recent meta-analysis by Etchell and colleagues (2018) looked at 46 studies that directly studied sex differences in language-related tasks in children who were regarded as typical in their development. The study found that the evidence for differences in brain development was inconsistent and that evidence for differences in structure and function were limited and conflictual. Whether or not sex differences were found depended largely on what was being measured and which areas of the brain were being studied. For example, one study of the inferior frontal gyrus found higher grey matter volume in boys than in girls (Blanton et al, 2004), while another study (Wilke et al, 2007) found the opposite. Likewise, studies of the corpus callosum have shown better inter-hemispheric connectivity in female brains but better intra-hemispheric connections in male brains (Ingalhalikar et al, 2014). To confuse matters further, another study showed no significant age-related differences whatsoever between the sexes in this area of the brain (De Bellis et al, 2001). This led the authors of the meta-analysis to conclude:

> There is inconsistent evidence of sex differences in brain structure/ function related to language. Although there may be statistically significant differences in brain structure and function between boys and girls, the practical significance of these differences seems to be negligible. (Etchell et al, 2018, p 16)

As in other areas where there have been assumptions about gender difference that have proved fallacious, differences in language development based on gender also seem problematic. Clearly this is an area that needs further research, but the contemporary view is that language differences based on gender in terms of brain structure and function are insignificant.

Summary

- Empiricist theories of language, such as those of Skinner and Bandura, emphasise that language is something that is acquired through learning.

- Nativist theories, such as those of Chomsky or Pinker, emphasise that language develops through an innate capacity.

- Social interactionist theories, such as that of Bruner, emphasise an innate capacity, together with a need for human interaction, as being necessary for language to develop.

- The early work of Paul Broca and Carl Wernicke established that the left temporal region of the brain is important for language processing.

- While it is now established that there is a preference for left temporal language processing, other areas of the brain are important for both speaking and listening.

- Brain plasticity allows children who have suffered damage to the left temporal region to use other areas for language.

- Early language processing allows infants to recognise and categorise the sounds of the languages they hear spoken around them.

- The ability to hear all the sounds of all the world's languages diminishes after the age of six months.

Revision questions

1. Match the theorists with the theories:
   a. Skinner; b. Bandura; c. Chomsky; d. Pinker
      (i) We learn by imitation.
      (ii) We have an internal mechanism for learning that already understands the universal rules of grammar.
      (iii) We are rewarded for doing this right and this encourages us to behave in this way.
      (iv) Children learn language creatively.
2. Which areas of the brain are involved in language development?
      a. Broca's area; b. Wernicke's area; c. anterior superior temporal lobe; d. middle temporal gyrus; e. middle temporal gyrus; f. the temporo-parietal junction; g. all of them.
3. What is the 'forbidden experiment'?
4. Can you explain the idea of equipotentiality?
5. What do we learn from the tragic case of Genie about the acquisition of language?

6. What are the consequences for language development of early damage to the left temporal region of the brain?
7. How does categorising the sounds of phonemes help us to learn language?
8. How does language develop in later childhood?
9. How does language develop during the teenage years?
10. What are the differences between the ways in which boys and girls develop language?

Discussion questions

1. Do animals other than humans use language?
2. What advice would you give to the parents of a newborn baby about how they can help their child develop language?
3. Given the advantages of multilingualism, should we encourage all children to learn at least one additional language?

Our answers

1. Some of us have probably had pets that seem to understand what we're saying or perhaps you have seen examples on YouTube of animals seeming to speak. We also know that some birds can mimic human speech. These appear to offer support for the idea that animals can use language but are really examples of rote learning. So, the simple answer to this question must be a definitive no. The development of language is something that is uniquely human. There are certainly examples of apes being taught to use some simplified forms of language. An ape called Kanzi managed to learn about 200 symbols, but it remains a matter of dispute whether this was simply rote learning and whether he understood language in the way a human understands it. The ability to think and reason in a language and to speak unique sentences that have understood meaning is a human attribute that is not shared in the rest of the animal kingdom.
2. Our advice would be, make sure you speak and listen to your baby. You don't have to teach children to use language in a deliberate and systematic way. Just speaking with them, interacting with them, reading to them and showing them love, giving them attention and using language where appropriate will be fine. Children learn language through experience. Hearing you speak will help them understand the sounds of language. They will hear the phonemes of the languages you speak. If you are a multilingual household, then use all the languages you speak. Infants might take a little longer to sort out all the different sounds and work out which belongs in which language, but they will do it and then have the wonderful advantages of being themselves multilingual.
3. We certainly should. There are massive advantages to being multilingual. Some are simple, such as being able to communicate with people from other countries. Others are more surprising. The advantage that still seems most unexpected is in the research that shows multilingualism protects against cognitive decline in our later years.

Notes

[1] One of the ways this debate is formulated is in the language we use. For those in the behaviourist tradition, such as Skinner and Bandura, it makes sense to talk about language *acquisition*; for those in the nativist tradition, the more appropriate term is language *development*.

[2] A voiceless consonant vibrates the vocal cords much, much less than a voiced consonant.

[3] We use the words bilingual and multilingual here interchangeably. Clearly there are differences. Bilingual refers to the ability to speak two languages; multilingual means the ability to speak three or more.

Further reading

Boynton, K.A. (2021) *Supporting Early Speech-Language Development: Strategies for Ages 0–8*, London: Routledge.

Curtiss, S. et al (1974) 'The linguistic development of Genie', *Language*, 50(3): 528–554.

Friedmann, N. and Rusou, D. (2015) 'Critical period for first language: The crucial role of language input during the first year of life', *Current Opinion in Neurobiology*, 35: 27–34.

Knowland, V. and Donlan, C. (2014) 'Language development', in D. Mareschal, B. Butterworth and A. Tolmie (eds) *Educational Neuroscience*, Chichester: John Wiley, pp 134–171.

Saxton, M. (2010) *Child Language: Acquisition and Development*, London: SAGE.

On our website

You can find lots more material on our website at https://policy. bristoluniversitypress.co.uk/child-development-and-the-brain/companion-website

This includes:

Podcasts on language development: https://policy.bristoluniversitypress.co.uk/child-development-and-the-brain/companion-website/podcasts-on-language-development

8

Literacy and numeracy development

This chapter:

- considers the theories of how we develop numeracy and literacy;

- evaluates what we know about the neuroscience of numeracy and literacy development;

- critically examines what we know about developmental dyslexia and developmental dyscalculia and how these affect brain development.

Literacy

Reading is one of the most unnatural things we do

While the learning of language might be a natural process, reading is a highly unnatural activity; in fact, according to David Wren (2002) it is one of the most unnatural things we do. Reading is a cultural activity, developed only about 5,500 years ago. For most children, many aspects of reading need to be explicitly taught (Johnston et al, 2005; Rose, 2006) and only improve with practice. Often, learning to read requires a lot of hard work. Exactly how the skills are taught remains controversial, even though in the United Kingdom one method, synthetic phonics, is now mandatory.

Keith Stanovich (1985) has noted that when it comes to reading ability, the more children do of it, the better they get at it. He termed this the 'Matthew effect' (Figure 8.1) because in literacy terms the rich always get richer and the poor always get poorer. Good readers tend to read more and so their reading improves. Poor readers tend to read less and so their reading falls further and further behind that of their more literate contemporaries.

Reading is a highly complex process involving several different areas of the brain, including visual and auditory processing areas as well as aspects of short-term memory. To read and understand a passage such as the one that you are now reading, a complex array of brain-based skills need to be utilised. These include regulation of eye movements, decoding a visual sign into a sound, making meaning from this sign and then holding this meaning in the memory. The first of these processes is about controlling the eye so that it travels from left to right, or right to left, or up to down, depending on which language you are reading.

Eye movements

It is only the central part of the eye, called the **fovea**, that provides the sharp vision that is necessary for us to be able to read words on a page. When we read a line of text it feels to us as though our eyes are making a continuous movement along the line. In fact, our eyes take little jumps from one group of letters to another. These jumps are called saccades. We are unaware of the blurring taking place as our eyes move from one group of letters to the next. Most of our reading takes place in the gaps between these jumps when our eyes are momentarily still. For experienced readers these still moments when reading takes place last between 200 and 250 milliseconds (Rayner, 1998). A millisecond is a thousandth of a second, so we are doing our reading in quick bursts lasting between one-fifth and one-quarter of a second.

Decoding

Next there is the problem of decoding. There has been considerable debate as to whether reading is a visual process or whether it involves phonological processes, that is, changing the visual image on the

> Please do not read this

page into a sound in the head. A study of readers aged from six to 22 years by Turkeltaub and colleagues (2003) showed that reading involves areas of the left temporal region that are usually associated with speech. The evidence is now quite strong that reading involves translating the squiggles that you see on the line into the sounds they represent. In slightly more technical language, we would say that the **graphemes** need to be converted into **phonemes**. In some senses this is what we mean by learning to read. We need to be able to decode and translate from the visual to the auditory and then make sense of what we have read. Studies to date of both children and adults reading single words have shown that this translation is also a very rapid process. Clearly there needs to be a similarity between the speed at which the eye jumps and the speed at which the brain does its processing. This is known as visual word recognition, which happens for both adults and children at between 160 and 180 milliseconds across most languages (see, e.g., Sauseng et al, 2004). Fluent readers learn to make this process of translation into something that happens automatically. You can see this for yourself. Look at any piece of writing that is in a language you understand. It is pretty much impossible not to read and comprehend what is written.

Comprehension and processing of reading

Reading is much more than just decoding. We do not read and understand words one at a time but, rather, derive our meaning from words at the level of both the sentence and the paragraph. At present there have been far more brain studies about individual word reading than there have been about text comprehension

(Perfetti and Bolger, 2004). Comprehension of what is read is a complex process that includes aspects of **syntax** and **semantics** as well as the ability to retain what has been read in the short-term working memory. Syntax is about the way we modify language to show whether we are talking about the past, the present or the future (tense) or whether we are referring to one or many (plural or singular). Semantics is the study of meaning in language.

The neuroscience of reading

> Other circuits can be recycled into a reading network

Just as we need to understand that reading is not a natural process, we also need to bear in mind that we do not have an area of the brain that has 'naturally' developed to facilitate reading. To paraphrase both Stephen Pinker and Maryanne Wolf, children's brains are wired for language, but reading is a bolt-on extra. Children can learn to read because of brain plasticity. This core feature of our brain means that areas that have evolved for other purposes, mainly visual and auditory circuits, can be recycled into what is now often termed a 'reading network'. This network has been identified as important across cultures and in many different languages and involves areas of the brain that are in the left hemisphere, specifically the frontal, temporo-parietal and occipitotemporal regions. This left lateralisation of reading develops over time. As readers become more proficient, activity in the left temporal and frontal areas of the brain increases.

The visual word form area

> The visual word form area plays a key role in reading, language processing and focusing attention

One part of the reading network that has been extensively studied has been called the visual word form area (VWFA) by Cohen and Dehaene (2004). This region of the brain is in the left occipitotemporal cortex area and involves a specific area called the **fusiform gyrus**. In adults, this region of the brain shows neural activity during reading. The way in which this part of the brain works seems to change as children develop their expertise in reading. As with other parts of the reading network, during the process of learning to read both the left and right hemispheres appear to be activated, whereas in mature readers the VWFA in the left hemisphere shows particularly strong neural activity (Schlaggar et al, 2002). As well as playing a key role in reading, the VWFA also plays a wider role in both language processing and focusing attention. A recent study (Chen et al, 2019) has found patterns of connectivity between the VWFA and the superior temporal sulcus, an area of the brain used in processing language and in social perception. The same study also confirmed evidence from other studies that the VWFA also plays a wider role in our capacity to choose on what and where we focus our attention.

Figure 8.1: The Matthew effect: the more children read, or are read to, the more their literacy improves

Source: Shutterstock Photo ID 1077765305

Memory

Storage in the memory areas of the brain is also a complex business that, according to Brooks and colleagues (2011), involves the storage of the sound patterns gained from reading. It also involves an inhibition process to stop thoughts straying and to sustain attention, as well as a certain amount of self-monitoring. Yet, as Kintsch and Rawson (2007) point out, working memory alone is not enough to account for the complex and often comparative processes that take place when comprehending and analysing a text. Kintsch and colleagues (Ericsson and Kintsch, 1995; Kintsch et al, 1999) suggest that long-term working memory is linked to conventional working memory by means of what they term 'retrieval structures'. We know that areas of the dorsolateral prefrontal cortex are used for working memory; however, many other areas of the brain are also important here, including the language areas of the left temporal cortex (Smith et al, 1998).

Comprehension

Brain studies show than many aspects of comprehension seem to be more distributed across the brain than is the case with decoding. The higher the level of the processing, the more distributed the functioning. For example, the left hemisphere is involved in dealing with vocabulary, syntax and semantics, but textual- and discourse-level analysis take place in both hemispheres of the brain (Hruby et al, 2011). The distributed nature of memory gives some clues as to how working memory and other storage areas might work together when higher-level thinking and processing of reading takes place.

Adolescent reading

Comprehending what is meant by a piece of writing is one thing: thinking about it, analysing it, critiquing it, is something else entirely. Once we have learned to read and to understand the meaning of a text, then we also need to learn how to think about it. According to Goldman (2012), effective readers need to learn how to process materials from a range of different sources (e.g., fiction, news, science texts), assess the relevance and reliability of such texts and then synthesise and evaluate these ideas. Wolf describes this as 'deep reading', 'characterized by the use of background knowledge, empathy, inference, analogical thinking, critical analysis and deliberation, contemplation, and – in its highest forms – insight and epiphany' (Wolf et al, 2016, p 153). As well as critical analysis, Wolf argues that two other processes are important: the ability to connect what is being read to other knowledge and so construct bridges between new knowledge and established knowledge; and empathy, or the capacity to imagine what another person is thinking and feeling. Goldman argues that such skills need to be learned and that this requires cross-disciplinary teaching as well as an emphasis on classroom-based discussion (Goldman and Snow, 2015). Adolescent reading is still a relatively new area of study and much more research is need into how adolescent brain development might affect the ability of teenagers to develop critical reading skills. The sensitivity of teenagers to reward, the significance of peer judgement and the tendency to engage with their peers, which we explore in Chapter 5, all seem relevant here, as does the capacity to process figurative language, which develops in late childhood and early adolescence.

Developmental dyslexia

Description and diagnosis

Developmental dyslexia is sometimes defined broadly to include all children who have problems with a range of reading and writing skills, including word identification, decoding and spelling. In this broad definition they may also have problems with word comprehension as well as word knowledge and syntax (Price and McCrory, 2007). It is also defined more narrowly as having difficulties solely with decoding (e.g., Peterson and Pennington, 2012). This is perhaps the most frequently used definition:

> Dyslexia is a specific learning disability that is neurobiological in origin. It is characterized by difficulties with accurate and/or fluent word recognition and by poor spelling and decoding abilities. These difficulties typically result from a deficit in the phonological

component of language that is often unexpected in relation to other cognitive abilities and the provision of effective classroom instruction. (Lyon et al, 2003, p 2)

> Dyslexia is a problem with phonological processing that does not correlate with other measures of ability

What is significant here is that it is identified as a specific problem with phonological processing, that is, in being able to decode the written word on the page into a sound, rather than a more general issue to do with language or cognitive processing. Also of significance is the unexpectedness of the problem, that is, it does not correlate with other measures of ability, particularly with IQ. It must be added that Lyon and colleagues also include in their definition the secondary consequences of dyslexia in that it can lead to problems with reading comprehension and a reduction in the amount that is read, which in turn can cause problems with vocabulary size and knowledge.

Prevalence

The prevalence of dyslexia depends on how you define it and, given the breadth of reading difficulties across populations, where you decide to put the cut-off point. Estimates across the world vary from 3% to 7% of the population (Wagner et al, 2020). There is also now evidence that dyslexia and other learning differences such as ADHD can overlap, although a recent systematic analysis (de Wit et al, 2018) suggests that better-quality research is needed to fully investigate the differences between the different conditions.

Dyslexia has also been shown to run in families. A male child with a dyslexic sibling or parent has a 50% chance of being dyslexic himself (Pennington et al, 1991).

Theories of dyslexia

There is no shortage of theories that attempt to account for why so many children have dyslexia. Here are just a few.

Critiquing the prevailing theory

The prevailing explanation of dyslexia is the phonological deficit hypothesis, namely that the reading problems associated with developmental dyslexia are about difficulties in translating written visual forms into word sounds. Children (and adults too for that matter) who have dyslexia have problems in storing, representing and retrieving speech sounds. This difficulty implicates both their short-term memory as well as the parts of the brain that are tasked with segmenting speech sounds into phonemes and, of course, the reverse process of

Table 8.1: Theories of dyslexia

Theory	Hypothesis
Phonological deficit theory (Stanovich, 1988)	It is problems with phonological processing, that is, turning words on the page into sounds in the head, that causes dyslexia.
Double-deficit hypothesis (Wolf and Bowers, 1999)	In this theory both phonological processing and slow processing speed cause dyslexia.
Speech rhythm deficit hypothesis (Goswami, 2002)	This sees the cause of dyslexia as originating in difficulties in detecting the rhythm of speech, particularly identifying the boundaries between speech sounds.
Magnocellular deficit hypothesis (Lovegrove et al, 1986)	Here the problem is seen as occurring in the magnocellular system causing interference with the motor/visual process of moving the fovea from one set of letters to the next.
Cerebellar deficit hypothesis (Nicolson and Fawcett, 1995)	The cerebellar connects to almost all other areas of the brain and contains half the neurons in the brain – this theory tries to subsume both the phonological and double-deficit theories.
The delayed neural commitment framework (Nicolson and Fawcett, 2019)	In this recent theory children with dyslexia take longer to build (and rebuild) the neural networks associated with reading.

joining up phonemes into words. While this may be the dominant theory, there are many others which point out the problems with this idea.

In an ideal world

It would be helpful if we could find the part of the brain that is responsible for dyslexia and then find a way of compensating for this neurological deficit. Of course, we'd need to be able to do this before the child started to read; that way, we would know this is a biological deficit and not caused by their experiences of trying to learn to read. These environmental issues complicate things further as ideally we'd like to know how the lived experience of the child improves or worsens a tendency towards reading difficulties.

Timing problems

Much of the controversy that surrounds the different theories of dyslexia arises from the fact that by the time the problem can be identified, children have already gone through the experience of being taught to read and will be at least five years old, if not considerably older. It then becomes very difficult to map out the developmental history that led to the diagnosis of the condition.

Brain imaging could help us to understand the neural correlates of dyslexia in children who have been found to have it, but such studies are to some extent hijacked by that most amazing quality of the brain, plasticity. By the time the child is identified as having a problem with reading and the brain scan is completed, the child will have already started to learn at least some of the basics of reading. The plasticity of the brain means that it will have adapted to the experience of struggling to read. However carefully we study the scan, it becomes impossible to separate out cause and effect.

Mapping

> It has not been possible to map one area of the brain that is responsible for dyslexia

Trying to find the area of the brain responsible for dyslexia has also proven difficult. Xi and colleagues (2017) have reviewed the current state of knowledge about the areas of the brain implicated in dyslexia. This includes the left temporo-parietal cortex, the left occipitotemporal cortex and the left inferior frontal gyrus. As we explored earlier, reading is an activity that involves a network of regions in the brain. It should be no surprise that difficulties in reading also implicate a wide network of neural regions.

Of significance here is that efficient and fluid reading relies on connections between multiple areas of the (mostly) left brain. This meta-analysis demonstrates that there is not a simple mapping exercise that can be undertaken to show where dyslexia resides in the brain. As Xi and colleagues also point out, reading is a developmental process, and how each of these regions develops in children with dyslexia as compared with children who do not have this condition will be different.

Early mapping

One of the ways of overcoming these problems is to look at the brains of children who have been identified as being 'at risk' of developing dyslexia because one or more of their parents has the condition. A Norwegian study (Clark et al, 2014) took 26 high-risk and 26 low-risk children and looked at their brains before they started to learn to read (in Norway this begins at ages six to seven), then they followed them until they were aged 11–12. The study found no structural differences in the 'reading network' areas of the brain in scans of the children before they started to read. They did, however, find that these children had a thinner cortex in the primary auditory and visual areas of the brain. As Goswami (2019) notes, this study demonstrates a sensory basis, a problem with basic auditory processing. This suggests that the under-activation of the 'reading network' reported in many other studies in children with dyslexia is a consequence of the fact that they do less reading rather than a cause of their dyslexia.

Another proposed solution to the problem can be found in the delayed neural commitment (DNC) proposed by Roderick Nicolson and Angela Fawcett's theory (2019).

The DNC framework

The DNC model is built on a 'minimal brain dysfunction' hypothesis. It supposes there is a slight difference in brain structure at birth, perhaps, for example, caused by abnormal neural migration in the early stages of development. It leads to just enough of a difference in brain structure to cause a difference in processing capacity, what is sometimes called a higher level of **processing noise**. Given that complex skills such as reading must become automatic if they are to be efficient, any difficulties with processing will impair this skill. Try reading this short paragraph to see this for yourself:

> I walked quickly down the street. Suddenly, I was a eguh gniyfirret retsnom.

Whatever your language skills, the fact that the latter part of the second sentence is written with each word spelled in reverse will be enough to stop the automaticity of your reading process! You cannot just pull the meaning effortlessly off the page. By the way, we are not suggesting that this example demonstrates the experience of reading with dyslexia, just that it shows how difficult it is to read if automaticity is absent.

As well as making the automaticity of reading more difficult, DNC is likely to cause some delay to the dual 'natural' processes of speech perception and production, leading to phonological problems that are at the heart of reading difficulties. DNC also leads to other learning difficulties such as making it harder to unlearn primitive reflexes that can interfere with more sophisticated learning and make it much tougher to move from decoding individual phonemes into whole word reading. Nicolson and Fawcett also cite evidence to show that children with dyslexia fail to develop a fully functioning visual word form area. This means that they fail to form fluent reading networks that can manage the phoneme to grapheme conversions that we referred to earlier.

Other theories also acknowledge the complexity of dyslexia. Maryanne Wolf (Wolf and Bowers, 1999), for example, argues that there are multiple factors that are responsible for a child developing dyslexia. Wolf argues that reading is both learned and unnatural. This means that we must repurpose existing circuits, primarily those in the auditory and visual cortices. One of the best means of achieving this for parents is to read to their children. Households where there is little or no exposure to books and stories produces children who fall behind their peers in reading.

Wolf also argues that this lack of exposure can lead to delays in the development of the brain's reading network, problems of connectivity between the component parts of the network and a lack of automaticity in any of these parts. These problems could be to do with phonological awareness, phoneme to grapheme conversion, or a limited ability to perform rapid automatised naming (RAN), such that once the phoneme is recognised it cannot be quickly matched to a word and a meaning stored in the memory of the brain. So, the letters C–A–T need to be linked to the word 'cat' stored in the child's lexicon, and that then needs to be linked to the concept *cat* that is stored in the child's memory. If the child has developed a capacity for RAN, then this can all happen in a millisecond. If this has not developed, then it will take longer and consequently reading will be much slower.

This slowness could also be linked to **orthographic knowledge**, that is, recognising that C–A–T spells the word 'cat'. It could be linked to **semantic knowledge**, that is, understanding that the word 'cat' refers to all sorts of cats, from Tiddles who is sleeping by the fire to the lion in the zoo to the leopard in the African savanna.

Concluding thoughts about dyslexia

Dyslexia continues to be the subject of considerable neurological research. Advances in techniques as well as advances in genetics should help us identify those children and those families where there is a history of dyslexia, and then we should be able to scan the brains of those children before they begin to read. This will help identify the brain areas that underlie dyslexia as well as help educators decide on the best techniques for helping children who have normal levels of intelligence but who struggle to read.

Numeracy

Calculating, like reading, is a learned skill, although, unlike literacy, there is some evidence to suggest that we might be born with a basic capacity to count. It is a complex process involving visual, spatial and language skills, the capacity to focus attention, as well as utilising both working and long-term memory.

There are two systems in humans and in other species for representing numbers: a rough and ready approximate system for big numbers and another, much more accurate system for small numbers, that is, those from one up to about four. There is evidence that these are present in some form in very young infants. We will look at the development of the big number system first.

The big-number system

> Our big-number system distinguishes between big amounts and small amounts

Human infants, as well as many animal species, have the capacity to distinguish between different amounts provided there is enough of a difference between the two quantities. There is considerable evidence to suggest that infants and adults do this by means of a process called **analogue magnitude representation** (AMR). AMR suggests that numbers are represented in our brain by means of an internal measure that allows us to hold a rough idea of magnitude. We do this by having a neural-based internal representation of size.

Let's look at the words 'magnitude' and 'analogue representation' in order to fully understand the concept.

The idea of magnitude refers to how much bigger or smaller one thing is than another thing. If I have two beans in a sack and then someone gives me another two, then this is a doubling of the number of beans in my sack. The ratio between what I had to start with and what I have afterwards is 2:1. If, however, I have 20 beans in my sack and someone gives me another two, then this is an addition of a much smaller magnitude, just 10% or a ratio of 10:1.

The term analogue representation suggests that there is an equivalent amount of neuronal activity that happens in our brain that equates with the magnitude of the numbers we are calculating. So, when we get twice as many beans (a ratio of 2:1) as we had before, there is much more neuronal activity than if we get just 10% more (a ratio of 10:1). This means we are likely to be much more accurate in our internal representations of numbers when the ratio is around 2:1 or more and much less accurate than when the ratios are 10:1 simply because we have more neurons firing away when the ratio is significant than when it is less so.

This approximate system seems to be reasonably well developed by the time infants are aged six months. Goswami (2019) presents evidence from studies which suggest that infants use AMR to make decisions about quantity. For example, Libertus and Brannon (2010) conducted an experiment with 80 infants with a mean age of six months. The infants were shown two visual displays, one showing a series of images in which the number of dots on a screen stayed the same and one in which the numbers changed. As we know, infants quickly become habituated (and thus disinterested) by things that stay the same but are more engaged with things that keep changing. In this experiment most of the infants looked longer at the changing display, and the greater the ratio of change between one screen in the display and the next, the longer they looked. Even young infants, it would seem, have a greater preference for big changes in ratios, such as 20 dots changing to ten dots, than they do for smaller ratios, such as 15 dots changing to 20 dots. Goswami argues that the infants' sensitivity to ratios can be accounted for by AMR. There is also evidence that this capacity becomes sensitised and that older children can better discriminate between smaller ratios than younger children.

The small-number system

Experiments with young infants have shown they have the capacity to accurately distinguish between different amounts so long as those amounts are quantitively small. Infants as young as five months can distinguish between one, two, three and four objects. In a classic experiment Wynn (1992) showed that infants with a mean age of around five months could understand basic addition and subtraction using three objects. Wynn's experiment shows

> Our small-number system helps us distinguish between one, two and three

Figure 8.2: Learning to count

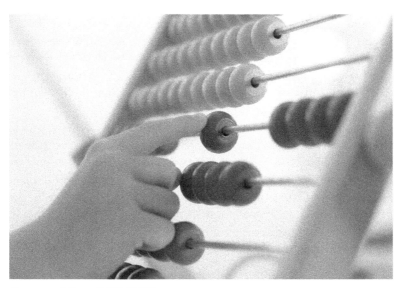

Source: Shutterstock Photo ID 563053258

that 'humans are innately endowed with arithmetical abilities' (1992, p 749) (Figure 8.2). Later experiments (e.g., Wakeley et al, 2000) disputed this finding but a recent meta-analysis of the significant studies (Christodoulou et al, 2017) found that Wynn's findings were still supported by most of the research.

Learning to count

Children begin to count when young and start using the language of counting often before they really understand the relationship between the words they are using and the quantities they are supposedly 'counting'. In other words, counting begins linguistically before children understand that numbers refer to precise quantities (cardinality) and that numbers progress upwards and downwards (ordinality). By the age of five most children can count from one to five (Gelman and Gallistel, 1978). Wynn (1990) suggests that at about the age of three and a half children begin to have a conceptual understanding of counting. Others suggest that there is a slower, more linear progression through the process of learning to count using larger and larger numbers (Carey et al, 2017).

Von Aster and Shalev (2007) suggest a four-stage model of mathematical competence. In stage 1 very young infants show the capacity to subitise, that is, to quickly grasp the difference in the number of items in a small set (up to four) of objects. In stage 2 young children learn to apply labels to words and gain the capacity to count. In stage 3 children will learn (most often at school) to read Arabic numbers (1, 2, 3, 4, etc.) and learn how to add and subtract using this

Figure 8.3: Intraparietal sulcus

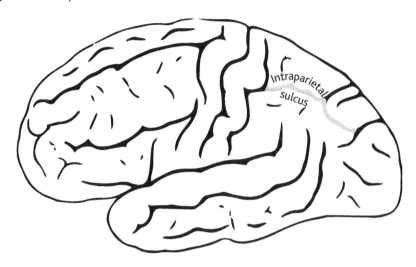

symbolic system with increasing speed and accuracy. In stage 4 they learn the numerical number line:

1	10	100	1,000	10,000

Rapin (2016) suggests it might take several years for children to develop the capacity to manipulate increasingly large numbers on the number line. Continued practice can lead to quick and accurate answers to frequently used combinations and a knowledge of multiplication tables, for example, 'seven fives are thirty-five'.

The neuroscience of numerical development

The evidence from brain imaging studies has homed in on an area of the brain in the parietal region, specifically the intraparietal sulcus (IPS) (Figures 8.3 and 8.2). We use different areas of the brain when we are learning how to carry out a mathematical procedure to those that are used when we are familiar with the process. Butterworth and Walsh (2011) discuss how when we do a new numerical calculation we use areas of the brain around the bilateral intraparietal sulcus and the frontal lobes; however, once we have learned the procedure, we start to use another part of the brain, the angular gyrus in the left parietal lobe, a part of the brain that is involved in memory retrieval.

The IPS is now widely agreed to be the area of the brain that deals with our conceptual understanding of magnitude. What is more, this capacity to be able to hold onto the idea of the bigness or the smallness of a number seems to be central to our capacity to perform arithmetical calculations. The importance of this area has been confirmed using both fMRI scans and EEG. The fMRI study (Cantlon et al, 2006) found that the right-hemisphere IPS was activated in four-year-old children who were asked to respond to differences in the numbers of circles or squares on a visual display. The EEG study asked children and adults to decide whether the numbers displayed on a screen were smaller or larger than the number five. Both groups produced very similar waveforms on the EEG display from the parietal area of the brain, although the response time of the adults was much faster than that of the children (Temple and Posner, 1998).

That is not to claim that this is only the area that deals with numbers. The IPS is part of a wider number network and counting relies on this network rather than just happening in one part of the brain. Doing maths is also a complex process involving short- and long-term memory, executive functioning and phonological processing. Typically, these involve areas in both hemispheres of the brain and include the dorsolateral and ventrolateral prefrontal cortex, the anterior cingulate, the occipito-ventral cortex and the medial temporal lobe (Peters and De Smedt, 2018). However, most studies suggest that problems with the IPS could well be the neural origin of dyscalculia.

Developmental dyscalculia

Developmental dyscalculia is a specific learning disability which results in children who are otherwise typical in their development struggling to learn mathematical skills. This might be, for example:

- understanding that the labels 'one', 'two', 'three' and so on refer to the number of items in a set;
- estimating approximate numbers of things;
- understanding that we can meaningfully count up the numbers of items in a set (cardinality); or
- understanding that numbers represent quantities going up or down, so that two is bigger than one and five is less than six (ordinality).

It is variously estimated that dyscalculia affects between 3% and 6% of the general population, so roughly the same prevalence as dyslexia. Despite this there are far fewer studies on dyscalculia than there have been on dyslexia. It occurs with regularity alongside other developmental disorders, particularly dyslexia and ADHD. There is also evidence of a genetic component to dyscalculia (Shalev et al, 2001). A 2005 report using data from two longitudinal studies argues that problems with numeracy are of more significance than problems with literacy, resulting in, for example, a greater likelihood of unemployment and mental health difficulties as well as a raft of other social disadvantages (Parsons and Bynner, 2005). It seems unlikely that this situation has changed much in the intervening years.

Theories of dyscalculia

There are two predominant theories about dyscalculia. The first theory is the core-deficit hypothesis and the second is the domain-general hypothesis.

Core-deficit hypothesis

The **core-deficit hypothesis** argues that many animal species including humans can distinguish between big amounts and small amounts. This is the capacity to process big numbers, the analogue magnitude representation we discussed earlier. It is a neat idea: if AMR is inbuilt, then children with dyscalculia must have problems making AMR-type judgements. The only problem with the idea is that much of the research fails to provide evidence to support it. Even those studies that do are often criticised on methodological grounds.

Goswami (2020) reviewed several recent studies. A study by Mussolin et al (2010), for example, showed that children with dyscalculia were slower than those in the control group at comparing quantities, whether those were shown as numbers, sticks or dots. This was taken as evidence of a deficit in the ANS. Goswami questions this finding on the basis that the group of children with dyscalculia were at a lower level of mathematical development than those in the control group and that this skews the data.

A recent study by Mammarella and colleagues (2021) tested the core-deficit model using a complex battery of tests on a large sample of children (n = 1,303) from 73 different classes across three different school grades. They found that none of their measures of basic number processing or of domain-general abilities, such as verbal ability and visuospatial short-term and working memory, detected any core deficits. Indeed, they state that looking for such a model may be 'simplistic' and that while children with mathematical difficulties might have problems both with processing numbers and with domain-general processing, neither of these is necessarily present.

The domain-general hypothesis

The **domain-general hypothesis** focuses more on problems associated with short-term or working memory and/or executive functions as an explanation for what they often prefer to term 'mathematical learning disability' (MLD), tending to avoid the term dyscalculia as it suggests a core deficit. A recent meta-analysis of 75 previous studies (Peng et al, 2018) found that children with MLD showed problems with a range of skills including general processing speed, phonological processing, short-term memory, executive functions and visuospatial skills. Mammarella and colleagues

> The domain-general model of dyscalculia focuses on issues around memory and executive control

(2021) are critical of some of the methods used in the studies included in the meta-analysis. They say, for example, that the studies vary in how they select children, particularly in the psychometric measure used to judge whether they should be considered as having MLD. They are also critical of the fact that many studies only use psychometric criteria and ignore broader criteria such as those proposed in the DSM V (American Psychiatric Association, 2013). Recently, Szűcs (2016) has suggested that MLD might be related to difficulties in visuospatial working memory alongside problems with short-term memory. This is clearly a field that requires much further investigation with the hope that once a specific problem has been identified, it will help to define a pathway to overcoming this problem that limits the life chances of many children throughout the world.

The neuroscience of dyscalculia

As we said earlier, most brain imaging research points to the area around the intraparietal sulcus as the part of the brain that is activated by mathematical activity. A longitudinal study by McCaskey and colleagues (2020) is starting to help us identify the brain network that is affected by dyscalculia. The study involved 35 children aged between eight and 11 years, 23 of whom had been identified as having dyscalculia. It showed that the children with dyscalculia performed less well than the other children in the study and that this reduced performance continues from childhood into adolescence. The study also showed reduced grey matter volumes in both parietal lobes as well as in the occipital, temporal and frontal areas of the brain. As we have seen, these areas of the brain are seen as significant in terms of the processing of numbers.

One of the criticisms that Goswami (2019) makes of the many studies into dyscalculia is that almost all of them fail to match typically developing children with those with dyscalculia in terms of ability. It is clear that children with dyscalculia are worse at numerical processing than other children of the same age. Perhaps a more effective study would take children who are matched for performance, so that older children with dyscalculia could be matched against younger children who do not have dyscalculia. They might then perform at the same level, but we would be able to see if there are differences in the way their brains function when they are carrying out mathematical operations. The McCaskey study does not do this, and we are still waiting for such a study to be published.

In the meantime, we can see that there is evidence of differences in the way children with dyscalculia process numerical data. It looks as though such differences persist over time. As well as longitudinal ability-matched studies, we also now urgently need research into how interventions might impact on brain development – we need to find out what works and what doesn't.

Summary

- Unlike speaking and listening, reading is an unnatural activity and one that many children need to be explicitly taught. While the exact mechanisms for achieving this remain the subject of considerable debate, the evidence now suggests that we translate the printed word into sound before we begin the process of comprehension.

- The visual word form area is seen as important in the process of reading, particularly in decoding.

- Comprehending and thinking about reading involves more areas of the brain than are used in decoding text.

- We are only just beginning to understand which areas of the brain might be implicated in developmental dyslexia. Some studies have focused on the left and right temporo-parietal regions; others have suggested areas such as the cerebellum, frontal lobe, caudate and thalamus.

- There are two systems of numeracy in humans and other animals. The first deals with big differences in magnitude and the second deals with small numbers.

- The intraparietal sulcus is involved in numerical calculations.

- There are two hypotheses to explain dyscalculia. The core-deficit model argues that it is all about our capacity for analogue magnitude representation. The domain-general hypothesis takes a wider view, focusing on memory and executive functions.

Revision questions
1. What are saccades?
2. What do we mean when we say that reading is not a natural process?
3. What parts of the brain are activated by reading?
4. What changes to how we read occur during adolescence?
5. What is the dominant theory of developmental dyslexia?
6. What are the main problems associated with this theory?
7. What areas of the brain are associated with developmental dyslexia?
8. What is analogue magnitude representation?
9. What part of the brain is most associated with numerical calculation?
10. What's the difference between the core-deficit hypothesis model of dyscalculia and the domain-general hypothesis of dyscalculia?

Discussion questions

1. What would be the impact of identifying the neural substrates for developmental dyslexia?
2. Why do we know so much more about dyslexia than we do about dyscalculia?
3. What has been the impact of social media on the literacy of children and teenagers?

Our answers

1. It could be argued that neuroscience does not offer us much. There is already a huge body of knowledge about dyslexia and an equally large knowledge base around helping young people with this specific learning difference. Brain science has also a made some contentious claims. For example, the 'brain-based' learning methods introduced in previous decades were often unhelpful to say the least. At the same time, as our discussion about dyslexia shows, understanding the neural origins of dyslexia could help us define the 'why' and the 'how' of this condition. In time, it will also help us develop new interventions or perhaps fine-tune existing ones.
2. The reasons are probably more social and cultural than scientific. It is more socially acceptable to be bad at maths than it is to be bad at reading. For example, you might hear someone say, 'Oh, I'm terrible at maths', whereas there is more shame in admitting that you struggle with reading. Being functionally illiterate is seen as a personal failure whereas being unable to do basic maths is somehow more allowable. Dyslexia research is also more established. Dyslexia was first described in the 1870s, while dyscalculia was not really described until the 1950s. The Dyscalculia Association was set up in the United Kingdom in 2018, whereas the Dyslexia Society and the Dyslexia Association were set up in the early 1970s.
3. We have looked elsewhere at some of the impacts of new technology on language and literacy. Here's another idea. According to Statistica (O'Dea, 2021) there are currently over six billion people on the planet with a smartphone and it is estimated that this will rise to 7.5 billion by 2026. Mobile phones bring with them education, particularly literacy. Literacy is seen by many as a way out of poverty. The Borgen Project (Phan, 2014), for example, suggests that mobile phone technology has helped those on the African continent improve their literacy rates from 52% in 2008 to 63% in 2014. More recent statistics suggest that this is continuing to rise. There are many media moral panics (see Chapter 5) around the impact of technology on the mental and physical health of young people, but it is likely that globally the impact on rates of literacy and poverty may be very positive.

Further reading

Butterworth, B., Varma, S. and Laurillard, D. (2011) 'Dyscalculia: From brain to education', *Science*, 332(6033): 1049–1053.

Costa, A. (2021) *The Bilingual Brain: And What It Tells Us about the Science of Language*, London: Penguin.

Kearns, D.M. et al (2019) 'The neurobiology of dyslexia', *Teaching Exceptional Children*, 51(3): 175–188.

Peters, L. and De Smedt, B. (2018) 'Arithmetic in the developing brain: A review of brain imaging studies', *Developmental Cognitive Neuroscience*, 30: 265–279.

Wolf, M. (2008) *Proust and the Squid: The Story and Science of the Reading Brain*, Thriplow: Icon Books.

Wolf, M. (2019) *Reader, Come Home: The Reading Brain in a Digital World*, New York: HarperCollins.

On our website

You can find lots more material on our website at https://policy.bristoluniversitypress.co.uk/child-development-and-the-brain/companion-website

9

Learning and memory

This chapter:

- explores the development of human memory and considers ideas about how these memory systems develop;

- explores several different ways of learning and looks at the brain systems that underpin them;

- considers some of the more questionable ideas about learning and the brain that have become popular in recent years.

A key theme in this book has been that brain development is dependent on experience. Of course, nowhere is this more obvious than when we consider learning and memory. In Chapter 2 we distinguished between experience-expectant development and experience-dependent development. In brief, experience-expectant development involves the overproduction of synapses; some of these are used and retained while others are pruned away. This process of synaptogenesis and pruning happens first in the visual and auditory parts of the brain, then in the parts devoted to language and lastly in the PFC. Experience-dependent development occurs over the course of the lifespan and equates to the process of learning and then storing in memory what has been learned. It involves the generation of new neural connections and the modification of existing connections.

We can see that learning and memory are highly interdependent. Explicit memory systems allow for the recall and reprocessing of experience. Learning is usually seen as a process that has the potential to change either knowledge or behaviour or, sometimes, both. There are many different ways of learning, and we explore some of them in this chapter. Likewise, human memory seems to be not one single system but a series of different systems, all of which operate and develop distinctively. In this chapter we begin by exploring the development of different types of memory systems and then go on to look at how these relate to different types of learning.

Memory

Memory is often divided into long-term and short-term memory, although there is considerable evidence that this division is too simple. There are at least three different temporal divisions that we can make: iconic memory, working memory and long-term memory; there is also a good case for what is termed intermediate memory.

Iconic memory

Iconic memory is visual and lasts for just a few seconds

Iconic memory is the name given to the shortest type of memory; it is sometimes also known as sensory memory. Iconic memory is purely visual. It refers to a memory system that lasts only fleetingly, perhaps for a matter of a few seconds; recent research suggests that it deteriorates quickly, dying a sudden death rather than fading gradually (Pratte, 2018). Iconic memory plays a key role in giving our visual experiences a sense of continuity. This is most obvious when we are watching television or viewing a film: it allows us to receive it as a continuous stream of images. In a broader sense, it allows us to detect changes in what we are seeing. If we are to see that a scene is different from how it was a moment ago, we must be able to hold in our minds the earlier image. A study by Blaser and Kaldy (2010) shows that iconic memory is formed by the age of six months. Blaser and Kaldy also suggest that it is adaptive, part of a versatile system that allows infants (and adults too, for that matter) to use limited resources in the brain to process lots of information and select out into more substantive memory systems the things that are important.

Working memory

Working memory stores small amounts of information for short periods of time. It is used to store and manipulate language, visual and spatial information. Working memory develops during childhood and adolescence. We have already discussed in some detail the development of working memory in relation to how ideas about Piaget's formulation of object permanence have changed as a result of new knowledge about the brain (for a full account see Chapter 3).

Intermediate memory

There is also some support for a third temporal division: **intermediate working memory**. This accounts for those items that we can remember for a while, but not for the long term. For example, you might remember what you had for breakfast today and yesterday but you are unlikely to be able to name what you had each day last week.

Infants tend to spend longer looking at new objects than they do looking at ones that are familiar. The conventional view here is that infants prefer novelty. The work of Bahrick and Pickens (1995), which measured infants' attention to moving objects, challenges this view and also tells us something about infant intermediate memory. They agree with the conventional view that three-month-old infants prefer novelty. This is typically measured in experiments where the delay between experiments is measured over a period of about one minute. However, when they lengthened the delay between experiments things changed. When the delay was between one day and two weeks infants showed that they had little preference for the familiar over the unfamiliar. This was seen as a result of intermediate memory. When the delay was increased to periods of one to three months, then infants reacted by being more interested in the familiar.

Later work (Bahrick et al, 2002) has shown that there are differences in memory retention of static as opposed to moving objects. As this discussion shows, links between our understanding of intermediate memory and our knowledge of what happens in the brain have not yet been made. This is an area that clearly needs further development.

Long-term memory

Long-term memory can be divided into implicit memory and explicit memory. Implicit memory is automatic, unconscious and non-verbal. Explicit memory is verbal and conscious.

The case of HM

Most of what we know about long-term memory was gained initially from the experiences of one man, known for most of his life as HM, although his real name was Henry Molaison (1926–2008). HM suffered from a very severe form of epilepsy. This meant that he experienced on average one major seizure a day. In 1953, at the age of 27, he had an operation that involved the removal of large parts of both temporal lobes, a bilateral medial temporal lobectomy. While HM was relieved of the worst of his epilepsy, he suffered a severe form of memory loss that meant that while he could remember events from before his operation, he was unable to form new long-term memories. He was effectively imprisoned in the present moment, not recognising friends or neighbours and unable to retain memories of what had happened earlier in the day.

You can learn more about HM and his brain at the HM Project, part of The Brain Observatory. https://www.thebrainobservatory.org/.

HM has been the subject of considerable study (e.g., Cohen and Squire, 1980; Squire and Zola-Morgan, 1991). These studies have helped neuroscientists to understand several important new ideas about memory. Firstly, the medial temporal lobes play a significant role in memory. Secondly, there are different types of memory, and these are stored in different places within the brain. These studies have shown us that we can divide long-term memory into two types. As we said earlier, the first of these is called implicit or non-declarative memory and the second is called explicit or declarative memory.

Development of implicit (non-declarative) memory

> We may not realise we have implicit memories, but they can still control our responses

Implicit memory happens outside our conscious control and the information stored there is not stored in the form of words. It might be a smell or a feeling or an image that we can recall, sometimes in a way that we might find puzzling. We may not realise that we have information stored in our implicit memory, but we will often behave in ways that demonstrate that it is there but outside our consciousness. We may not remember why we have a liking for particular sounds or colours or tastes, but unconscious memories stored in the parts of our brain that deal with this memory system are prompting us to express such preferences.

Our knowledge of how implicit memory develops is very incomplete. There is agreement that it develops within the first few months of life (Mandler, 1988) and that once we have reached the age of three years it does not get any better. It is also thought to be more important than explicit memory during the first two years of life (Johnson and de Haan, 2010).

There have been many psychological studies of implicit memory (e.g., Graf and Schacter, 1985; Schacter, 1995) that have established the existence of this memory system. We will mention just a few of these studies here. Carroll and colleagues (1985) showed children (aged five to ten years) and adults sets of pictures and then, after a period of time, showed them these same pictures plus some new ones. Implicit memory was measured by comparing reaction times in naming the familiar pictures with reaction times in naming the new ones. They concluded that implicit perceptual memory is different from the more explicit recognition memory. They also showed, by comparing the results for the adults and the children, that implicit memory does not develop with age.

Non–Verbal *a feeling*
Implicit a smell
memory
a sense
UnConscious

There have also been several studies of what are termed 'fragment completion tasks'. These tasks are often completed in two stages. In the first stage children are familiarised with some of the words or pictures that will be used in the second stage of the test. For example, they might be asked to name a set of pictures. In the second stage of the task children are shown these words or pictures in a fragmented form. The fragments gradually form into recognisable pictures. Implicit memory can be measured by means of whether they recognise the familiar pictures more quickly than those that are unfamiliar. Some examples of the use of this paradigm can be found in the research of Bullock Drummey and Newcombe (1995), Russo and colleagues (1995) and Perez and colleagues (1998).

These studies all support the idea that implicit memory develops much earlier than explicit memory and reaches its developmental peak in early childhood.

All these studies use perceptual memory. There have also been studies that look at olfactory memory, that is, the memory we retain of smell. One study, for example, has looked at the development of odour memory in young babies. This study (Allam et al, 2010) took advantage of the fact that lactating mothers were encouraged to rub a camomile balm onto their nipples as a means of mitigating soreness. The study traced the retention of this odour by testing infants' preference for it at seven and 21 months. Infants who had been exposed to the camomile odour during breastfeeding showed a marked preference for it at both ages.

While there have been several studies of implicit memory by cognitive psychologists, neuroimaging studies have been much thinner on the ground. Most of the studies have looked at how we develop our capacity to recall faces. Some studies with animals (e.g., McCormick et al, 1982) have shown that conditioned responses such as blinking an eye in response to a gentle tap on the forehead might be linked to the cerebellum. Other studies suggest that the parts of the brain used for storage and retrieval of implicit memories may change as the child develops. One example of this is the work of Thomas and colleagues (2004), whose fMRI study looked at the differences between adults and children aged seven to 11 years. In this study participants were required to press a button on a set of keys to indicate location in response to a visual sequence displayed on a screen. Sometimes these sequences were random and at other times they followed a pattern. Participants were not aware of these patterns. These types of tests are used quite frequently to test implicit memory. Usually, the response of the participants gets faster on the sequences where there is a pattern, and this shows evidence of implicit, unconscious memory. In the study by Thomas and colleagues it was found that the children used subcortical areas of the brain, whereas the adults tended to use parts of the cerebral cortex. There is also some evidence that the striatum, which is situated in the subcortical region of the forebrain, might be linked to implicit memory in adults and children. Finally, a recent study of older people who had damage to the hippocampal areas of the brain (Addante, 2015) suggested that damage to this area affects implicit memory in the same way as it affects explicit, conscious memory.

Development of explicit (declarative) memory

Explicit memory is conscious and verbal. It is stored in parts of the brain to which we have access; in other words, explicit memory can be consciously recalled. We are also usually able to explain in words things that are stored in our explicit memory.

We know much more about the development of explicit memory than we do about the development of implicit memory. This form of memory develops

Explicit memory

Conscious
Accessible
Verbal

much later than implicit memory. This links to ideas about infant amnesia, an idea, first propounded by Sigmund Freud (2002), that we are unable to remember events from our early childhood. One reason we are not able to consciously recall events before about the age of three years is that our explicit memory systems have not developed sufficiently until this age.

Tests of explicit memory

Tests of explicit memory tend to be based around infants' preferences for novel stimulation. Babies are much more interested in things they have not seen or heard before than they are in things with which they are familiar. In this paradigm (that is, experimental procedure) infants are first habituated to a particular stimulus. They might be played a sound, or presented with a pattern, picture or toy. This is repeated until the amount of time they spend looking or listening is reduced by about 50%. They are then presented with a novel stimulus, such as a new sound, a new pattern or a new toy. Paying more attention to the new stimulus clearly shows that they have a memory of the old one. The visual paired comparison is the most straightforward of these tasks, where infants are familiarised with a pair of identical stimuli. After a delay the familiar stimulus is then paired with a novel stimulus and the amount of time that the infant spends looking at each is measured. Longer looking at the novel stimulus indicates that knowledge of the familiar one has been retained in memory. The classic variation of this is called the delayed non-match to sample task, in which the infant is presented with an object that requires them to use one sense and which they have previously been familiarised with when using another sense.

Studies of the adult brain of HM (Scoville and Milner, 2000) showed that the medial temporal lobe (MTL) is central to the long-term storage of explicit memories. The MTL system consists of the hippocampus and other organs in the hippocampal region, including the perirhinal, entorhinal and parahippocampal cortices.

Schacter and Moscovitch (1984) suggested that this adult storage system does not develop until the child reaches about two years of age. However, experiments with both monkeys and children have shown that there is some ability to remember visual events before this age. Nelson (1995) has hypothesised that there might be what he terms a pre-explicit memory system, essentially a primitive version in the brain of what later becomes explicit memory. This memory system might be in existence when we are born. It relies on parts of the hippocampus that develop earlier than other parts of the medial temporal lobe.

Some studies have suggested that parts of the hippocampus may be important in novelty recognition, that is, the process of distinguishing what is new from what is familiar. Strange and colleagues (1999), for example, used fMRI scanning to find evidence of hippocampal processing of novelty in adults.

> **Improvements in explicit memory happen at age four to five and are linked to developments in the frontal cortex**

As children age beyond infancy, explicit memory systems continue to develop. Much of the improvement in memory that happens as children start school, at an average age of four to five years, has to do with developments in the prefrontal cortex. This allows children to process memory more consciously and to think about strategies for remembering things. There are also developments in semantic encoding. This is about processing and storing ideas that have inherent meaning. We can remember things better if we have a context and a reason for remembering them. For example, it is usually much easier to remember what you received as a present on your birthday than it is to store the names of the kings and queens of England – unless, that is, you have a particular interest in regal succession! The process for semantic encoding, which takes place in the frontal regions of the brain, is essential for this type of thinking and is therefore important in the development of long-term memory. The PFC is particularly important here, although we are less sure about which parts of the PFC are important in encoding memory and which parts help us to retrieve memories.

Explicit memory development in adolescence

There is some evidence to show that adolescence is a sensitive period for explicit memory. As discussed earlier, we are very likely to have strong recollections of events that happened in the period around adolescence than we do of events at other periods in our lives (the reminiscence bump). Studies have

> **The reminiscence bump describes the strong memories we form in adolescence**

shown that this is a cross-cultural phenomenon (Figure 9.1). In a 2005 study (Conway et al, 2005), 208 participants in their 40s and 50s (mean age 52 years) from Bangladesh, China, England, Japan and the United States took part in a study asking them to recall memories (see Figure 9.1). Most memories from all the participants were from the 10- to 30-year-old period of their lives. The content of the memories varied, with the US group recalling events that had a self-focus and the Chinese group more of a group focus, but the period in which most memories were recalled stayed much the same across nationalities. Fuhrmann and colleagues (2015) also report that memories of books, music and films from this period are of significance and that even what we may see as mundane, everyday events have a greater chance of being recalled and thus being significant if they originate in this period.

Figure 9.1: Lifespan retrieval curves from five countries

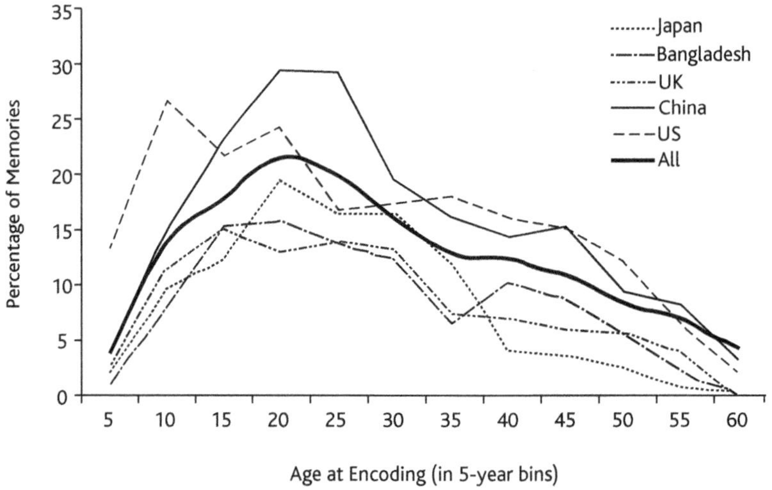

Source: Conway et al 2005, Figure 2, page 743. Reproduced with permission of SAGE

The intriguing question here is why this period is so universally recalled and the events of the period so significant. There have been several explanations offered and a meta-analysis (Munawar et al, 2018). These include the idea that late adolescence is when adult identity emerges and that many of the events that occur in this period can be seen as self-defining. Further, it may well be that this period becomes crucial to us as a means of defining and developing a stable sense of self.

Learning

Goswami defines learning as 'the modification of behaviour in the light of experience' (2019, p 79), reminding us that even the much-studied sea slug, the *Aplysia*, learns in this way. Just as there are several different types of memory, we can also see that there are many ways in which we learn. At the simplest level, much like the *Aplysia*, we learn through habituation and sensitisation. In the former we learn not to respond to a stimulus, whereas in the latter we become more sensitive and respond more quickly or even more fully to the stimulus. This type of learning seems to be useful when playing certain types of digital games. Behaviourist accounts of learning (Skinner, 1953) stress the way in which we learn to respond to the environment, emphasising the importance of positive reward for learning the correct response. Piagetian models of learning stress the way in which we construct knowledge through the development and expansion of schemas, a concept that was built on by Athey (2007) and Nutbrown (2006).

We have an inbuilt capacity to learn from experience and, as we will see at the end of this chapter, our brains respond dynamically and structurally to new experiences. Learning in an educational setting usually implies that there is both a purpose behind the learning and some sort of structure to what is being learned. Curricula are structured to help make learning easier, even if there is considerable disagreement about exactly what sort of curriculum

> We need repetition and practice if we are to sustain our learning

might best achieve that purpose. This might range from a traditional, formal curriculum to a broader set of principles, as outlined in the current statutory framework for early years education (Department for Education, 2017). Early years settings that practice 'free flow' play have put in place a set of resources that provide a structured environment in which learning can take place. Learning within an educational framework is also usually something that is sustained over a time – hence the link with memory. Few of us can learn and sustain our learning without repetition and practice. We can also clearly see this in infants. Learning to walk takes quite some time, a great deal of practice and numerous failures along the way. In this chapter we look at several different types of infant and child learning and show how our knowledge of the brain is helping us to understand these processes.

There are many ways of describing different types of learning – you might like to think of the different ways in which you yourself learn. There is, for example, learning through experimentation, learning through receiving instructions, intuitive learning, dialogical learning and learning by means of self-reflection, to name just five.

Goswami (2019) categorises several different ways of learning, including statistical learning, learning by imitation, learning by analogy and explanation-based learning. We have used some of these headings in this chapter to explore the relationship between brain science and learning.

Learning by imitation

One of the expedient models of learning is learning by imitation, that is, copying someone else's behaviour, an idea exemplified initially in Bandura's (1977) social learning yourself theory. This method of learning is now seen as essential for the development of infant cognition. Meltzoff and Marshall (2018) describe children as 'imitative generalists', in that they imitate pretty much everything they experience, and have shown they can do so both from immediate experience, what they are seeing or hearing, as well as from memory. It is also, they argue, a highly effective means of cultural transmission in which babies and children learn how to engage with the practices, skills and customs of their culture. It is also something that humans do far better than any other species on the planet (Tomasello, 2019).

In a series of increasingly ingenious experiments, Meltzoff (1985, 1988b, 1988c, 1995) traced the development of imitative learning in young children. His experiments involved activities such as an infant watching a toy being pulled apart by an experimenter several times. After a gap of 24 hours the infant was given the toy. Their success at pulling it apart was measured against that of an infant who had not seen the experiment the day before. Infants who had seen the experiment and who could imitate the actions of the experimenter were much more proficient than those who had not seen it.

The neuroscience of learning by imitation

Some recent studies have suggested that learning by imitating an action or behaviour may involve utilising the **mirror neuron system** (MNS). This is still a very controversial idea, with some neuroscientists (e.g., Dinstein et al, 2008; Hickok, 2009) suggesting that our ideas on this are still too speculative. Despite these reservations there is a growing body of evidence to support the idea of an MNS. This system is thought to contain neurons that fire in the brain when we watch an action being performed in much the same way as they do when we perform the action ourselves. The system has been found to operate in both humans and monkeys. There have been some initial studies on the development of this MNS in infants.

> Learning by imitation may involve the mirror neuron system

The use of images obtained by EEG have allowed researchers to start investigating the development of this MNS in infants (Marshall and Meltzoff, 2011). The EEG studies have shown that watching someone perform an action produces changes in both infants and adults in what are termed **mu waves**. These are synchronised rhythmical waves of electrical activity involving large numbers of neurons in the motor cortex. When an activity is performed there is a desynchronisation of the mu rhythm. This occurs both when the subject is performing a task themselves and when they are watching an activity being performed by someone else.

Statistical learning

This type of learning is automatic, implicit and unconscious. We live in a world that is full of sensory stimulation – noise, smells, language and vision. Statistical learning allows us to unconsciously process all this stimulation and extract from it a pattern that can be used for learning. It often takes place over long periods of time, although there is also evidence that it can be done rapidly. In their review of statistical learning Schapiro and Turk-Browne (2015) describe the many different areas in which statistical learning is used, including language, non-linguistic sounds, shapes, tactile stimuli and spatial locations.

As we have seen in Chapter 7, which looked at language development, one of the ways in which babies' brains benefit from statistical learning is through the unconscious processing of the language sounds they hear from their immediate environment. Just as language is initially learned by listening to the sounds of the native language and developing an ability to place these sounds into different categories, so the brain can process other sorts of information received through the senses and begin the process of categorisation. Statistical learning happens when the brain calculates probabilities based on the

> Statistical learning happens when the brain calculates probabilities

number of times it has heard or seen one sound or action following another. Kirkham and colleagues (2002) have demonstrated that babies as young as two months can undertake this kind of statistical processing of pictures. In their experiment, babies aged two months, five months and eight months were shown six shapes in different colours (turquoise square, blue cross, yellow circle, pink diamond, green triangle and red octagon) on a computer screen. After a period of habituation, the infants were shown pairs of shapes sometimes in a familiar order and sometimes in a novel order. Infants of all ages looked longer at the novel sequences than the familiar ones. This experiment shows that the brains of even very young babies have a propensity for statistical learning. This sort of learning is neither deliberate nor conscious but seems to be one of the ways in which the human infant is pre-programmed to learn through engaging with the world around them.

The neuroscience of statistical learning

Two of the important areas of the brain that are involved in statistical learning are the superior temporal gyrus (STG) and the inferior frontal gyrus (IFG) (Figure 9.2).

The STG is activated when it detects regular sequences such as those produced by speech patterns, particularly phoneme regularities. The IFG is involved in detecting regularities in both sound and vision. We have explored statistical learning when we discussed language processing in Chapter 7 and developmental dyslexia in Chapter 8.

Learning by analogy

Learning by analogy occurs when we learn how to do one thing and then find that this learning helps us with other tasks because we understand there are similarities. To give a simple example, learning how to put on gloves can be used when learning how to put on socks. Quite a lot of mathematical reasoning is about noticing patterns between one set of numbers (or shapes, sizes, weights) and another. We use analogy in our everyday thinking when we say, 'Doing *this* reminds me of *that*'. We also use it when we speak or think metaphorically: 'I feel like I'm a spider in a giant web …'. It is something that is also a common feature of many intelligence tests. Several psychological experiments have established that some form of learning by analogy can be achieved even by babies aged only three months (Greco et al, 1990). Studies by Sanchez and colleagues (2001) have

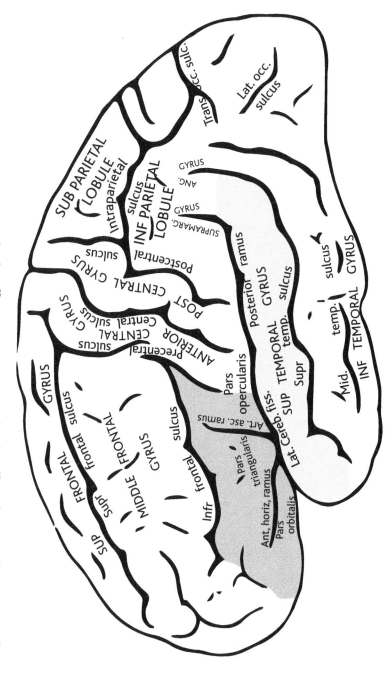

Figure 9.2: The superior temporal gyrus (STG) and the inferior frontal gyrus (IFG)

confirmed that some infants aged ten to 13 months are able to use analogical thinking to solve problems. Memory is clearly a key component of learning by analogy: to utilise previous experience in a novel situation requires both memory recall and analytic processing.

The neuroscience of learning by analogy

> The PFC plays a major role in analogical reasoning

The PFC is important when undertaking reasoning. Several brain-imaging studies of adults have identified one specific area of the brain that plays a major role in analogical reasoning, the rostral prefrontal cortex (Volle et al, 2010). This area of the brain develops more slowly than other regions and continues to develop throughout childhood and adolescence (Dumontheil et al, 2008). Studies show that several changes occur in the structure of this region in late childhood/early adolescence (Klingberg et al, 1999; Sowell et al, 2004). The study by Sowell and colleagues also shows that this area of the brain develops very substantially in children between the ages of five and eleven. A more recent study (Whitaker et al, 2018) has shown that there is likely to be a wider network which includes regions in the frontal, parietal and occipital regions of the brain that play a key role in analogous learning. The study found that the left lateral PFC played an increasing role in such learning and that the anterior left inferior PFC is more engaged as children grow older.

The video deficit effect

We have moved into an age where remote learning is becoming increasingly popular. While Meltzoff's (1988a) work showed that young infants can imitate behaviour that they see modelled on television, other modes of learning may not be as effective when delivered remotely. Many studies have shown that infants as well as toddlers and preschool children all learn less from a television demonstration than from a live one, a phenomenon that has been called the **video deficit effect**. Many reasons have been suggested for this anomaly, which are summarised in a recent meta-analysis by Strouse and Samson (2021). Firstly, there are fewer perceptual clues from a two-dimensional presentation that has less depth and texture than real life; this may result in children encoding less detailed memories. It may also be more cognitively demanding to try and learn from a digital image. Furthermore, there is less social information. For example, it is harder to see where an on-screen presenter is looking than it would be with a face-to-face teacher. Strouse and Samson conclude that, on average and across all age ranges and types of presentation, children learned more from face-to-face learning than they did from teaching presented by video. The difference is reduced as children get older because of factors such as improvements in working memory and a greater capacity to use referential clues to help learning.

Learning during adolescence

As we have explored in other sections of this book, there are developmental changes that happen in the brain that extend into adolescence and some that occur because of puberty. The brain does not grow in volume during adolescence: it reaches its peak volume by the end of childhood.

Brain development does not proceed in a linear fashion: temporal and frontal areas of the brain continue to develop into and beyond adolescence. For example, neurons in the frontal area of the brain become more myelinated during adolescence. Myelin insulates the axons of the neuron, speeding up the transmission of electrical impulses as they travel from one neuron to the next. This mean that it is likely that the neurons in our frontal cortex (the area responsible for executive functions) get faster during adolescence. There is also a decrease in the synaptic density of the brain. This does not begin in the frontal cortex until after puberty and continues during adolescence.

As we discussed earlier in the book, it is thought that there is a developmental mismatch in adolescence. The frontal areas of the brain responsible for executive control lag behind the subcortical areas of the brain that are implicated in emotional processing. This can lead to a propensity for more risky behaviour.

Adolescents learn better when they get rewards for their learning

Does any of this, or the other changes we have noted in adolescence, mean that adolescents learn better than adults and children? There is some evidence that it does, or at least that they are better at certain types of learning. Davidow and colleagues (2016) studied a group of 41 teenagers aged 13 to 17 and compared them with 31 adults. The study used a reinforcement learning task that rewarded correct answers to simple questions. The study found that the adolescents were better than the adults at learning from tasks where they achieved a positive result. The participants' brain activities were also studied using fMRI. This showed that two areas of the brain, the striatum (the brain's reward centre) and the hippocampus, were both involved in this activity, suggesting that the brain was both noting the positive result in the striatum and remembering this event by means of the hippocampus.

The fact that the brain is still developing and that it can make structural and functional changes in response to the environment means that adolescents in this sensitive period are also highly receptive to learning from experience. It is experience-expectant, meaning it is programmed to learn. The idea that we should continue to educate young people during adolescence and into early adulthood is still a relatively new idea. In the United Kingdom the school-leaving age was raised to 16 in 1972, to 17 in 2014 and to 18 the following year. In the United States the minimum age for completing mandatory education varies from 16 to 18. Across Europe it also varies, from 16 in France and Italy to 18 in Germany.

There is a need for far more research into changes to the structure and function of the brain and a need to provide a better match between how we encourage young people to learn and the development of their brains. For example, if adolescent brains are more sensitive to success and reward, does this mean they are also super-sensitise to failure? If risk taking is appealing, can we find ways to safely incorporate moderate risk taking into educational programmes at school, college and university? If working memory is dependent on good sleep patterns, then should we change the pattern of the teaching day?

Learning and memory at the level of the neuron

How neurons learn

Neuroscientists are starting to understand some of the ways in which learning takes place at the level of the individual neuron. Much of the work on these neural mechanisms of memory is based on animal experiments. There are clearly issues around comparing human brain mechanisms with those of other species (see the Introduction for more on this). At the same time, at the neuronal level humans share very similar structures and processes with other species. Quite a lot of work on neuronal learning, for example, has been based on the way in which neurons operate in the sea slug, *Aplysia*. *Aplysia* has far fewer neurons than we have and many of them are also much bigger, so they are easier to observe. Kandel (2007) showed that changes in the way in which *Aplysia* responds to stimuli can be observed and measured as changes in the ways in which neurons communicate with each other. In other words, as the sea slug learns to respond differently to stimuli, this learning is reflected in changes in the physical structure and chemistry that determine communication between individual neurons.

You may recall from Chapter 1 that neurons communicate with each other by firing an action potential (a brief electrical signal) down the length of the axon. This is then converted into a chemical signal by the synapse. This chemical messenger, or

> Learning changes
> the ways
> neurons communicate

neurotransmitter, travels across the synaptic cleft to the receiving neuron and binds to receptors, creating a small electrical charge in the receiving neuron. Experiments on the sea slug and several other animals have shown that learning produces changes in the ways in which these neurons communicate. Our understanding of these changes, and how they relate to learning and memory, can be traced back to the theories of Donald Hebb (1949). He suggested that when one neuron repeatedly responds to the firing of another the synaptic connection between them will become stronger. This is often captured in the expression 'cells that fire together, wire together'.

Exactly what changes take place when learning occurs seem to be quite varied. The process of learning involves the stimulation of neurons, resulting in several possible actions affecting both the presynaptic and postsynaptic cells. For example, a new learning experience might result in more neurotransmitters being released from the presynaptic axon. Or it could be that the postsynaptic membrane (that is, the part of the dendrite that receives the neurotransmitter signal) becomes enlarged or more sensitive. As learning continues, new synaptic connections will be formed. Learning physically affects the structure of the brain. If an area of the brain is being stimulated, in other words if the neurons involved are firing more frequently, then the number of connections between those neurons will increase. This capacity of the brain to form new synaptic connections is part of what is meant by the idea of **neural plasticity**.

Neural plasticity and learning

As we have shown throughout this book, the brain is highly experience-dependent. Learning is a particular form of experience that is explicitly directed at making changes to behaviour or knowledge. As such, learning strengthens the synaptic connections between individual neurons. If what is learned continues to be used, then these synaptic connections become stronger.

Conversely, of course, if this learning is not used, then the synaptic connections become weaker. This neurological explanation fits with the experiences that most of us have in relation to our own learning. For example, we may learn how to speak a second (or third, or fourth) language at school, but if we do not use that knowledge it grows weaker. Charles Nelson puts it this way:

> Neural plasticity can best be thought of as a subtle but orchestrated dance that occurs between the brain and the environment; specifically, it is the ability of the brain to be shaped by experience and, in turn, for this newly remoulded brain to facilitate the embrace of new experiences, which leads to further neural changes, ad infinitum. (Nelson, 1999, p 42)

Brain plasticity is a quality that we maintain throughout our lives, although, as we have seen in Chapter 2, it is a quality of the brain that is at its most spectacular during childhood. There are many studies exploring the area of adult brain plasticity. For example, Draganski and colleagues (2004) used fMRI scans to study the effects on the adult brain of learning to juggle. They found that learning this skill changes the volume of grey matter in the mid-temporal and left posterior intraparietal sulcus. What was particularly telling here was that when these adults stopped juggling, the amount of grey matter decreased. The study indicated that learning affects the physical structure of the brain.

Long-term potentiation

The capacity to retain memory capacity over time by means of increasing the effectiveness of synaptic connections is called **long-term potentiation** (LTP)

Figure 9.3: Long-term potentiation

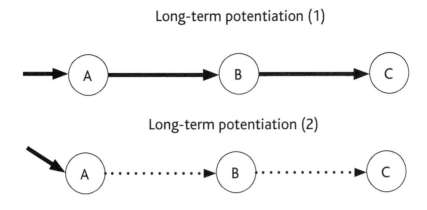

(Figure 9.3). The process of forming and retaining memories is enacted at the cellular level. If we look at this in terms of just three neurons it is easier to understand, although in reality the process will involve many thousands of cells (Figure 9.3).

Cell A, in response to a signal from elsewhere in the brain, fires off a chemical signal to cell B. Cell B in response fires off a chemical signal to another neuron, cell C. Once a cell has received a signal from another cell, this causes chemical changes to take place in the receiving cell. As a result, cell B becomes sensitised to the possibility of receiving another chemical signal from cell A. Cell A will now need to send only a weak signal to cell B in order for it to fire off a signal to cell C. Of course, cell C has also become sensitised to receiving a signal from cell B.

If cell A keeps firing and cell B keeps inevitably responding, the connection between them will strengthen such that whenever cell A fires it will trigger cell B. If this happens often enough then a permanent pathway will have been formed from cell A to cell B to cell C. In this way a memory is formed.

Almost all the experiments in this field have used non-human populations and there is a need to be wary about translating the results into a discussion about human development. However, there has been a considerable amount of work on young animals (e.g., Yasuda et al, 2003) that has shown that the mechanisms that are responsible for adult long-term potentiation are different from those observed in infant animals. We provide here just a small sample of the extensive work that has been carried out into this field.

Experiments with rats (Bliss and Lømo, 1973; Schwartzkroin and Wester, 1975) and rabbits (Weisz et al, 1984) have shown that LTP certainly occurs in some parts of the hippocampus, the area of the brain that is known to be important in the formation of long-term memories. In these experiments a high-frequency electrical stimulation is applied to certain neurons in the hippocampal region. A means of recording postsynaptic activity is also implanted into the brains of the rats used in the experiment. The rats are then put through a series of tasks involving learning and memory. The experiments show that there is a measurable increase in the LTP of the neurons that equates with the rats' increased ability to perform the tasks required. LTP seems to be something that affects some areas of the brain more than others. Areas such as the hippocampus and the amygdala seem to have the most LTP, whereas other areas, such as the sensory and motor systems, have less of it. Teyler and Fountain (1987) suggest that these areas that do not seem to show much evidence of LTP may act as a stable baseline against which the faster-acting areas of the brain can work.

As well as LTP, there are other kinds of plasticity including long-term depression, which is the weakening of synaptic responses – considered by some (e.g., Cordo et al, 1997) to be important in motor learning and memory formation.

Three neuromyths about learning

Learning styles

> There is no scientific evidence to support the idea of learning styles

Ideas about learning styles developed in the 1970s and 1980s and can be traced to several influences. For example, Howard Gardner's (1983) theories about multiple intelligences suggested that we each have a different range of capacities that are akin to different intelligences. According to Gardner's work, we can help individuals to develop separate intelligences. Those who advocate this theory (e.g., Prashnig, 2004) argue that all children have a dominant learning style. The different theories advocate a range of different styles. In Honey and Mumford's (2006) work, for example, there are four styles: activist, reflector, theorist and pragmatist. The most popular version with children is the Visual-Auditory-Kinesthetic (VAK) model (Fleming, 1995; Fleming and Baume, 2006), which argues that we are all visual, auditory or kinaesthetic learners. It would follow, therefore, that we learn best when we are able to use our dominant learning style. Unfortunately, despite its considerable popularity among some educators, there is absolutely no scientific evidence whatsoever to support the idea of learning styles. In fact, the evidence from neuroscience points to the opposite conclusion, that learning depends on neural networks distributed across multiple brain regions: visual, auditory and kinaesthetic (Goswami and Bryant, 2007, p 4).

There are many in the neuroscience community who have argued that the brain does not work in the segmented way that VAK and other ideas about learning styles suggest (e.g., Goswami, 2004; Corballis, 2012). Input into the brain, it is argued, is interlinked (Geake, 2008). We can see this most clearly in early infant development, where there is considerable evidence that processing for the senses is not yet separated. The neonatal-synaesthesia hypothesis argues that sound and vision, for example, are intertwined such that sounds will be seen and vision will be heard during early infancy. This gradually subsides during the course of normal development (Maurer, 1993). There is also a lot of evidence (e.g., Meltzoff and Borton, 1979) to show that infants use a range of senses to understand and interpret the world around them. Focusing children's attention on their learning from just one sense would seem to deny them access to learning from their other senses.

A study published in the *Journal of Neuroscience* (Kraemer, Rosenberg and Thompson-Schill, 2009) presented evidence that verbal and visual learning use separate parts of the brain. In the brain-imaging part of the study participants were asked to perform a task that utilised either verbal reasoning or visual processing. The images were compared with ratings from a verbal/visual questionnaire that had been completed by participants. The study showed that activities that require visual processing utilised the fusiform gyrus, the part of the brain associated with visual processing, and that verbal tasks used the supramarginal gyrus, the part of the brain used in phonological processing. This was a small-scale study of 18 adult subjects.

It looks as though the debate is likely to continue, although the majority view at the moment seems to be that most studies have not established enough evidence to support the claim for separate learning styles. For those who want to read further, a study by Pashler and colleagues (2008) examines the evidence.

The left brain is rational, and the right brain is creative

Since the earliest days of neuroscientific research there has been much speculation and discussion about the fact that the brain has two separate hemispheres. One idea that seems to have developed a specific – if misplaced – credibility is the notion that the right brain is a centre for creativity, imagination and passion, while the left brain is dominant in scientific, rational and analytical thinking. Unfortunately, this idea is largely false. Pretty much everything we do requires us to use both hemispheres of the brain. There is no scientific evidence at all to support the idea that creativity is particularly right-brained or that rational thought is an activity that exclusively uses areas of the left brain. Educational programmes that seek to try to foster aspects of the creative right brain are, in the words of Lindell and Kidd (2011, p 121), 'half-witted'.

Brain Gym

Brain Gym was devised in the United States by Paul and Gail Dennison during the 1980s (Dennison and Dennison, 1994). The programme makes some impressive claims about the way in which 'moving with the intention leads to optimal learning' (Breakthroughs International: The Brain Gym Program, 2022). The programme advocates a series of movements to stimulate brain activity and so facilitate learning. A number of different exercises are expounded in the programme. These include advocating that children be taught to touch points between their hairline and eyebrows, which will increase the blood flow from the hypothalamus to the frontal lobes; undertake exercises that extend the motion of the spinal column to improve communication between the brain and the CNS; and rub an area of the chest that is identified as housing the 'brain buttons' to improve communication between the right hemisphere of the brain and the left part of the body. There have been quite a lot of critical comments on Brain Gym from neuroscientists and educationalists. The most extensive examination of the claims has been carried out by Keith Hyatt (2007). Hyatt examines the theoretical foundation of the Brain Gym programme: neurological repatterning, cerebral dominance and perceptual motor training. Hyatt reports that neurological repatterning is based on the Doman-Delcato theory, which argues that we need to acquire motor skills at the appropriate age as we develop. If any of these are missed, neurological development will be affected. In order to overcome this problem children are given specific exercises to repattern the neurons. Hyatt states that most research has shown that this idea simply does not work and in any case lacks empirical evidence to support it. Cerebral dominance, the theory that one or the other hemisphere of the brain is dominant and that this has an impact on learning, is likewise dismissed by Hyatt as having been refuted by research. Perceptual motor training is more difficult to define; it refers to the idea that there are links between perception, movement and learning and that learning difficulties can be overcome by a combination of movement and developing perceptual skills. Hyatt again notes that research has served only to demonstrate that these techniques do not work. He writes:

> Neurological repatterning has been described as fraudulent, cerebral dominance has not been linked to learning, and perceptual-motor training has not withstood rigorous scientific investigation. (Hyatt, 2007, p 120)

Summary

- There are different systems of memory: implicit and explicit; long-term, intermediate-term and short-term.

- Implicit memory happens automatically and below the level of consciousness whereas explicit memory can be consciously and verbally recalled.

- We are only just starting to understand the neurological basis of implicit memory. It is thought to be present from birth. It is the most important form of memory during the first years of life. There is some evidence that subcortical processing is an important aspect of implicit memory.

- Explicit memory develops later, although there is some evidence that babies have a primitive version of explicit memory, called a pre-explicit memory system, that is based in the hippocampus.

- The developing PFC allows children to begin to process and take control over some aspects of explicit memory.

- Adolescence is often seen as a sensitive period for memory, with events from this period being recalled more often and with greater significance in later life.

- Learning makes physical changes to the brain at the neuronal level, strengthening connections between neurons as well as altering the structure of the neurons themselves.

- The ability of the brain to reshape itself is called neural plasticity and it is a quality that the brain has throughout life.

- Long-term potentiation refers to the way in which synaptic connections alter as a result of experience.

- Babies learn through imitation and have a preference for imitating real human beings rather than a televised image.

- We learn by processing data from our senses and unconsciously detecting patterns in this data.

- We can also learn to perform new actions by understanding the similarities between one situation and the next, and so learning by analogy.

- There are quite a few neuromyths that have developed around learning. There is no neuroscience evidence to support the idea that the right side of the brain is the seat of creativity or that we each have a preferred learning style.

Test your knowledge
1. True or false?
   a. Iconic memory lasts for only a few seconds.
   b. Iconic memory continues developing into late childhood.
   c. Iconic memory is purely a visual system.

2. True or false?
   a. Implicit memory develops in the first few months of life.
   b. Implicit memory is very important in the first years of our life.
   c. We can recall implicit memories whenever we like.
3. True or false?
   a. Explicit memory is very reliable.
   b. The medial temporal lobe is important for storing explicit memories.
   c. Explicit memory improves once the frontal cortex has developed.
4. True or false?
   a. Adolescence might be a sensitive period for developments in explicit memory.
   b. We often remember events from our adolescence better than other times in our life.
   c. The reminiscence bump helps us forget embarrassing moments from our teens.
5. What is the mirror neuron system?
6. How does statistical learning help us to learn things that we might not even remember learning?
7. Which area of the brain is important in helping us to learn by analogy?
8. What do you understand by the idea that there is a developmental mismatch in brain development during adolescence?
9. How does the idea of neural plasticity relate to learning?
10. What is long-term potentiation?

Answers to questions 1–4
1. (a) true; (b) false; (c) true.
2. (a) true; (b) true; (c) false.
3. (a) false; (b) true; (c) true.
4. (a) true; (b) true; (c) false.

Discussion questions
1. What's your memory like? Here are two sequences of numbers; give yourself a couple of minutes and see how many digits you can recall. Take a ten-minute break and then see if your recall has deteriorated.
   a. 3.14159 26535 8979323 846264 338327 950288 419716 939937 510582 097494 459230 781640 628620 899862 803482 534211 706798 214808 6513282 306647 093844 6095505 822317 2535940
   b. 1.4142 13562 37309 50488 01688 72420 96980 78569 67187 53769 48073 17667 97379
2. Here's another memory exercise. Again, take a couple of minutes and see if you can learn this sequence.
   581215192226293337
3. Given what we are learning about the adolescent brain, what changes would you make to the way students are taught in further and higher education?

Our answers

1. The first of these numbers is pi and the second is the square root of two. When we have conducted this experiment with undergraduate students, we have found the results differ massively. Some students can recall 15–20 digits, while others struggle to recall five. They are asking you to use your short-term memory and there is huge variability across the population. We also found that our students' memories deteriorated over time. According to Guinness World Records, Rajveer Meena holds the word record: in 2015 he recalled pi to a total of 70,000 digits, taking over seven hours to recite the numbers (Guinness World Records: Most pi Places memorised, 2023).

2. Some of our students understood this problem very quickly and realised that there was a pattern to these numbers. This meant they could recall them perfectly and even extend the sequence further. Table 9.1 shows the pattern.

   Rather than relying on memory, once you have understood the pattern you can use a different sort of learning to 'recall' and predict the pattern.

Table 9.1: Number pattern for memory test

5		8		12		15		19		22		26
	3		4		3		4		3		4	

3. Here are three suggestions:
   a. Make the teaching day start time later. There is some evidence that delaying the start of the teaching day can improve performance. Likewise, it can lead to a decrease in both tardiness and disruptive behaviour. There is also evidence that allowing adolescents to sleep in can improve their driving skills (Dahl, 2008).
   b. Ensure that adolescents are not shamed by teachers, particularly in front of their contemporaries. We know that teenagers are highly sensitive to the opinions of their peers. Anything which makes them look or feel foolish in the eyes of their contemporaries will have an adverse effect on their learning and their mental health.
   c. We also know that adolescents are attracted to novel experiences and responsive to meaningful rewards. Perhaps these two tendencies could be utilised to create more exciting and stimulating learning?

Further reading

Frewin, K., McEwen, E., Gerson, S., Bekkering, H. and Hunnius, S. (2019) 'What's going on in babies' brains when they learn to do something?', *Frontiers for Young Minds*, Available from: https://www.frontiersin.org/articles/10.3389/frym.2019.00044/pdf [Accessed 31 January 2023].

Goswami, U. (2019) *Cognitive Development and Cognitive Neuroscience: The Learning Brain* (2nd edn), London: Routledge.

Gülgöz, S. (ed). (2020) *Autobiographical Memory Development: Theoretical and Methodological Approaches*, Abingdon: Routledge.

Henry, L. (2011) *The Development of Working Memory in Children*, Los Angeles: SAGE.

Jensen, E.P. and McConchie, L. (2020) *Brain-Based Learning: Teaching the Way Students Really Learn* (3rd edn), Thousand Oaks, CA: Corwin.

On our website

You can find lots more material on our website at https://policy.bristoluniversitypress.co.uk/child-development-and-the-brain/companion-website

This includes:

A quiz on neuromyths: https://policy.bristoluniversitypress.co.uk/child-development-and-the-brain/companion-website/quiz

10

Genetics and neurodevelopmental disorders

This chapter:

- gives an overview of how genes work;

- describes the following neurodevelopmental disorders: ADHD, fragile X, ASD, Down's syndrome, Williams syndrome, Turner syndrome and Prader-Willi syndrome;

- describes each condition, the prevalence and the criteria for diagnosis;

- reviews the neuroscience of each condition;

- provides details of where you can find further information.

Chromosomes and genes

Our understanding of genetics has developed substantially over the last hundred years or so, particularly since the publication of the human genome, a project that began in 1990 and was completed in 2003. We now know that genes determine which traits we inherit from our parents. Genes are located on chromosomes, coiled double helix pieces of DNA (deoxyribonucleic acid).

We inherit our genes from our mother and father. Human sexual reproduction means that the cells from the male sperm and those from the female egg are combined in such a way that the genes contained within each chromosome are shuffled around to produce a unique recombination.

Humans have 23 pairs of chromosomes. One half of each pair comes from the mother and the other half from the father. These genes determine our physical appearance – whether, for example, our eyes are green, blue or brown, whether our hair is blonde or brown, whether we are right- or left-handed. Genes also play a central role in determining our behavioural characteristics. None of this is controlled by a single gene.

Eye colour, for example, seems to be dependent on two genes on chromosome 15, but there are also about 14 other genes that play a part in it (White and Rabago-Smith, 2010). Genes are also not the only influence on our characteristics. Medland and colleagues (2009) studied over 25,000 Australian and Dutch twins and their siblings and established that handedness was less than 25% dependent on genetic factors, with environmental influences accounting for the remaining 75%. Even so, however much we struggle as we grow older to not turn into our mothers or fathers, the odds are probably stacked against us, considering that we contain a strong genetic inheritance from both!

Almost all – that is, 99% – of our DNA sequence is shared by everyone on the planet. It is only the remaining 1% of base pairs of DNA that are different and that define our individuality. Most of the research on heritability has been conducted through twin studies. Identical, or monozygotic, twins will

> Only 1% of our DNA defines individual difference

share 100% of their DNA. They are most usually also brought up in the same household and so will also share an environment. The Minnesota Study of Twins Reared Apart (see, e.g., Bouchard et al, 1990), which has found and followed over 100 sets of twins and triplets who have been raised in different households, has provided some particularly rich data here in helping to determine differences between genetic and environmental influence.

Our genetic template

Our genes contain a template for our development. We can perhaps understand this better by considering how genes work on a smaller scale. At the cellular level, genes contain instructions for making proteins. The instructions contained within genes are made up of strands of DNA. You can think of these as being like sentences, each one of which contains a set of instructions for making particular proteins. In fact, when geneticists write them down, they look rather like sentences made up of only four letters, with each sentence providing a specific set of instructions:

CGC AGC TGG CAT TAT GTT GAA CCC AAG TTT TTA AAC AAG GCT TTT GAA GTT GCA

The human genome project has allowed us to identify individual genes and we can begin to see how they affect development. This work is at the very early stages but is already producing some fascinating results. We know, for example, that a gene called MCI R is important in regulating skin and hair colour (Rees, 2003). We know that fragile X is caused by a mutation on the FMR1 gene on the X chromosome and we even know the exact position of this gene on the chromosome.

BOX: Gregor Mendel and his peas

Our understanding of genetics begins with the biologist Gregor Mendel (1822–1884), who studied the process of inheritance in the pea plant (Mendel, 1967). The peas that Mendel used had either brown seeds or white seeds, but never a mixture of both.

He looked at what are called dichotomous traits, that is, traits that occur only on their own, never in combination. An example of this would be tall/short or, in this case, brown or white. He began by establishing that the plants he was using would breed true. That is, he established that when he did no cross-breeding and bred only brown seeds with brown seeds and white seeds with white seeds, the brown-seeded varieties would always produce brown-seeded offspring, and likewise the white seeds would always produce peas with white seeds. He then began cross-breeding brown-seeded peas with white-seeded peas. He found that their offspring all had brown seeds. He then took this first generation of cross-bred seeds and bred them with another batch of the same generation. He found that about three-quarters of the second-generation cross-bred peas had brown seeds and about a quarter had white seeds. He discovered that there was what he called a dominant trait, which appeared in all the first generation of cross-bred seeds, and alongside this was what he named a recessive trait. Brown was the dominant trait, hence all the seeds of the first generation were brown. White was the recessive trait and so only appeared in the second generation of the seeds. Of central significance here is the fact that recessive traits can be passed on through a generation that do not appear to possess that trait themselves.

Sometimes problems with chromosomes mean that we inherit genetic disorders. These disorders can be caused by problems affecting a single gene or pair of genes – for example, phenylketonuria (PKU) or fragile X syndrome. There are also disorders that are caused by a combination of several different genes. These are called polygenic disorders and include both autism spectrum disorder (ASD) and dyslexia. In addition, there are inherited disorders that are caused by problems with an entire chromosome, such as Down's syndrome, or parts of a chromosome, such as Williams syndrome. Tager-Flusberg (2003) lists several recent developments in the genetics of developmental disorders that show that the pattern of inheritance may in fact be more complicated than this. She describes a pattern in which not all cells are affected by the inherited abnormality. This is known as **mosaicism** and often gives rise to a milder form of the disorder. There is also the phenomenon of **anticipation**, which affects those with single-gene disorders such as fragile X syndrome. Here the DNA sequences that cause the mutation increase in number as they are passed from one generation to the next, which means that later generations experience more severe manifestations of the condition.

Tager-Flusberg (2003) points out that we know a great deal more about single-gene disorders than we do about polygenic disorders. There is likely to be a complex interplay between genetic inheritance and the environment and untangling this to establish the appropriate causality of a condition can often be very difficult. Studies of monozygotic (that is, identical) twins can be used to show the heritability of a condition. However, as twins who share the same genes also tend to share the same environment, separating the one from the other in scientific studies can be quite difficult.

Genetic disorders and very early development

Several serious problems can occur when genetic disorders impact upon the early development of the brain. These include conditions that affect the development of the neural tube, which is formed during the initial stages of brain development, and that can result in failure of the neural tube to close either at the front (anterior) or at the back (posterior). When the anterior part of the tube fails to close, this gives rise to a condition called **anencephaly** (pronounced an-en-kef-aly). This is a fatal condition that affects about one in 10,000 births in the United Kingdom (Public Health England, 2020). When the posterior of the neural tube fails to close, this gives rise to a condition called **myelomeningocele**, a form of **spina bifida**. Infants with this condition may be born with the spinal sac protruding from the lower to middle back, a condition that can be treated through surgery. If an infant with myelomeningocele has developed hydrocephalus (fluid on the brain) they may also need to be fitted with a ventriculoperitoneal shunt to drain the fluid.

Disorders associated with neurogenesis fall into two categories: those that produce a small brain (microcephaly) and those that produce a large brain (macrocephaly). Both conditions can lead to termination of the foetus; if the baby survives, they will usually have some form of both physical and cognitive problems. The two conditions can be brought about by a range of factors, including the mother having rubella or overconsumption of alcohol.

Neurodevelopmental disorders

Attention-deficit/hyperactivity disorder

Description and diagnosis

There are three dimensions to attention-deficit/hyperactivity disorder (ADHD): inattention, inhibition and self-regulation. The extent to which a particular child is affected by each of these varies and the point at which it is considered a 'disorder' depends on how it is diagnosed. According to the DSM V (American Psychiatric Association, 2013), ADHD is diagnosed on the basis of a range of behavioural symptoms that are divided into two different categories: inattention and hyperactivity/impulsivity. In children, six or more of the symptoms from the two categories need to be evident for at least six months before a diagnosis can be made. In the United Kingdom, diagnosis is based on meeting the DSM V criteria plus experiencing 'moderate psychological, social and/or educational or occupational impairment' as well as this being pervasive in both the home and other aspects of a person's life (NICE, 2018).

Prevalence

ADHD is the most widely diagnosed neurodevelopmental condition, affecting children in many different countries across the globe. Estimates of the numbers of children suffering from this condition vary considerably and depend on how this is measured. The community prevalence of the condition describes how many people are affected by ADHD in a representative population and probably gives a more helpful figure than, for example, the numbers prescribed medication. Sayal and colleagues (2018) describe seven systematic review articles on the community prevalence of ADHD. The studies vary in their methodology and the exact age range of children they describe. Overall, they give a global figure of between 2.2% and 7.2% for the prevalence of ADHD in children.

Causes of ADHD

The causes of ADHD are complex and multiple. Genetics are thought to play an important role while many different environmental factors are also seen as significant. Of the two, genetics is seen by most commentators as being the most significant factor (Barkley, 2015). ADHD runs in families. If a parent has ADHD, then there is a likelihood that their children will also have ADHD. However, as Barkley points out, there are other ways that genetics can affect inheritance. For example, mutations can occur in both sperm and eggs that can lead to mutations in the gene of the child even if these are not present in the genes of the parents. There are a range of environmental factors that can also contribute to ADHD. Premature birth, perinatal hypoxia, poor nutrition, pesticide exposure and exposure to heavy metals have all been suggested as causal factors (Núñez-Jaramillo et al, 2021).

The neuroscience of ADHD

Neuroimaging studies have shown that there are often abnormalities in the brain structure of people with ADHD. The main areas identified include parts of the higher 'executive functioning' areas of the frontal brain, that is, the fronto-striato-parietal and fronto-cerebellar networks. Rubia (2018) uses

> We are still unsure which parts of the brain are implicated in ADHD

the terminology developed by Zelazo and Carlson (2012) to distinguish between the 'hot' and 'cool' executive functioning networks. Hot functioning is where there is an emotional significance to the processing, whereas cool functioning is where there is a more neutral context. Both are affected by ADHD. The most consistent deficits are found in cool executive functioning. This includes working memory, inhibiting motor response and estimating how long it might take to do a task. Hot functions such as controlling motivation and making decisions based on rewards are also affected but at a less consistent rate.

Many fMRI studies have shown that in children with ADHD the prefrontal striatal circuits are underactivated in inhibitory tasks, for example, computer-based tasks that ask the child to press a button to stop a particular sequence of events that they view on the screen. Studies are also showing wider issues in the lateral prefrontal cortex, the medial prefrontal cortex and the orbito-frontal regions (Rubia, 2018). As is so often the case in neuroscience studies, the results from meta-analyses are mixed. A 2019 meta-analysis of 96 studies involving 1,914 children and adolescents found 'no significant convergent across structural and functional regional alterations in ADHD' (Samea et al, 2019, p 11). This could be because of differences in methodology or different populations of children or publication bias, but it could also point to 'a more distributed, network-based pathology lacking a consistent expression at any particular location' (Samea et al, 2019, p 11). While very few researchers now dispute the existence of ADHD, there is still no clear consensus on exactly which parts of the brain are implicated in the condition, although there is much greater agreement on what aspects of executive control are compromised.

Fragile X

Description and diagnosis

Fragile X is an inherited genetic condition. It is linked to a particular gene, known as the FMR1 gene, which is one of the genes associated with synaptogenesis. Since the discovery of the FMR1 gene in 1991 (Verkerk et al, 1991), the condition can now be diagnosed by means of a simple blood test.

There are many ways in which fragile X can affect children. Boys will often have learning difficulties, which can range from mild to severe. About a third of girls will also be affected in this way, again ranging from mildly to severely. This means that about two-thirds of girls with the condition will be seen as having a normal range of intelligence. Both boys and girls with the condition can have difficulties with attention span and may also suffer from restlessness and overactivity. Whether or not they have learning difficulties, girls may be very shy and find social situations quite difficult. Both boys and girls may also suffer from delays in the acquisition of language.

Prevalence

As boys have only one X chromosome, they are more likely to be affected than girls. Girls have two X chromosomes, and so if one of them is affected the other is likely to compensate. Some girls may carry the condition in their genes without being aware that they have it. This also means that parents can unknowingly pass the condition on to their children. According to the National Fragile X Foundation (2021) the prevalence of fragile X is between one in 4,000 and one in 7,000 in males, and between one in 6,000 and one in 11,000 in females.

Causes

The condition gets its name from the appearance of the X chromosome, the tip of which, when examined under the microscope, looks as if it is in the process of breaking off. The effect of this is to stop the gene from working, which means that it does not produce the protein that is necessary for brain growth through synaptogenesis.

The neuroscience of fragile X

As we discussed in Chapter 2, during early development cells in the cerebral cortex are created by a process of active cell migration. The creation of this part of the brain is a highly complex process in which neurons are created from neural stem cells which then form neural networks. When things go wrong in this process the result is likely to be a neurodevelopmental disorder. Neuroscientists at Tohoku University, using animal models, have identified some of the molecules that are responsible for such disorders. One of these is the fragile X mental retardation protein. Researchers at Tohoku University hope that by uncovering the molecular mechanisms that are responsible for fragile X in the foetal brain they will be able to provide an essential resource for further research.

Autism spectrum disorder

Description and diagnosis

The term autism spectrum disorder (ASD) covers a very broad range of behaviours (Figure 10.1). As we do not know what causes it, we identify and diagnose the condition by means of a range of behaviours. It is now seen as a form of neurodiversity in which the brain is simply wired in a slightly different way (Figure 10.1). Diagnosis is reliant on a range of observed behaviours that are not really apparent until at least the age of two. In reality this means that the condition is not diagnosed until the child is three or older. Brain-imaging studies are increasingly able to make much earlier diagnoses.

Wing and Gould's (1979) criteria of a triad of impairments remains of diagnostic value today and reflects aspects of the current definition of the American Psychiatric Association. In the DSM V, the diagnostic criteria for ASD discuss the presence of markedly abnormal development of social interaction and communication; problems in matching communication to context; problems with following rules; and difficulties in understanding non-literal language such as idioms, metaphors and jokes (American Psychiatric Association, 2013). Conditions that were previously described as **Asperger's** and **pervasive developmental disorder not otherwise specified** are now included in the ASD spectrum.

Wing and Gould (1979) specified that individuals with ASD have impairments in social behaviours and difficulties in relating to others. Such individuals often

Figure 10.1: Autism spectrum disorder (ASD)

Source: Shutterstock, Photo ID 280931180

have impairments in verbal and non-verbal communication, for example, parroting others and misunderstanding a range of communicative signs. They may exhibit a narrow range of interests, often showing resistance to change. ASD is viewed as a spectrum of conditions crossing all degrees of severity. The severity and course can change at different development times, can present at the same time as other conditions such as ADHD and can be influenced by a range of external factors such as individual temperament and education (Ward, 2012).

Cognitive psychologists have sought to understand the causes and the behaviour of individuals, particularly children, with ASD. In the next section we examine these theories while representing neuroscientific findings that have increased our understanding of the functional correlates of this complex spectrum disorder.

Theory of mind

It has been suggested that certain social impairments may arise from a lack of theory of mind, namely a lack of understanding that other people's minds exist in terms of the beliefs, desires, thought and emotions of others. An example of this can be found in pretend play. Leslie (1987) proposed that pretend play is an expression of such understanding; as other minds cannot be perceived directly, they are recognised through the imagination required for pretend play. A lack of the imagination required for pretend play could explain why children with ASD struggle when it comes to recognising the minds of others. The term 'mentalising' is often used to describe the mental process of holding and manipulating in the mind ideas about the mental states of other people.

Figure 10.2: The modified unexpected-transfer task

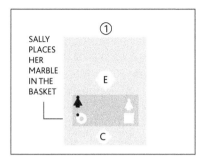
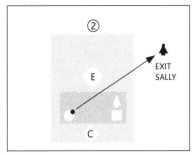
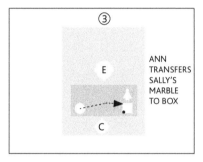
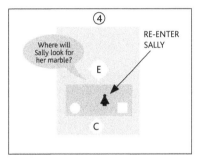

Source: Baron-Cohen et al, 1985, figure 1, page 41. Reproduced with permission of Elsevier

One ability inherent in understanding other people's minds is the understanding that people's behaviour is governed by simple factual beliefs. The false-belief paradigm was developed to assess whether children understood this principle, on the basis that if a child understands that a false belief can be held, then they will also have an understanding that correct beliefs exist. The modified unexpected-transfer task, shown in Figure 10.2 (Baron-Cohen et al, 1985), has revealed that 80% of children with ASD fail the target question while typically developing children pass.

Some authors have argued that there is a relationship between children's verbal mental age and the ability to pass false-belief tasks (e.g., Sparrevohn and Howie, 1995), possibly because proficient language use enables more understanding of the subtleties of other people's minds. While difficulties with the false-belief task are not exclusive to children with ASD – for example, hearing- and visually impaired children have problems with the task – it does seem that these children's problems with communication affect their understanding of the minds of others.

Weak central coherence theory

Other theorists have argued that the cognitive patterns exhibited by children with ASD may arise from problems with integrating information so as to think about a coherent whole (Frith and Frith, 2003), together with related difficulties in understanding meaning in communication and perception. In simple terms, those on the autism spectrum may be better at processing the separate parts of something, but not so good at seeing the whole pattern. This inability to integrate an array of information may be partly responsible for difficulties in social functioning and communication which require information to be integrated for comprehension and expression. More recent studies have questioned weak coherence theory. For example, a small-scale study (Delli et al, 2017) did not find evidence to support the theory. Likewise, an analysis of the neuroscience findings (Scher and Shyman, nd) has suggested that it might be that children with ASD are better at local processing than other children.

Empathising and systematising

More recently, theorists have tried to account for the processing styles that can potentially differentiate the profiles of individuals with ASD. Baron-Cohen and colleagues (2003) proposed that all people combine two qualitatively different kinds of cognitive processing, namely empathising and systematising. Empathising is when we can understand another person's thoughts and feelings, and systematising is our ability to analyse and understand rules. They suggest that people without ASD use a mixture of styles in nearly equal degrees, whereas individuals with ASD are positioned at the high end of systematising and have a lack of empathising. Baron-Cohen (2002) proposed that a lack of empathising could account for the social impairments and difficulties with theory-of-mind tasks in individuals with ASD and that high-end systematising could account for their ability to follow rules, their narrow range of interests and their focus on detail, and could even account for a tendency to perseverate, that is, to repeat responses even after the event.

These classic and more recent explanations of the pattern of impairments remain the subject of debate and continued empirical examination. However, we can see that children with ASD have particular patterns of inflexibility of thought and socio-communicative difficulty, including problems of inhibition and, often, a delayed understanding of mind.

Prevalence

The incidence in the population is about one in every 100 and it is three times more common in males than in females (Hill and Frith, 2003). A commonly applied diagnostic criterion categorises children as high- or low-functioning ASD. The latter includes about 40% of individuals with ASD who have an IQ of 70 or lower (Baird et al, 2000).

The neuroscience of ASD

Genetics

It has become apparent in recent years that there is a strong genetic competent to ASD. A meta-analysis in 2016 showed that ASD is between 64% and 91% heritable (Tick et al, 2016). In an article for *The Lancet*, Catherine Lord and colleagues (2018) report that there is an increased risk in families where one child already has an ASD diagnosis and an even greater risk where there are two older siblings with ASD. While the exact genetic components remain unknown, Lord and colleagues report that over 100 genes have been identified as having deletions or duplications and they say that many doctors are now recommending that every child with ASD should be genetically tested. In an article published in *Spectrum*, which reviews news and studies on ASD, Jessica Wright (2019) describes the four different tests that can be used to detect autism. Of these the most comprehensive (and hence most expensive) is to sequence the whole genome, although she warns that there is as yet no readily available means of reliably testing for ASD.

Brain size

> Expansion of the cortex in early development might be a biomarker for ASD

While there has in the past been considerable focus on specific areas of the brain that may be implicated in ASD, one of the most replicated areas of research involves differences in brain volume between children with ASD and other children. Work at the University of North Carolina (Hazlett et al, 2017) has shown that infants who develop ASD have an increased brain volume that appears as early as six months, that is, well before any diagnosis based on behaviour. Further studies have looked at differences in surface area and cortical thickness in children with a high risk of developing ASD. These studies have found that from six to 12 months the surface area of the cortex expands in high-risk infants and that this is followed by an increased growth rate in total volume between 12 and 24 months. This is an exciting development as it might indicate a biomarker for ASD.

Other developmental differences

Shen and Piven (2017) have reviewed the developments in the neuroscience of ASD. As well as the developments in measuring brain size, they also detail three other significant findings from imaging studies of infants. Firstly, infants who were later diagnosed with ASD had increased amounts of cerebrospinal fluid in the subarachnoid space surrounding the cortical surface of the brain (Shen et al, 2013). Secondly, infants with a high risk of developing ASD have been found to have significant differences in white matter tracts in the corpus collosum (Wolff et al, 2015). Thirdly, an MRI brain study of functional connectivity of infants at six months of age successfully predicted which infants would be diagnosed with ASD at 24 months (Emerson et al, 2017).

Treatment and ASD

Taken together, it looks as though we are now close to being able to at least diagnose ASD at an earlier age. The question of whether we should be seeking a 'treatment' for the condition remains controversial and the idea that we should find a 'cure' is even more controversial, especially for those with the condition and their families. There are no approved pharmacological treatments for ASD for children in the United Kingdom. Despite this, many of them are prescribed a range of medications including sleeping pills, psychostimulants and antipsychotics (Murray et al, 2014). However, there are therapies and treatments that can help children with ASD. For example, **applied behaviour analysis** offers several interventions which are shown to be beneficial to young children. The Early Start Denver Model, when used with children aged 18–30 months, showed improvements in a range of behaviours when followed up two years later (Estes et al, 2015).

Down's syndrome

Description and diagnosis

Down's syndrome is also known as trisomy 21 (Figure 10.3). Trisomies occur when an extra copy of a chromosome is present and are caused by the non-disjunction (that is, the failure to separate) of a chromosome during meiosis (cell division). In the case of Down's syndrome, it is caused by a trisomy of chromosome 21. Other trisomies are much less common than Down's syndrome and include Edward syndrome (trisomy of chromosome 18) and Patau syndrome (trisomy of chromosome 13).

Down's syndrome is associated with a range of physiological and mental difficulties. These include an altered physical appearance, language delays, learning difficulties, an increased risk of congenital heart disease, sight and hearing problems and an increased possibility of the early onset of Alzheimer's disease. Some decades ago the lifespan for those with Down's was often reduced. Today the average lifespan is 50–60 years.

The NHS in the United Kingdom provides a screening test for Down's syndrome between weeks ten and 14 of pregnancy. The test includes both ultrasound and a blood test. As part of the scan, the fluid at the back of the baby's neck is measured to determine the 'nuchal translucency', that is, the appearance of the fluid under the skin behind the foetal neck.

Figure 10.3: Down's syndrome

Source: Shutterstock, Photo ID 369646874

Prevalence

According to the Down's Syndrome Medical Interest Group (Lakhanpaul, 2020), the prevalence of Down's syndrome in the United Kingdom in 2018 was 25 in every 10,000. This is lower than the 2017 rate because of a change in criteria. They estimate the number of babies born with Down's in England and Wales in 2018 at 762. Studies have shown that the risk rises slowly as maternal age increases, and there has been an increased prevalence in mothers aged over 35 across Europe. Environmental factors have been suggested, including the possibility that a combination of smoking and use of oral contraceptives can have an adverse effect (Loane et al, 2013).

The neuroscience of Down's syndrome

Perhaps surprisingly, given the prevalence of Down's, there have been relatively few neural-imaging studies, resulting in a lack of knowledge about the brain development of children with this syndrome. Some 20 years ago Capone (2001) summarised the

> We need more brain-based research into Down's syndrome

findings from brain studies over the preceding 80 years. He wrote that post-mortem studies have shown that the brain structure of children with Down's syndrome differs from that of children without the condition. Both the size and the weight of the brain are often reduced, with the frontal lobes being one of the areas affected. The few studies done more recently have critiqued that view. Neuroscientists at the Centre for the Developing Brain at King's College London (Baburamani et al, 2019) report that neurodevelopment in children with Down's varies considerably. When compared with typically developing children there might only be very limited delays in learning and cognitive ability that are apparent before the age of two. So, for example, early language skills such as babbling might be comparable to those of neurotypical children. However, after this age there is evidence of delayed development.

A meta-analysis (Hamner et al, 2018) of the available studies shows that both children and adolescents with Down's syndrome have a smaller cerebellum volume. This is an area of the brain that is important in motor control. In contrast, the analysis shows that there is no consistent evidence for reduced hippocampus size across the age range. There is very mixed evidence for reductions in brain size in areas of the cortex. For example, while all studies included in Hamner's meta-analysis report a reduction in volume in frontal regions, they vary considerably in terms of statistical significance. Their conclusion is that there needs to be more developmental research into this area, with a particular need for longitudinal studies showing how the brains of those with Down's develop from infancy into adolescence.

Williams syndrome

Description and diagnosis

Williams syndrome (WS) is caused by the deletion of a specific and limited range of genes on the long arm of chromosome 7. It is a neurodevelopmental disorder that often causes cognitive difficulties, with typical IQ scores of around 60, although there is considerable variation in scores between different sub-tests (Bellugi et al, 1999). However, people with WS often have excellent musical skills and nearly perfect pitch, as well as often a great enthusiasm for communicating through music. Despite their limited scores in cognitive ability tests, many WS children have excellent language skills and can often be very sociable. The condition does cause problems with some of the more intuitive aspects of communication, and subjects do not do well in theory-of-mind tests (Tager-Flusberg, 2003). Children with this condition can also suffer from poor attention and increased anxiety, as well as a tendency to be overly friendly with people they do not know (Gosch and Pankau, 1994). There are also physical health problems associated with WS. The heart is particularly affected, with many children experiencing difficulties, particularly **supravalvular aortic stenosis**, a narrowing of the blood vessels that carry oxygenated blood from the heart to the body.

Prevalence

A Norwegian study (Strømme et al, 2002) has estimated that WS occurs in one in 7,500 of all births.

The neuroscience of WS

A study of 14 young adults with WS showed a reduction in brain size of about 13% compared with a control group of children without WS (Reiss et al, 2006). However, this reduction is uneven across the brain. For example, brain stem tissue was very reduced, whereas the cerebellum was much less affected. Likewise, white matter in the brain was much more affected than grey matter.

There is currently quite a lot of research into the exact genetic sequence that causes WS, including mapping of the genes and the matching of these to specific aspects of the disorder. There is also research into which parts of the brain are responsible for cognitive and behavioural aspects of the condition (Tager-Flusberg, 2003). In one such recent animal study (Osso and Chan, 2019) researchers found that deleting a WS gene (Gtf2i) from a mouse brain resulted in a deficit of myelin, resulting in few neurons being myelinated and a decrease in the thickness of the corpus callosum. This resulted in a highly increased level of sociability and reduced motor skills, both associated with WS.

Phenylketonuria

Description and diagnosis

PKU or phenylketonuria (pronounced fen-il-key-to-new-ree-uh) was first identified by a Norwegian doctor named Foiling in 1934. Følling (1934) noticed a strange odour in the urine of several of his 'mentally retarded' patients. He found that the urine of these patients contained high levels of the chemical phenylketone, hence the name of the condition: phenylketone + uria. Babies who are born with PKU have high levels of an amino acid called phenylalanine in their blood. This amino acid is found in many high-protein foods such as chicken, fish, peanuts, some nuts, milk and cheese. PKU is caused by a mutation on the PAH gene on chromosome 12. When it is working properly this gene produces an enzyme that can metabolise (change) phenylalanine into another amino acid called tyrosine, which is involved in synthesising the neurotransmitter dopamine. The mutation means that subjects with this disorder cannot metabolise phenylalanine. If the level of phenylalanine in the blood gets too high it can cause brain damage, resulting in intellectual processing difficulties, with IQ levels of about 50.

Prevalence

The number of cases reported across the world varies considerably. This ranges from Japan, with an incidence of one in 108,822, to Turkey, with a rate of one in 6,000 (Shoraka et al, 2020). In Europe the incidence rate is about one in 10,000

(Genomics Education Programme, 2019). In the United States it is around one in 10,000–15,000 (National Library of Medicine, 2021).

The neuroscience of PKU

In the 1950s it was discovered that brain damage that is caused by PKU could be avoided by very strict dietary control supplemented by a protein drink. Removing phenylalanine from the diet, particularly in the first two years of life, prevented the brain damage caused by PKU. Many countries have since developed a screening programme to test all newborn babies for the condition (Guthrie and Susi, 1963).

> Managing PKU means living on a carefully controlled diet

Reviewing progress of our understanding of this condition, Tager-Flusberg (2003) describes how, by the 1960s, it looked as if we had the condition under control: scientists were able to detect it in newborn infants and then treat it with a special diet that prevented brain damage. However, she shows that by the 1990s our understanding had developed further. Clearly, a balance needs to be achieved between preventing phenylalanine from reaching toxic levels and dealing with an absence of tyrosine. It is not possible to completely remove all phenylalanine from children's diets, and many children find it a struggle to keep to the diet and to tolerate the taste of the protein drink supplement. Studies have shown that it is important to sustain the diet throughout the subject's life. Huijbregts and colleagues (2002) have suggested that variations in the level of phenylalanine in the blood may also be dangerous.

Diamond and Amso (2008) review the contribution that more recent neuroscience has made to our understanding of PKU. They explain that the dopamine system in the frontal cortex has higher firing rates and higher requirements for dopamine than other brain areas. It is thus more sensitive to levels of tyrosine than other parts of the brain. A reduction in the amount of tyrosine in the brain will affect the prefrontal area of the brain but not the rest of it.

Turner syndrome

Description and diagnosis

As you will recall, there are 23 sets of chromosomes. The last of these, pair 23, determines sex. Because we inherit one chromosome from each of our parents' pairs of chromosomes, for pair 23 we will inherit either two X chromosomes, in which case we will be a girl, or an X and a Y chromosome, in which case we will be a boy. Some babies have only a single X chromosome. When this happens, they will develop Turner syndrome (TS). There are, of course, some variations on this. Sometimes the second chromosome will be incomplete. There will also be cases of mosaicism, where the X chromosome is missing from only some of the cells. There is also a possibility that a small part of the Y chromosome will be present in TS: this is a condition known as **mixed gonadal dysgenesis**. As the condition is marked by an absence of the Y chromosome, TS affects only girls.

Turner syndrome is named after the man who first identified the condition in 1938, the American endocrinologist Dr Henry Turner (1938). A German paediatrician, Dr Otto Ullrich, had identified the same condition slightly earlier, and Turner syndrome is sometimes referred to as Ullrich-Turner syndrome.

The condition has several physical characteristics, which include a tendency to be short, with a short, webbed neck and broad chest. The condition also affects sexual development. Girls with TS do not develop ovaries and so are infertile. The condition has quite specific effects on measured intelligence tests. Girls with TS tend to score within the normal range on verbal IQ tests but do not do so well on those tests requiring visuospatial ability. Typically, they may also exhibit problems with non-verbal memory and executive function and may have difficulties with maintaining attention (Van Dyke et al, 1991). There can also be broader problems, including difficulty in relationships with others and lack of self-esteem. This may at least in part be due to their appearance, leading to teasing and bullying behaviours from other children.

Prevalence

While the condition had been identified in the 1930s, it was not until the late 1950s that science had developed sufficiently for the missing sex chromosome to be identified. TS affects about one in 2,500 –3,000 live female births (Sybert and McCauley, 2004).

The neuroscience of Turner syndrome

Both MRI studies and other more advanced imaging methods show that children with TS have reduced grey matter density or volume in both the parietal and occipital lobes. For example, a study by Brown and colleagues (2002) compared 26 girls with TS (17 with a fully missing X chromosome and nine with a mosaic version of the condition) with 26 girls without the condition and showed differences in the parietal, occipital and cerebellar regions. This study, like an earlier one by Reiss and colleagues (1995), showed a reduction in the amount of grey matter in both the right and left parietal regions. Also consistent with earlier studies was the finding that the parietal lobes were smaller in girls with TS. This may explain the problems with visuospatial skills, executive functioning and attention in girls with TS.

Many studies have also shown differences in volume of the amygdala and the hippocampus when compared with children without the condition. This is thought to be associated with some of the difficulties around affective processing such as reading emotion from facial expression.

There is likely to be a complex interplay in TS between inherited genetic problems, hormonal difficulties resulting from a lack of oestrogen and/or androgen (Ross et al, 2006) and social/environmental factors (McCauley et al, 1986).

Prader-Willi syndrome

Description and diagnosis

Prader-Willi syndrome (PWS) is a complex disorder with a wide range of symptoms. It was first described in the 1950s (Prader et al, 1956) and is diagnosed by several specific symptoms that can be confirmed by genetic testing. It is caused by the deletion of several genes on chromosome 15, specifically the genes that are inherited from the father. Identical deletion of the genes inherited from the mother on the same chromosome leads to Angelman syndrome. Although the two syndromes have almost identical deletions on the same chromosome, Angelman syndrome and PWS are entirely different disorders with entirely different physical and psychological symptoms (Kaplan et al, 1987).

There is an excellent clinical case study of an 11-year-old girl with PWS which we would recommend (Martin et al, 1998). It shows the range of difficulties that children with this condition experience as well as the problems they present for parents, carers and educators. Babies with the condition are usually seen as suffering from hypotonia, meaning they have no muscle tone, with the result that their movements are lethargic and their ability to suck may be limited. Poor food intake at this early age is contrasted with obsessive eating when they are older, a condition known as hypophagia, often leading to excessive weight gain and obesity. The sexual organs of these children do not grow properly and puberty is often considerably delayed. Stunted growth and consequent small stature are other features of the condition. There are also several behavioural problems associated with PWS, including obsessive-compulsive behaviours, temper tantrums and stubbornness (Cassidy, 1997; Martin et al, 1998).

Prevalence

Estimates of the prevalence of PWS seem to vary widely although it is still regarded as a rare genetic condition. One widely cited study in North Dakota suggests that PWS has a prevalence rate of about one in 16,000 (Burd et al, 1990).

The neuroscience of Prader-Willi syndrome

There are several factors that affect the brain development of children with PWS. There is some evidence to suggest that the hypothalamic paraventricular nucleus, part of the hypothalamus associated with the regulation of appetite, may be smaller in those with PWS than in the general population

(Swaab et al, 1995). Swaab (1997) also suggests that the lack of growth hormone-releasing hormone may be responsible for the problems with physical growth and that the hypothalamus may also be implicated in the decreased levels of sex hormones. Another study (Ogura et al, 2011) has shown that there are smaller amounts of grey matter (neurons that have not been myelinated) in several regions of the brain, including the orbitofrontal cortex, caudate nucleus, inferior temporal gyrus and cerebellum. The study suggests that some of the behaviours associated with PWS may be related to structural abnormalities in these regions of the brain.

More information

More information on the conditions discussed in this chapter can be found at the sources listed below.

National Attention Deficit Disorder Information and Support Service
    ADDISS PO Box 340
    Edgware
    Middlesex
    HA8 9HL
    Tel: 020 8952 2800
    Website: http://wwwaddiss.co.uk/

    Fragile X Society
    Rood End House
    6 Stortford Road
    Great Dunmow
    Essex
    CM6 1DA
    Tel: 01371 875100
    Email: info@fragilex.org.uk
    Website: wwwfragilex.org.uk/

National Autistic Society
    393 City Road
    London
    EC1V 1NG
    Tel: 020 7833 2299
    Email: nas@nas.org.uk
    Website: http://www.ASD.org.uk/

Down's Syndrome Association
    Langdon Down Centre
    2a Langdon Park

Teddington
Middlesex
TW11 9PS
Tel: 0333 1212 300
Email: info@downs-syndrome.org.uk
Website: http://www.downs-syndrome.org.uk/

Williams Syndrome Foundation (UK)
Box 103
Charter House
Lord Montgomery Way
Portsmouth
PO1 2SN
Tel: 0208 567 1374
Email: enquiries@williams-syndrome.org.uk
Website: http://www.williams-syndrome.org.uk

National Society for Phenylketonuria
NSPKU (UK) Ltd.
PO Box 6046
Sheffield
S12 9ET
Tel: 030 3040 1090
Email: info@nspku.org
Website: http://www.nspku.org/

Turner Syndrome Support Society (UK)
12 Simpson Court
11 South Ave
Clydebank Business Park
Clydebank
G81 2NR
Tel: 0141 952 8006
Website: http://www.tss.org.uk/

Prader-Willi Syndrome Association (UK)
125a London Road
Derby
DE1 2QQ
Tel: 01332 365676
Email: admin@pwsa.co.uk
Website: http://pwsa.co.uk/

Further reading

Barclay, R. 'Fact Sheets': http://russellbarkley.org/factsheets.html [Accessed 31 January 2023].

Carvajal, I.F. and Aldridge, D. (2011) *Understanding Fragile X Syndrome: A Guide for Families and Professionals*, London: Jessica Kingsley.

Irving, M. (2019) *The Human DNA Manual: Understanding Your Genetic Code*, Sparkford: Haynes.

OpenLearn (nd) 'Understanding ADHD', Available from: https://www.open.edu/openlearn/health-sports-psychology/understanding-adhd/content-section-0 [Accessed 31 January 2023].

Shen, M.D. and Piven, J. (2017) 'Brain and behavior development in autism from birth through infancy', *Dialogues in Clinical Neuroscience*, 19(4): 325–334.

Wall, K. (2009) *Autism and Early Years Practice* (2nd edn), London: SAGE.

On our website

You can find lots more material on our website at https://policy.bristoluniversitypress.co.uk/child-development-and-the-brain/companion-website

This includes:

How to read difficult academic papers: https://policy.bristoluniversitypress.co.uk/child-development-and-the-brain/companion-website/how-to-read-difficult-academic-papers

Brain development in the news: https://policy.bristoluniversitypress.co.uk/child-development-and-the-brain/companion-website/brain-development-in-the-news

Finding material about brain development: https://policy.bristoluniversitypress.co.uk/child-development-and-the-brain/companion-website/finding-materials-about-brain-development

Glossary

Accommodation: This process is where new information is accommodated by mental schemas. Existing schemas change and new ones develop as the cognitive system reorganises to accommodate conflicting new information.

Action potentials: Waves of electrical activity that are conducted along the body of the neuron.

Adrenal glands: Glands that sit above the kidneys and that release hormones in response to stress.

Amygdala: The left and right amygdalae are situated in the temporal lobes. They play a role in the production and processing of emotions and in the processing of memories.

Assimilation: This process occurs when new knowledge fits in with an existing schema and does not entail any restructuring of the existing schema.

Astrocytes: Glial cells that reside in the brain and spinal cord. Their functions include the maintenance of the chemical environment to facilitate neural signalling.

Attachment: An inbuilt set of behaviours designed to keep the infant close to their primary carer by means of establishing a strong emotional relationship.

Axon: The part of the neuron that carries the action potential.

Binocular parallax: Objects appear in different locations when viewed separately with one eye from the same position. This parallax is an important depth cue when the information from both eyes is combined during visual processing.

Brain stem: This plays an important function in regulating reflex activities such as heart rate, blood-sugar levels and breathing. Together with the medulla, pons and midbrain, it also plays a role in relaying information between the brain and the spinal cord.

Broca's area: This is an area in the frontal lobe of one hemisphere usually associated with functions of speech production. Typically this area is in the left hemisphere.

Categorical speech perception: The ability to categorise the language sounds we hear, such that we can distinguish, for example, between the phonemes /b/ and /p/.

Central nervous system (CNS): Collective term for the brain and the spinal cord.

Cerebellum: Sometimes called the 'little brain'. This is involved in planning and controlling movement, although damage to this region also affects language use and decision-making abilities, so it clearly has several functions.

Cerebrum: The part of the brain that contains the cerebral cortex and some parts of the subcortical brain including the hippocampus and the olfactory bulb.

Cingulate cortex: This is important in emotional processing as well as learning and memory. It is situated just above the corpus callosum.

Cognitive complexity: A view of cognition being on a continuum from simple to complex thought processes.

Computed tomography: Often just called CT scans, these are X-rays that are computer processed to produce images of the brain.

Corpus callosum: The thick layer of neural fibres that connects the two hemispheres of the brain.

Cortisol: A hormone released as part of the daily diurnal rhythm and also in response to stress.

Dendrite: The part of the neuron that receives synaptic input.

Depth perception: The ability to assess the distance of stimuli from the viewer and in spatial relation to other stimuli, for example to see whether or not objects are closer or farther away than other objects.

Diffusion tensor imaging (DTI): An MRI process that allows the diffusion of molecules to be mapped.

Diurnal: A daily repeating pattern.

Electroencephalography: A means of recording electrical activity in the brain by placing electrodes on the scalp.

Electrophysiological: This term refers to the electrical components of cells and tissues and changes in the voltage or current that are measured to assess a range of activities. The methods involve a wide range of techniques from single-cell to whole-organ recording to assess healthy biological function.

Emotional regulation: The ability to monitor and manage feelings.

Equilibration: Piaget's idea that cognitive balancing is obtained through this process where new information is balanced with existing knowledge through the processes of assimilation and accommodation of new information into existing schemas.

Equipotentiality: The idea that if one part of the brain is damaged another part can take over the functions of that area.

Executive function: The cognitive capacities that allow control of thought and behaviour.

Explicit memory: Verbal and conscious memory system.

Fixation: In relation to vision, this refers to involuntary gaze on one location.

Frontal lobe: The largest lobe of the brain, which is involved in a great number of higher functions.

Functional magnetic resonance imagery (fMRI): Images of the brain, which show us the moment-by-moment activity of the brain as the person does things such as reading or thinking.

Fusiform face area: Part of the fusiform gyrus that is specialised for human face recognition.

Fusiform gyrus: This is part of the temporal lobe and occipital lobe and is also sometimes referred to as the occipitotemporal gyrus.

Glia or glial cells: Cells that support the work of neurons. They include astrocytes, oligodendrocytes and microglial cells.

Grey matter: Areas of the brain and CNS that have lots of unmyelinated neurons. This contrasts with white matter, which includes neurons with myelinated axons and which communicate between areas of the cerebrum.

Gyrus (plural = gyri): The hills that make up the crinkly surface of the brain (Greek = ring or circle).

Habituation: A reduction in response to a stimulus that has been repeatedly presented. It is generally taken as a sign that the stimulus has become familiar. The process is used extensively in research with infants to get them accustomed to perceptual stimuli.

Hippocampus: This is situated in the medial temporal cortex. It is a part of the brain that is used in the formation of memory.

Hormone: A chemical messenger.

Hypothalamic-pituitary-adrenocortical Axis (HPA Axis): A system in the body that is used to control the response to stress.

Hypothalamus: A small collection of clusters of neurons that sit just below the thalamus. It controls functions such as body temperature, feeling hungry or thirsty and sleep.

Iconic memory: Visual memory that lasts only fleetingly and is used to give us a sense of continuity.

Implicit memory: Non-verbal memory system that we do not control and are unable to recall, as it is in the unconscious part of the brain.

Insula or **insula cortex:** Part of the cerebral cortex.

Intermediate working memory: Used to store memory over a matter of days.

Lateral geniculate nucleus (LGN): Part of the thalamus, a section of the brain that acts as a relay for information from the retina to all parts of the brain.

Limbic system: Term that is used for the parts of the cortical and subcortical brain that control emotions.

Long-term potentiation (LTP): Increases in the effectiveness of synaptic connections that occur because of experience. This allows us to learn from our experiences.

Magnetic resonance imaging (MRI): Using an MRI scanner, which produces a strong magnetic field, to detect signals from excited hydrogen atoms that are present in water.

Magnetoencephalography: A neuroimaging technique that directly measures the magnetic activity that is produced by electrical currents in the brain.

Medulla: The lower part of the brain stem, which controls functions such as heart rate and breathing.

Mesocorticolimbic pathway: This has lots of dopamine-releasing neurons. It links the ventral striatum of the basal ganglia in the forebrain to the ventral tegmental area in the midbrain. It is associated with the rewarding effect of pleasures including eating, drugs and sex.

Metacognition: The executive process of thinking about and examining our own thinking. Metacognitive processes are those which we are aware of and understand, for example, knowing how to memorise a list of numbers or how to solve a mathematical problem.

Microglia: A type of cell found in the brain and CNS. Microglia cells repair and maintain other brain cells.

Midbrain: This is situated below the cerebral cortex. It is also known as the mesencephalon.

Mirror neuron system (MNS): The system that fires neurons in the brain when we watch an action that mirrors those that would fire if we performed the action ourselves.

Motion parallax: This is a depth cue that results from our motion. As we move, objects that are closer to us appear to move farther across our field of view than objects that are in the distance.

Myelination: In this process glial cells provide a layer of fatty tissue that wraps and insulates axons. It acts to increase the speed of communication within neurons.

N170: A negative electrical signal that can be measured in the occipital to temporal region of the scalp in response to human faces.

Near-infrared spectroscopy: An imaging technique that measures the near-infrared spectrum to show changes in blood flow in the brain.

Neocortex: This is the six-layered, largest part of the cerebral cortex.

Neural plasticity: The way in which the brain is capable of being reshaped by experience, as well as the rewiring in early years that is not necessarily reliant on experiential learning.

Neural substrates: Term used in neuroscience to describe the systems in the brain that respond to a particular activity.

Neuroanatomical: Anatomical studies in the discipline that investigate and describe the nervous system and seek to understand the typical and atypical functioning of the neural structure of an organism.

Neuroconstructivism: Broad theory of cognitive development that takes into account the interactions between genes, neural connections in the brain and the environment.

Neurogenesis: The production of new neurons.

Neurons: The nerve cells of the central and peripheral nervous systems, which includes those in the brain. Neurons transmit small electrical signals containing information and so form the building blocks of the nervous systems of the body.

Nodes of Ranvier: Gaps in the myelinated sheath of an axon that allow the exchange of ions and so recharge the action potential of the neuron.

Object permanence: This is the understanding that objects exist independent of ourselves and have continuous properties even when they cannot be seen.

Occipital cortex: This is where a lot of visual processing takes place.

Occipital lobe: This is the main area for processing visual data when it first reaches the cortex. It is situated at the anterior region of the cerebral cortex.

Ocular dominance columns: Stripes of neurons that process the distinctive inputs from each eye and are sensitive to the different information that each eye receives.

Oculomotor skills: The ability to track moving objects.

Oligodendrocytes: Cells found in the brain and central nervous system. Their main role is the laying down of myelin.

Orbitofrontal cortex: Part of the frontal cortex that sits just behind the eye sockets. It plays a central role in emotional processing.

Paradigm: A set of approaches and methods in scientific enquiry that is adopted at a particular time and/or within a particular context of inquiry.

Left Parahippocampal region: An area in the brain's limbic system involved in encoding memories and recalling visual scenes.

Parietal lobe: The area of the brain that deals with a lot of sensory information as well as controlling aspects of movement.

Perception: This occurs when sensory information is identified, organised and actively interpreted by the nervous system. In visual perception, light hits the retina and is interpreted actively by our brain. Top-down processes, including memory and learning, can guide this interpretation, as do bottom-up processes such as sensation.

Peripheral nervous system (PNS): The PNS is the nerves and the associated fibres that lie beyond the brain and connect the central nervous system to the rest of the body. The PNS also controls functions such as breathing and digestion.

Pituitary gland: A pea-sized gland that sits at the base of the hypothalamus. It produces a number of hormones, including corticotrophins and growth hormones.

Pons: One of the three components of the brain stem. It acts as a relay for signals having to do with functions such as sleep, breathing, taste and eye movements.

Positron emission tomography (PET): After being injected with a radioactive tracer into the bloodstream, positrons are released; when these collide with electrons they release a photon which can be detected by a scanner.

Preferential looking: A method that is usually used in developmental psychology to understand if infants have discriminated between two visual stimuli. Typically, an infant is habituated to a stimulus and then shown a new one. If the child looks longer at the second stimulus it is usually inferred that they have discriminated between the two stimuli. Looking time is taken as the measure of preference.

Prefrontal cortex: The executive area of the brain. It is involved in planning, memory, personality and decision making and is also the area where emotional reactions are thought through.

Primary emotions: The emotions that develop early in infancy. They are usually seen as including joy, fear, anger, distress, sadness, interest and disgust.

Reminiscence bump: The period in adolescence that is most often recollected in later life. Memories from this period are better remembered and have more significance than memories from other periods.

Saccades: Rapid and jerky movements of the eye that are typically used for reading.

Schema: The way we understand something as a pattern of repeatable behaviour. A schema can act as an organising mental structure through which we organise new information.

Secondary emotions: More complex emotions that develop around the second year of life and that include pride, jealousy, shame, guilt and empathy.

Selective attention: The ability to focus on specific information amid an array of sensory information.

Sensation: In developmental psychology this refers to the effect of stimuli on the senses. It is seen as the neurological and biochemical events that act on the sensory receptor cells.

Shape constancy: The tendency to perceive the shape of an object as constant despite differences in the viewing angle (and consequent differences in the shape of the pattern projected on the retina of the eye).

Short-term memory: The ability to maintain information that is available for use for a short period of time.

Stereopsis: Where two separate images from the two eyes are successfully combined into one image in the brain to give a three-dimensional view of the world.

Sulcus (plural = sulci): The valleys that make up the crinkly surface of the brain (Latin = furrow).

Superior temporal sulcus: Area of the brain activated during gazing. It is also a part of the brain that is used to process faces.

Synaptic cleft: The gap between two neurons. It allows for the release and the reception of a chemical (or sometimes electrical) signal, known as a neurotransmitter, which communicates between the two cells.

Synaptogenesis: The connecting together of the brain, most of which occurs postnatally.

Temporal lobes: There are two of these, one on each side of the head. They play a role in the processing of sound. The temporal lobe in the left hemisphere is where most people process speech.

Thalamus: This sits on top of the brain stem and also has a relay function, receiving and processing signals from most of the sensory receptors in the body and then relaying them to the appropriate parts of the cortex.

Transcranial magnetic stimulation: The use of electromagnetic induction to stimulate areas of the brain.

Ventral and dorsal pathways: Once visual information has been processed in the occipital lobe it can be processed by two main pathways that project differently from the occipital lobe. The dorsal pathway projects information to the parietal lobe, while the temporal lobe receives information via the ventral pathway. Researchers investigate the extent to which the ventral stream processes information about object identification and the dorsal stream processes spatial information from the viewer's perspective.

Visual acuity: This refers to the discrimination of the eye to fine detail. The process depends upon the clarity of focus within the retina. Visual acuity in infants is studied extensively as a baseline for using infant gaze to infer their cognitive abilities.

Visual cortex: This area, responsible for processing visual data, is in the occipital lobe in both hemispheres. The term is usually used to refer to the primary visual cortex, also referred to as the striate cortex V1, connecting to the further visual cortical areas that are extra striate, known as V2, V3, V4 and V5.

Visual orientation: This is the ability to move the head and the eyes in anticipation of, or in response to, a new sensory stimulus.

Visual word form area (VWFA): An area of the brain in the occipitotemporal cortex area. In adult readers the left VWFA is activated, whereas in immature readers this region in both the left and right hemispheres is active.

White matter: This is the tissue in the brain containing nerve fibres that send important nerve signals. Many of these fibres are covered in myelin fat which makes the tissue look white.

Working memory: The limited cognitive system capacity that enables information to be used primarily in reasoning and behavioural decisions.

References

Adair, L.S. (2008) 'Child and adolescent obesity: Epidemiology and developmental perspectives', *Physiology & Behavior*, 94(1): 8–16.

Adams, S. and Beckford, M. (2018) 'Nine in ten teens at drug clinics are being treated for marijuana use', *Mail Online*, 22 April, Available from: http://www.dailymail.co.uk/news/article-5642917/Nine-ten-teens-drug-clinics-treated-marijuana-use.html [Accessed 21 October 2019].

Addante, R.J. (2015) 'A critical role of the human hippocampus in an electrophysiological measure of implicit memory' *NeuroImage*, 109: 515–528.

Administration for Children and Families. (2019) 'Child maltreatment 2019', Available from https://www.acf.hhs.gov/cb/report/child-maltreatment-2019 [Accessed 30 January 2023].

Ainsworth, M.D.S., Bell, S.M. and Stayton, D.J. (1974) 'Infant–mother attachment and social development: "Socialisation" as a product of reciprocal responsiveness to signals', in M.P.M. Richards (ed) *The Integration of a Child into a Social World*, New York: Cambridge University Press, pp 99–135.

Ainsworth, M.D.S., Blehar, M.C., Waters, E. and Wall, S. (1978) *Patterns of Attachment: A Psychological Study of the Strange Situation*, Hillsdale, NJ: Erlbaum.

Aksan, N. and Kochanska, G. (2004) 'Heterogeneity of joy in infancy', *Infancy*, 6(1): 79–94.

Al Odhayani, A., Watson, W.J. and Watson, L. (2013) 'Behavioural consequences of child abuse', *Canadian Family Physician*, 59(8): 831–836.

Alcohol Policy Team, Department of Health. (2016) *How to Keep Health Risks from Drinking Alcohol to a Low Level: Government Response to the Public Consultation*, London: Department of Health.

Allam, D.-E., Soussignan, R., Patris, B., Marlier, L. and Schaal, B. (2010) 'Long-lasting memory for an odor acquired at the mother's breast', *Developmental Science*, 13(6): 849–863.

Allen, G. (2011a) *Early Intervention: Smart Investment, Massive Savings. The Second Independent Report to Her Majesty's Government*, London: The Stationery Office.

Allen, G. (2011b) *Early Intervention: The Next Steps. An Independent Report to Her Majesty's Government by Graham Allen MP*, London: The Stationery Office.

American College of Obstetricians and Gynecologists. (2017) 'Marijuana use during pregnancy and lactation', Available from: https://www.acog.org/Clinical-Guidance-and-Publications/Committee-Opinions/Committee-on-Obstetric-Practice/Marijuana-Use-During-Pregnancy-and-Lactation [Accessed 28 September 2021].

American Psychiatric Association. (2013) *DSM-V: Diagnostic and Statistical Manual of Mental Disorders* (5th revd edn), Washington, DC: American Psychiatric Press.

Anblagan, D., Jones, N.W., Costigan, C., Parker, A J.J., Allcock, K., Aleong, R., ... and Gowland, P.A. (2013) 'Maternal smoking during pregnancy and fetal organ growth: A magnetic resonance imaging study', *PLoS One*, 8(7) 1–7.

Andalib, S., Emamhadi, M.R., Yousefzadeh-Chabok, S., Shakouri, S.K., Høilund-Carlsen, P.F., Vafaee, M.S. and Michel, T.M. (2017) 'Maternal SSRI exposure increases the risk of autistic offspring: A meta-analysis and systematic review', *European Psychiatry*, 45: 161–166.

Anderson, V.A., Anderson, P., Northam, E., Jacobs, R. and Catroppa. C. (2001) 'Development of executive functions through late childhood and adolescence in an Australian sample', *Developmental Neuropsychology*, 20(1): 385–406.

Andrade, S.E., Reichman, M.E., Mott, K., Pitts, M., Kieswetter, C., Dinatale, M., … and Toh, S. (2016) 'Use of selective serotonin reuptake inhibitors (SSRIs) in women delivering liveborn infants and other women of child-bearing age within the U.S. Food and Drug Administration's Mini-Sentinel program', *Archives of Women's Mental Health*, 19(6): 969–977.

Arbel, I., Kadar, T., Silbermann, M. and Levy, A. (1994) 'The effects of long-term corticosterone administration on hippocampal morphology and cognitive performance of middle-aged rats', *Brain Research*, 657(1–2): 227–235.

Athey, C. (2007) *Extending Thought in Young Children* (2nd edn), London: Paul Chapman.

Azevedo, F.A.C., Carvalho, L.R.B., Grinberg, L.T., Farfel, J.M., Ferretti, R.E.L., Leite, R.E.P., Lent, R. and Herculano-Houzel, S. (2009) 'Equal numbers of neuronal and nonneuronal cells make the human brain an isometrically scaled-up primate brain', *Journal of Comparative Neurology*, 513(5): 532–541.

Azhari, A., Truzzi, A., Neoh, M.J.-Y., Balagtas, J.P.M., Tan, H.H., Goh, P.P., Ang, X.A., Setoh, P., Rigo, P., Bornstein, M.H. and Esposito, G. (2020) 'A decade of infant neuroimaging research: What have we learned and where are we going?', *Infant Behavior and Development*, 58: 101389.

Baburamani, A.A., Patkee, P.A., Arichi, T. and Rutherford, M.A (2019) 'New approaches to studying early brain development in Down syndrome', *Developmental Medicine and Child Neurology*, 61(8): 867–879.

Baddeley, A.D. and Hitch, G.J. (1975) 'Working memory', in G.H. Bower (ed) *The Psychology of Learning and Motivation*, Vol. 8, London: Academic Press, pp 47–90.

Bahrick, L.E. and Pickens, J.N. (1995) 'Infant memory for object motion across a period of three months: Implications for a four-phase attention function', *Journal of Experimental Child Psychology*, 59(3): 343–371.

Bahrick, L.E., Gogate, L.J. and Ruiz, I. (2002) 'Attention and memory for faces and actions in infancy: The salience of actions over faces in dynamic events', *Child Development*, 73(6): 1629–1643.

Baillargeon, R. (1993) 'The object concept revisited: New directions in the investigation of infants' physical knowledge', in C.E. Granrud (ed) *Visual Perception and Cognition in Infancy*, Hillsdale, NJ: Erlbaum, pp 265–315.

Baillargeon, R., Spelke, E.S. and Wasserman, S. (1985) 'Object permanence in five-month-old infants', *Cognition*, 20: 191–208.

Baird, A.A., Kagakn, J., Gaudette, T., Walz, K.A., Hershlag, N. and Boas, D.A. (2002) 'Frontal lobe activation during object permanence: Data from near infrared spectroscopy', *Neuroimage*, 16(4): 1120–1126.

Baird, G., Charman, T., Baron-Cohen, S., Cox, A., Swettenham, J., Wheelwright, S. and Drew, A. (2000) 'A screening instrument for autism at 18 months of age: A 6-year follow-up study', *Journal of the American Academy of Child & Adolescent Psychiatry*, 39(6): 694–702.

Bandura, A. (1969) 'Social learning theory of identificatory processes', in D.A. Goslin (ed) *Handbook of Socialization Theory and Research*, Chicago, IL: Rand McNally, pp 213–262.

Bandura, A. (1977) *Social Learning Theory*, London: Prentice-Hall.

Barkley, R.A. (2015) *Attention-Deficit Hyperactivity Disorder: A Handbook for Diagnosis and Treatment*, New York: Guilford.

Baron-Cohen, S. (2002) 'The extreme male brain theory of autism', *Trends in Cognitive Sciences*, 6(6): 248–254.

Baron-Cohen, S., Richler, J., Bisarya, D., Gurunathan, N. and Wheelwright, S. (2003) 'The systemizing quotient: An investigation of adults with Asperger syndrome or high-functioning autism, and normal sex differences', *Philosophical Transactions of the Royal Society of London. Series B: Biological Sciences*, 358(1430): 361–374.

Baron-Cohen, S., Leslie, A.M. and Frith, U. (1985) 'Does the autistic child have a "theory of mind"', *Cognition*, 21(1): 37–46.

Barrett, L.F. (2006) 'Solving the emotion paradox: Categorization and the experience of emotion', *Personality and Social Psychology Review*, 10(1): 20–46.

Barsalou, L.W., Simmons, W.K., Barbey, A. and Wilson, C.D. (2003) 'Grounding conceptual knowledge in modality-specific systems', *Trends in Cognitive Sciences*, 7: 84–91.

Bartolotti, J. and Marian, V. (2012) 'Language learning and control in monolinguals and bilinguals', *Cognitive Science*. 36: 1129–1147.

Bates, E., Bretherton, I., Beeghly-Smith, M. and McNew, S. (1982) 'Social bases of language development: A reassessment', *Advances in Child Development and Behavior*, 16: 7–75.

Bates, E., Roe, K., Nelson, C. and Collin, M. (2001) 'Language development in children with unilateral brain injury', in C. Nelson and M. Luciana (eds) *Handbook of Developmental Cognitive Neuroscience* (2nd edn), Cambridge, MA: MIT Press, pp 281–302.

Battista, C., Evans, T.M., Ngoon, T.J., Chen, T., Chen, L., Kochalka, J. and Menon, V. (2018) 'Mechanisms of interactive specialization and emergence of functional brain circuits supporting cognitive development in children', *Science of Learning*, 3(1): 1–11.

Battle, C.L., Uebelacker, L.A., Magee, S.R., Sutton, K.A. and Miller, I.W. (2015) 'Potential for prenatal yoga to serve as an intervention to treat depression during pregnancy', *Women's Health Issues*, 25(2): 134–141.

Belfort, M.B., Anderson, P.J., Nowak, V.A., Lee, K.J., Molesworth, C., Thompson, D. K., … and Inder, T.E. (2016) 'Breast milk feeding, brain development, and neurocognitive outcomes: A 7-year longitudinal study in infants born at less than 30 weeks' gestation', *Journal of Pediatrics*, 177: 133–139.

Bell, M.A. and Fox, N.A. (1992) 'The relations between frontal brain electrical activity and cognitive development in infancy', *Child Development*, 63: 1142–1163.

Bell, M.A. and Wolfe, C.D. (2007) 'Changes in brain functioning from infancy to early childhood: Evidence from EEG power and coherence during working memory tasks', *Developmental Neuropsychology*, 31(1): 21–38.

Bellugi, U., Mills, D., Jernigan, T., Hickok, G. and Galaburda, A (1999) 'Linking cognition, brain structure, and brain function in Williams syndrome', in H. Tager-Flusberg (ed) *Neurodevelopmental Disorders*, Cambridge, MA: MIT Press, pp 111–136.

Benítez-Bribiesca, L., De la Rosa-Alvarez, I. and Mansilla-Olivares, A. (1999) 'Dendritic spine pathology in infants with severe protein-calorie malnutrition', *Pediatrics*, 104(2): e21–e21.

Bernard, K., Frost, A., Bennett, C.B. and Lindhiem, O. (2017) 'Maltreatment and diurnal cortisol regulation: A meta-analysis', *Psychoneuroendocrinology*, 78: 57–67.

Bhatt, R.S. and Quinn, P.C. (2011) 'How does learning impact development in infancy? The case of perceptual organization', *Infancy*, 16(1): 2–38.

Biddulph, S. (2006) *Raising Babies: Should under Threes Go to Nursery?*, London: Harper Collins.

Bishop, K.M. and Wahlsten, D. (1997) 'Sex differences in the human corpus callosum: Myth or reality?', *Neuroscience & Biobehavioral Reviews*, 21(5): 581–601.

Bjorklund, D.F. (1987) 'How age changes in knowledge base contribute to the development of children's memory: An interpretive review', *Developmental Review*, 7(2): 93–130.

Blakemore, S.-J. (2008) 'The social brain in adolescence', *Nature Reviews Neuroscience*, 9(4): 267–277.

Blakemore, S.-J. (2012) 'Imaging brain development: The adolescent brain', *Neuroimage*, 61(2): 397–406.

Blakemore, S.-J. (2019) *Inventing Ourselves: The Secret Life of the Teenage Brain*, London: Black Swan.

Blakemore, S.-J. and Choudhury, S. (2006) 'Development of the adolescent brain: Implications for executive function and social cognition', *Journal of Child Psychology and Psychiatry*, 47(3–4): 296–312.

Blanton, R.E., Levitt, J.G., Peterson, J.R., Fadale, D., Sporty, M.L., Lee, M., To, D., Mormino, E.C., Thompson, P.M. and McCracken, J.T. (2004) 'Gender differences in the left inferior frontal gyrus in normal children', *Neuroimage*, 22(2): 626–636.

Blaser, E. and Kaldy, Z. (2010) 'Infants get five stars on iconic memory tests: A partial-report test of 6-month-old infants' iconic memory capacity', *Psychological Science*, 21(11): 1643–1645.

Blasi, A. et al (2011) 'Early specialization for voice and emotion processing in the infant brain', *Current Biology*, 21(14): 1220–1224.

Bliss, T.V. and Lømo, T. (1973) 'Long-lasting potentiation of synaptic transmission in the dentate area of the anaesthetized rabbit following stimulation of the perforant path', *Journal of Physiology*, 232(2): 331–356.

Bostock, J. (1962) 'Evolutionary approaches to infant', *Lancet*, 1: 1033–1035.

Bouchard, T.J., Lykken, D.T., McGue, M., Segal, N.L. and Tellegen, A. (1990) 'Sources of human psychological differences: The Minnesota study of twins reared apart', *Science*, 250(4978): 223–228.

Bowers, J.M. and Moyer, A. (2017) 'Effects of school start time on students' sleep duration, daytime sleepiness, and attendance: A meta-analysis', *Sleep Health*, 3(6): 423–431.

Bowlby, J. (1969) *Attachment and Loss*, Vol. 1: *Attachment*, London: Hogarth Press.

Bowlby, J. (1973) *Attachment and Loss*, Vol. 2: *Separation*, London: Hogarth Press.

Bowlby, J. (1980) *Attachment and Loss*, Vol. 3: *Loss*, London: Hogarth Press.

Breakthroughs International: The Brain Gym Program (2022). Available from: https://breakthroughsinternational.org/programs/the-brain-gym-program/ [Accessed 31 January 2023].

Bremer, A.A. and Lustig, R.H. (2012) 'Effects of sugar-sweetened beverages on children', *Pediatric Annals*, 41(1): 26–30.

Broca, P. (1861) 'Remarks on the seat of the faculty of articulated language, following an observation of aphemia (loss of speech)', in G. von Bonin (ed) *Some Papers on the Cerebral Cortex*, Springfield, IL: Charles C. Thomas, pp 199–220.

Brooks, A.D., Berninger, V.W. and Abbott, R.D. (2011) 'Letter naming and letter writing reversals in children with dyslexia: Momentary inefficiency in the phonological and orthographic loops of working memory', *Developmental Neuropsychology*, 36(7): 847–868.

Brown, Q.L., Sarvet, A.L., Shmulewitz, D., Martins, S.S., Wall, M.M. and Hasin, D.S. (2017) 'Trends in marijuana use among pregnant and non-pregnant reproductive-aged women, 2002–2014', *JAMA*, 317(2): 207–209.

Brown, R. and Hanlon, C. (1970) 'Derivational complexity and the order of acquisition in child speech', in J.R. Hayes (ed) *Cognition and the Development of Language*, Hoboken, NJ: Wiley, pp 11–53.

Brown, W.E., Kesler, S.R., Eliez, S., Warsofsky, I.S., Haberecht, M., Patwardhan, A., Ross, J.L., Neely, E.K., Zeng, S.M., Yankowitz, J. and Reiss, A.L. (2002) 'Brain development in Turner syndrome: A magnetic resonance imaging study', *Psychiatry Research*, 116(3): 187–196.

Bruer, J.T. (1999) *The Myth of the First Three Years: A New Understanding of Early Brain Development and Lifelong Learning*, New York: Simon & Schuster.

Bruner, J.S. (1983) *Child's Talk: Learning to Use Language*, Oxford: Oxford University Press.

Bullock Drummey, A. and Newcombe, N. (1995) 'Remembering versus knowing the past: Children's explicit and implicit memories for pictures', *Journal of Experimental Child Psychology*, 59(3): 549–565.

Bunea, I.M., Szentágotai-Tătar, A. and Miu, A.C. (2017) 'Early-life adversity and cortisol response to social stress: A meta-analysis', *Translational Psychiatry*, 7(12): 1–8.

Bunge, S.A., Dudukovic, N.M., Thomason, M.E., Vaidya, C.J. and Gabrieli, J.D. (2002) 'Immature frontal lobe contributions to cognitive control in children: Evidence from fMRI', *Neuron*, 33(2): 301–311.

Burd, L., Vesely, B., Martsolf, J. and Kerbeshian, J. (1990) 'Prevalence study of Prader-Willi syndrome in North Dakota', *American Journal of Medical Genetics*, 37(1): 97–99.

Butterworth, B. and Walsh, V. (2011) 'Neural basis of mathematical cognition, *Current Biology*, 21(16): R618–R621.

Bywaters, P., Bunting, L., Davidson, G., Hanratty, J., Mason, W., McCartan, C. and Steils, N. (2016) *The Relationship between Poverty, Child Abuse and Neglect: An Evidence Review*, London: Joseph Rowntree Foundation.

Caldji, C., Tannenbaum, B., Sharma, S., Francis, D., Plotsky, P.M. and Meaney, M.J. (1998) 'Maternal care during infancy regulates the development of neural systems mediating the expression of fearfulness in the rat', *Proceedings of the National Academy of Sciences*, 95(9): 5335–5340.

Calem, M., Bromis, K., McGuire, P., Morgan, C. and Kempton, M.J. (2017) 'Meta-analysis of associations between childhood adversity and hippocampus and amygdala volume in non-clinical and general population samples', *NeuroImage: Clinical*, 14: 471–479.

Campagne, D.M. (2019) 'Antidepressant use in pregnancy: Are we closer to consensus?', *Archives of Women's Mental Health*, 22(2): 189–197.

Campos, J.J. and Barrett, K.C. (1984) 'Emergent themes in the study of emotional development and emotion regulation', in C.E. Izard and R.B. Zajonc (eds) *Emotions, Cognition and Behavior*, New York: Cambridge University Press, pp 229–263.

Cantlon, J.F., Brannon, E.M., Carter, E.J. and Pelphrey, K.A. (2006) 'Functional imaging of numerical processing in adults and 4-y-old children', *PLoS Biology*, 4(5), e125.

Capone, G.T. (2001) 'Down syndrome: Advances in molecular biology and the neurosciences', *Journal of Developmental & Behavioral Pediatrics*, 22(1): 40.

Carey, S., Diamond, R. and Woods, B. (1980) 'Development of face recognition: A maturational component?', *Developmental Psychology*, 16(4): 257.

Carey, S., Shusterman, A., Haward, P. and Distefano, R. (2017) 'Do analog number representations underlie the meanings of young children's verbal numerals?', *Cognition*, 168: 243–255.

Carrion, V.G., Haas, B.W., Garrett, A., Song, S. and Reiss, A.L. (2009) 'Reduced hippocampal activity in youth with posttraumatic stress symptoms: An FMRI study', *Journal of Pediatric Psychology*, 35(5): 559–569.

Carrion, V.G. and Wong, S.S. (2012) 'Can traumatic stress alter the brain? Understanding the implications of early trauma on brain development and learning', *Journal of Adolescent Health*, 51(2): S23–28.

Carroll, M., Byrne, B. and Kirsner, K. (1985) 'Autobiographical memory and perceptual learning: A developmental study using picture recognition, naming latency, and perceptual identification', *Memory & Cognition*, 13(3): 273–279.

Casey, B.J., Getz, S. and Galvan, A. (2008) 'The adolescent brain', *Developmental Review*, 28(1): 62–77.

Casey, B.J., Jones, R.M. and Hare, T.A. (2008) 'The adolescent brain', *Annals of the New York Academy of Sciences*, 1124: 111–126.

Casey, B.J., Tottenham, N., Liston, C. and Durston, S. (2005) 'Imaging brain development: What have we learned about cognitive development?', *Trends in Cognitive Sciences*, 9(3): 104–110.

Cassidy, S.B. (1997) 'Prader-Willi syndrome', *Journal of Medical Genetics*, 34(11): 917.

Castro-Caldas, A. and Reis, A. (2003) 'The knowledge of orthography is a revolution in the brain', *Reading and Writing: An Interdisciplinary Journal*, 16: 81–97.

CDC (Centers for Disease Control and Prevention). (2018) 'Alcohol use in pregnancy', 17 July, Available from: https://www.cdc.gov/ncbddd/fasd/alcohol-use.html [Accessed 14 October 2019].

CDC (Centers for Disease Control and Prevention). (2019a) 'Breastfeeding report card', Available from: https://www.cdc.gov/media/releases/2018/p0820-breastfeeding-report-card.html [Accessed 28 September 2021].

CDC (Centers for Disease Control and Prevention). (2019b) 'Childhood obesity facts', https://www.cdc.gov/obesity/data/childhood.html [Accessed 31 January 2023].

CDC (Centers for Disease Control and Prevention). (2019c) 'Adverse childhood experiences (ACEs)', Available from: https://www.cdc.gov/violenceprevention/aces/index.html [Accessed 28 September 2021].

Charlton, R.A., Jordan, S., Pierini, A., Garne, E., Neville, A.J., Hansen, A.V., … and den Berg, L. de J. (2015) 'Selective serotonin reuptake inhibitor prescribing before, during and after pregnancy: A population-based study in six European regions', *BJOG: An International Journal of Obstetrics & Gynaecology*, 122(7): 1010–1020.

Chasnoff, I.J., Burns, W.J., Schnoll, S.H. and Burns, K.A. (1985) 'Cocaine use in pregnancy', *New England Journal of Medicine*, 313(11): 666–669.

Chen, L., Wassermann, D., Abrams, D.A., Kochalka, J., Gallardo-Diez, G. and Menon, V. (2019) 'The visual word form area (VWFA) is part of both language and attention circuitry', *Nature Communications*, 10(1): 5601.

Cheour, M., Shestakova, A., Alku, P., Ceponiene, R. and Näätänen, R. (2002) 'Mismatch negativity shows that 3–6-year-old children can learn to discriminate non-native speech sounds within two months', *Neuroscience Letters*, 325(3): 187–190.

Children's Society. (2018) 'What is child poverty?', Available from: https://www.childrenssociety.org.uk/what-we-do/our-work/ending-child-poverty/what-is-child-poverty [Accessed 16 September 2019].

Chomsky, N. (1957) *Syntactic Structures*, The Hague: Mouton.

Chomsky, N. (1968) *Language and Mind*, New York: Harcourt Brace and World.

Christodoulou, J., Lac, A. and Moore, D.S. (2017) 'Babies and math: A meta-analysis of infants' simple arithmetic competence', *Developmental Psychology*, 53(8): 1405.

Chugani, H.T., Behen, M.E., Muzik, O., Juhász, C., Nagy, F. and Chugani, D.C. (2001) 'Local brain functional activity following early deprivation: A study of postinstitutionalized Romanian orphans', *Neuroimage*, 14(6): 1290–1301.

Clark, K.A., Helland, T., Specht, K., Narr, K.L., Manis, F.R., Toga, A.W. and Hugdahl, K. (2014) 'Neuroanatomical precursors of dyslexia identified from pre-reading through to age 11', *Brain*, 137(12): 3136–3141.

Clarke, L.E. and Barres, B.A. (2013) 'Emerging roles of astrocytes in neural circuit development', *Nature Reviews Neuroscience*, 14(5): 311.

Clouchoux, C., Guizard, N., Evans, A.C., du Plessis, A.J. and Limperopoulos, C. (2012) 'Normative fetal brain growth by quantitative in vivo magnetic resonance imaging', *American Journal of Obstetrics and Gynecology*, 206(2): 173e1–173e8.

Cohen, L. and Dehaene, S. (2004) 'Specialization within the ventral stream: The case for the visual word form area', *Neuroimage*, 22(1): 466–476.

Cohen, N.J. and Squire, L.R. (1980) 'Preserved learning and retention of pattern-analyzing skill in amnesia: Dissociation of knowing how and knowing that', *Science*, 210(4466): 207–210.

Cohen, S. (2002) *Folk Devils and Moral Panics: The Creation of the Mods and Rockers*, London: Routledge.

Cole, P.V., Hawkins, L.H. and Roberts, D. (1972) 'Smoking during pregnancy and its effects on the fetus', *BJOG: An International Journal of Obstetrics & Gynaecology*, 79(9): 782–787.

Comasco, E., Rangmar, J., Eriksson, U.J. and Oreland, L. (2018) 'Neurological and neuropsychological effects of low and moderate prenatal alcohol exposure', *Acta Physiologica*, 222: 1–18.

Conway, M.A., Wang, Q., Hanyu, K. and Haque, S. (2005) 'A cross-cultural investigation of autobiographical memory: On the universality and cultural variation of the reminiscence bump', *Journal of Cross-Cultural Psychology*, 36(6): 739–749.

Corballis, M. (2012) 'Educational double-think', in S. Della Sala and M. Anderson (eds) *Neuroscience in Education: The Good, the Bad and the Ugly*, Oxford: Oxford University Press, pp 22–229.

Cordero, M.E., D'Acuña, E., Benveniste, S., Prado, R., Nuñez, J.A. and Colombo, M. (1993) 'Dendritic development in neocortex of infants with early postnatal life undernutrition', *Pediatric Neurology*, 9(6): 457–464.

Cordo, P.J., Bell, C.C. and Harnad, S.R. (1997) *Motor Learning and Synaptic Plasticity in the Cerebellum*, Cambridge: Cambridge University Press.

Corrow, S., Granrud, C.E., Mathison, J. and Yonas, A. (2012) 'Infants and adults use line junction information to perceive 3D shape', *Journal of Vision*, 12(1) : 1–7.

Cowell, R.A., Cicchetti, D., Rogosch, F.A. and Toth, S.L. (2015) 'Childhood maltreatment and its effect on neurocognitive functioning: Timing and chronicity matter', *Development and Psychopathology*, 27(2): 521–533.

Coyne, S. M., Rogers, A. A., Zurcher, J. D., Stockdale, L. and Booth, M (2020) 'Does time spent using social media impact mental health? An eight-year longitudinal study', *Computers in Human Behavior*, 104: 106160.

Crane, N.A., Schuster, R.M., Fusar-Poli, P. and Gonzalez, R. (2013) 'Effects of cannabis on neurocognitive functioning: Recent advances, neurodevelopmental influences, and sex differences', *Neuropsychology Review*, 23(2): 117–137.

Crystal, D. (2003) *The Cambridge Encyclopedia of the English Language* (2nd edn), Cambridge: Cambridge University Press.

Cuevas, K. and Bell, M.A. (2010) 'Developmental progression of looking and reaching performance on the A-not-B task', *Developmental Psychology*, 46: 1363–1371.

Cuevas, K. and Bell, M.A. (2011) 'EEG and ECG from 5 to 10 months of age: Developmental changes in baseline activation and cognitive processing during a working memory task', *International Journal of Psychophysiology: Official Journal of the International Organization of Psychophysiology*, 80(2): 119–128.

Curtiss, S., Fromkin, V., Krashen, S., Rigler, D. and Rigler, M. (1974) 'The linguistic development of Genie', *Language*, 50(3): 528–554.

Curtiss, S., Fromkin, V., Rigler, D., Rigler, M. and Krashen, S. (1975) 'An update on the linguistic development of Genie', in D.P. Dato (ed) *Developmental Psycholinguistics: Theory and Applications*, Washington, DC: Georgetown University School of Languages and Linguistics, pp 145–158.

Dahl, R.E. (2008) 'Biological, developmental, and neurobehavioral factors relevant to adolescent driving risks', *American Journal of Preventive Medicine*, 35(3): S278–S284.

Daily Mirror. (2012) 'Internet addiction disrupts nerve wiring in teenagers' brains, study finds', 12 January, Available from: https://www.mirror.co.uk/news/tec hnology-science/technology/internet-addiction-disrupts-nerve-wiring-171964 [Accessed 26 August 2020].

Davidow, J.Y., Foerde, K., Galván, A. and Shohamy, D. (2016) 'An upside to reward sensitivity: The hippocampus supports enhanced reinforcement learning in adolescence', *Neuron*, 92(1): 93–99.

Dean, D.C., Planalp, E.M., Wooten, W., Schmidt, C.K., Kecskemeti, S.R., Frye, C., Schmidt, N.L., Goldsmith, H.H., Alexander, A.L. and Davidson, R.J. (2018) 'Investigation of brain structure in the 1-month infant', *Brain Structure and Function*, 223(4): 1953–1970.

De Bellis, M.D., Keshavan, M.S., Beers, S.R., Hall, J., Frustaci, K., Masalehdan, A., Noll, J. and Boring, A.M. (2001) 'Sex differences in brain maturation during childhood and adolescence', *Cerebral Cortex*, 11(6): 552–557.

Defoe, I.N., Dubas, J.S., Figner, B. and van Aken, M.A. (2015) 'A meta-analysis on age differences in risky decision making: Adolescents versus children and adults', *Psychological Bulletin*, 141(1): 48–84.

Dehaene-Lambertz, G., Dehaene, S. and Hertz-Pannier, L. (2002) 'Functional neuroimaging of speech perception in infants', *Science*, 298(5600): 2013.

De Haan, M., Johnson, M.H. and Halit, H. (2003) 'Development of face-sensitive event-related potentials during infancy: A review', in M. De Haan (ed) *Infant EEG and Event-Related Potentials*, Hove: Psychology Press, pp 77–100.

Dekaban, A.S. and Sadowsky, D. (1978) 'Changes in brain weights during the span of human life: Relation of brain weights to body heights and body weights', *Annals of Neurology: Official Journal of the American Neurological Association and the Child Neurology Society*, 4(4): 345–356.

Delli, C.K.S., Varveris, A. and Geronta, A. (2017) 'Application of the theory of mind, theory of executive functions and weak central coherence theory to individuals with ASD', *Journal of Educational and Developmental Psychology*, 7(1): 102–122.

Dennis, M. and Whitaker, H.A. (1976) 'Language acquisition following hemidecortication: Linguistic superiority of the left over the right hemisphere', *Brain and Language*, 3(3): 404–433.

Dennison, P.E. and Dennison, G. (1994) *Brain-gym*, Ventura, CA: Edu-Kinesthetics.

Department for Education. (2017) 'Statutory framework for the early years foundation stage: Setting the standards for learning, development and care for children from birth to five, Available from: https://www.gov.uk/governm ent/publications/early-years-foundation-stage-framework--2 [Accessed 28 September 2021].

DePrince, A.P., Weinzierl, K.M. and Combs, M.D. (2009) 'Executive function performance and trauma exposure in a community sample of children', *Child Abuse & Neglect*, 33(6): 353–361.

Dettling, A.C., Parker, S.W., Lane, S., Sebanc, A. and Gunnar, M.R. (2000) 'Quality of care and temperament determine changes in cortisol concentrations over the day for young children in childcare', *Psychoneuroendocrinology*, 25(8): 819–836.

Dewey, K.G. and Begum, K. (2011) 'Long-term consequences of stunting in early life', *Maternal & Child Nutrition*, 7(s3): 5–18.

de Wit, E., van Dijk, P., Hanekamp, S., Visser-Bochane, M.I., Steenbergen, B., van der Schans, C.P. and Luinge, M.R. (2018) 'Same or different: The overlap between children with auditory processing disorders and children with other developmental disorders: A systematic review', *Ear and Hearing*, 39(1): 1–19.

Diamond, A. (1991) 'Neuropsychological insights into the meaning of object concept development', in S. Carey and R. Gelman (eds) *The Epigenesist of Mind: Essays on Biology and Cognition*, Hillsdale, NJ: Erlbaum, pp 67–110.

Diamond, A. (2001) 'Looking closely at infants' performance and experimental procedures in the A-not-B task', *Behavioral and Brain Sciences*, 2(1): 38–41.

Diamond, A. (2002) 'A model system for studying dopamine in prefrontal cortex during early development in humans', in M.H. Johnson, Y. Munakata and R. Gilmore (eds) *Brain Development and Cognition: A Reader*, Oxford: Blackwell, pp 441–493.

Diamond, A. (2013) 'Executive functions', *Annual Review of Psychology*, 64: 135–168.

Diamond, A. and Amso, D. (2008) 'Contributions of neuroscience to our understanding of cognitive development', *Current Directions in Psychological Science*, 17(2): 136–141.

Diamond, A., Cruttenden, L. and Nederman, D. (1994) 'AB with multiple wells: I. Why are multiple wells sometimes easier than two wells? II. Memory or memory + inhibition', *Developmental Psychology*, 30: 192–205.

References

Dienlin, T. and Johannes, N. (2020) 'The impact of digital technology use on adolescent well-being', *Dialogues in Clinical Neuroscience*, 22(2): 135.

Dinstein, I., Thomas, C., Behrmann, M. and Heeger, D.J. (2008) 'A mirror up to nature', *Current Biology*, 18(1): R13–R18.

Dirnhuber, J. (2018) 'Radiation from SMARTPHONES could cause memory loss in teenagers, new study reveals', *The Sun*, 20 July, Available from: http//www.thesun.co.uk/tech/6831084/smartphone-radiation-causes-memory-loss-teenagers/ [Accessed 26 August 2020].

Donaldson, M. (1978) *Children's Minds*, New York: W. W. Norton.

Downey, A. (2018) 'Scans reveal the shocking impact extreme neglect has on toddler's brains', *The Sun*, 20 November, Available from: https://www.thesun.co.uk/fabulous/4825334/brain-sizes-different-children-emotional-abuse-study/ [Accessed 13 April 2020].

Draganski, B., Gaser, C., Busch, V., Schuierer, G., Bogdahn, U. and May, A. (2004) 'Neuroplasticity: Changes in grey matter induced by training', *Nature*, 427(6972): 311–312.

Dubois, J., Dehaene-Lambertz, G., Kulikova, S., Poupon, C., Hüppi, P.S. and Hertz-Pannier, L. (2014) 'The early development of brain white matter: A review of imaging studies in fetuses, newborns and infants', *Neuroscience*, 276: 48–71.

Duchaine, B.C. and Nakayama, K. (2006) 'Developmental prosopagnosia: A window to content-specific face processing', *Current Opinion in Neurobiology*, 16(2): 166–173.

Dumontheil, I. (2014) 'Development of abstract thinking during childhood and adolescence: The role of rostrolateral prefrontal cortex', *Developmental Cognitive Neuroscience*, 10: 57–76.

Dumontheil, I., Burgess, P.W. and Blakemore, S.-J. (2008) 'Development of rostral prefrontal cortex and cognitive and behavioural disorders', *Developmental Medicine & Child Neurology*, 50(3): 168–181.

Durston, S. (2005) 'Integrating neurodevelopmental imaging and genetic designs', *Psychiatry*, 4(12): 35–37.

Eimas, P.D., Siqueland, E.R., Jusczyk, P. and Vigorito, J. (1971) 'Speech perception in infants', *Science*, 171(3968): 303.

Ekblad, M., Gissler, M., Korkeila, J. and Lehtonen, L. (2013) 'Trends and risk groups for smoking during pregnancy in Finland and other Nordic countries', *European Journal of Public Health*, 24(4): 544–551.

Ekblad, M., Korkeila, J. and Lehtonen, L. (2015) 'Smoking during pregnancy affects foetal brain development', *Acta Paediatrica*, 104(1): 12–18.

Ekmekcioglu, C., Wallner, P., Kundi, M., Weisz, U., Haas, W. and Hutter, H.-P. (2018) 'Red meat, diseases, and healthy alternatives: A critical review', *Critical Reviews in Food Science and Nutrition*, 58(2): 247–261.

El-Rafie, M.M., Khafagy, G.M. and Gamal, M.G. (2016) 'Effect of aerobic exercise during pregnancy on antenatal depression', *International Journal of Women's Health*, 8: 53.

Emerson, R.W., Adams, C., Nishino, T., Hazlett, H.C., Wolff, J.J., Zwaigenbaum, L., Constantino, J.N., Shen, M.D., Swanson, M.R. and Elison, J.T. (2017) 'Functional neuroimaging of high-risk 6-month-old infants predicts a diagnosis of autism at 24 months of age', *Science Translational Medicine*, 9(393): 1–19.

English, L.K., Fearnbach, S.N., Lasschuijt, M., Schlegel, A., Anderson, K., Harris, S., ... and Keller, K.L. (2016) 'Brain regions implicated in inhibitory control and appetite regulation are activated in response to food portion size and energy density in children', *International Journal of Obesity*, 40(10): 1515–1522.

Ericsson, K.A. and Kintsch, W. (1995) 'Long-term working memory', *Psychological Review*, 102(2): 211.

Eriksen, B.A. and Eriksen, C.W. (1974) 'Effects of noise letters upon the identification of a target letter in a nonsearch task', *Perception & Psychophysics*, 16(1): 143–149.

Ernst, M., Nelson, E.E., Jazbec, S., McClure, E.B., Monk, C.S., Leibenluft, E., Blair, J. and Pine, D.S. (2005) 'Amygdala and nucleus accumbens in responses to receipt and omission of gains in adults and adolescents', *Neuroimage*, 25(4): 1279–1291.

Eslinger, P.J., Flaherty-Craig, C.V. and Bentonb, A.L. (2004) 'Developmental outcomes after early prefrontal cortex damage', *Brain and Cognition*, 55: 84–103.

Estes, A., Munson, J., Rogers, S.J., Greenson, J., Winter, J. and Dawson, G. (2015) 'Long-term outcomes of early intervention in 6-year-old children with Autism spectrum disorder', *Journal of the American Academy of Child and Adolescent Psychiatry*, 54(7): 580–587.

Etchell, A., Adhikari, A., Weinberg, L.S., Choo, A.L., Garnett, E.O., Chow, H.M. and Chang, S.-E. (2018) 'A systematic literature review of sex differences in childhood language and brain development', *Neuropsychologia*, 114: 19–31.

Falkingham, M., Abdelhamid, A., Curtis, P., Fairweather-Tait, S., Dye, L. and Hooper, L. (2010) 'The effects of oral iron supplementation on cognition in older children and adults: A systematic review and meta-analysis', *Nutrition Journal*, 9(1): 4.

Farroni, T., Chiarelli, A.M., Lloyd-Fox, S., Massaccesi, S., Di Merla, A., Gangi, V., Mattarello, T., Faraguna, D. and Johnson, M.H. (2013) 'Infant cortex responds to other humans from shortly after birth', *Scientific Reports*, 3(1): 1–5.

Fehér, O., Wang, H., Saar, S., Mitra, P.P. and Tchernichovski, O. (2009) 'De novo establishment of wild-type song culture in the zebra finch', *Nature*, 459(7246): 564–568.

Feldstein Ewing, S.W., Sakhardande, A. and Blakemore, S.-J. (2014) 'The effect of alcohol consumption on the adolescent brain: A systematic review of MRI and fMRI studies of alcohol-using youth', *NeuroImage: Clinical*, 5: 420–437.

Felipe, R. de M. and Ferrão, Y.A. (2016) 'Transcranial magnetic stimulation for treatment of major depression during pregnancy: A review', *Trends in Psychiatry and Psychotherapy*, 38(4): 190–197.

Felleman, D.J. and Van Essen, D.C. (1991) 'Distributed hierarchical processing in the primate cerebral cortex', *Cerebral Cortex*, 1(1): 1–47.

Fernald, A. (1985) 'Four-month-old infants prefer to listen to motherese', *Infant Behavior and Development*, 8(2): 181–195.

Flak, A.L., Su, S., Bertrand, J., Denny, C.H., Kesmodel, U.S. and Cogswell, M.E. (2014) 'The association of mild, moderate, and binge prenatal alcohol exposure and child neuropsychological outcomes: A meta-analysis', *Alcoholism: Clinical and Experimental Research*, 38(1): 214–226.

Flatley, J. (2016) 'Abuse during childhood: Findings from the crime survey for England and Wales, year ending March 2016', Office for National Statistics, Available from: https://www.ons.gov.uk/peoplepopulationandcommunity/crimeandjust ice/articles/abuseduringchildhood/findingsfromtheyearendingmarch2016crimes urveyforenglandandwales [Accessed 28 September 2021].

Fleming, N.D. (1995) 'I'm different; not dumb. Modes of presentation (VARK) in the tertiary classroom', in A. Zelmer (ed) *Research and Development in Higher Education, Proceedings of the 1995 Annual Conference of the Higher Education and Research Development Society of Australasia*, 18: 308–313.

Fleming, N.D. and Baume, D. (2006) 'Learning styles again: VARKing up the right tree!', *Educational Developments*, 7(4): 4.

Fletcher, S., Elklit, A., Shevlin, M. and Armour, C. (2017) 'Predictors of PTSD treatment response trajectories in a sample of childhood sexual abuse survivors: The roles of social support, coping, and PTSD symptom clusters', *Journal of Interpersonal Violence*, 36(3–4): 1283–1307.

Følling, A. (1934) 'Excretion of phenylpyruvic acid in urine as a metabolic anomaly in connection with imbecility', *Nord Med Tidskr*, 8: 1054–1059.

Fonagy, P., Gergely, G., Jurist, E. L. and Target, M. (2018) *Affect Regulation, Mentalization, and the Development of the Self*, London: Routledge.

Fontes, M.A., Bolla, K.I., Cunha, P.J., Almeida, P.P., Jungerman, F., Laranjeira, R.R., Bressan, R.A., and Lacerda, A.L. (2011) 'Cannabis use before age 15 and subsequent executive functioning', *The British Journal of Psychiatry*, 198(6): 442–447.

Freud, S. (2002) *The Psychopathology of Everyday Life* (A. Bell, Translator), London: Penguin Classics.

Friedmann, N. and Haddad-Hanna, M. (2014) 'The comprehension of sentences derived by syntactic movement in Palestinian Arabic speakers with hearing impairment', *Applied Psycholinguistics*, 35(3): 473.

Friedmann, N. and Rusou, D. (2015) 'Critical period for first language: The crucial role of language input during the first year of life', *Current Opinion in Neurobiology*, 35: 27–34.

Friemel, C.M., Spanagel, R. and Schneider, M. (2010) 'Reward sensitivity for a palatable food reward peaks during pubertal developmental in rats', *Frontiers in Behavioral Neuroscience*, 4: 39.

Frith, U. and Frith, C.D. (2003) 'Development and neurophysiology of mentalizing', *Philosophical Transactions of the Royal Society of London. Series B: Biological Sciences*, 358(1431): 459–473.

Fuhrmann, D., Knoll, L.J. and Blakemore, S.-J. (2015) 'Adolescence as a sensitive period of brain development', *Trends in Cognitive Sciences*, 19(10): 558–566.

Fuster, J.M. (2002) 'Frontal lobe and cognitive development', *Journal of Neurocytology*, 31(3–5): 373–385.

Galvan, A., Hare, T., Voss, H., Glover, G. and Casey, B.J. (2007) 'Risk-taking and the adolescent brain: Who is at risk?', *Developmental Science*, 10(2): 8–14.

Gao, W., Alcauter, S., Smith, J.K., Gilmore, J. and Lin, W. (2015) 'Development of human brain cortical network architecture during infancy', *Brain Structure & Function*, 220(2): 1173–1186.

Gardner, H. (1983) *Frames of Mind: The Theory of Multiple Intelligences*, New York: Basic Books.

Gavaghan, C. (2009) '"You can't handle the truth": Medical paternalism and prenatal alcohol use', *Journal of Medical Ethics*, 35(5): 300–303.

Geake, J. (2008) 'Neuromythologies in education', *Educational Research*, 50(2): 123–133.

Geary, J.W. (2002) 'Reappraising MacLean's triune brain concept', in G.A. Cory and R. Gardner (eds) *The Evolutionary Neuroethology of Paul MacLean: Convergences and Frontiers*, Santa Barbara, CA: Greenwood, pp 9–27.

Gelman, R. and Gallistel, C.R. (1978) *The Child's Concept of Number*, Cambridge, MA: Harvard University Press.

Gendron, M., Roberson, D., van der Vyver, J.M. and Feldman Barrett, L. (2014) 'Perceptions of emotion from facial expressions are not culturally universal: Evidence from a remote culture', *Emotion*, 14(2): 251.

Genomics Education Programme. (2019) 'Phenylketonuria', Available from: https://www.genomicseducation.hee.nhs.uk/documents/phenylketonuria/ [Accessed 29 June 2021].

Genovez, M., Vanderkruik, R., Lemon, E. and Dimidjian, S. (2018) 'Psychotherapeutic treatments for depression during pregnancy', *Clinical Obstetrics and Gynecology*, 61(3): 562–572.

Geoffroy, M.-C., Côté, S.M., Parent, S. and Séguin, J.R. (2006) 'Daycare attendance, stress, and mental health', *Canadian Journal of Psychiatry. Revue Canadienne De Psychiatrie*, 51(9): 607–615.

Gerhardt, S. (2014) *Why Love Matters: How Affection Shapes a Baby's Brain* (2nd edn), London: Routledge.

Giedd, J.N., Blumenthal, J., Jeffries, N.O., Castellanos, F.X., Liu, H., Zijdenbos, A., Paus, T., Evans, A.C. and Rapoport, J.L. (1999) 'Brain development during childhood and adolescence: A longitudinal MRI study', *Nature Neuroscience*, 2(10): 861.

Gilbertson, M.W., Shenton, M.E., Ciszewski, A., Kasai, K., Lasko, N.B., Orr, S.P. and Pitman, R.K. (2002) 'Smaller hippocampal volume predicts pathologic vulnerability to psychological trauma', *Nature Neuroscience*, 5(11): 1242–1247.

Gillies, V., Edwards, R. and Horsley, N. (2017) *Challenging the Politics of Early Intervention: Who's 'Saving' Children and Why*, Bristol: Policy Press.

Gilman, J.M., Kuster, J.K., Lee, S., Lee, M.J., Kim, B.W., Makris, N., van der Kouwe, A., Blood, A.J. and Breiter, H.C. (2014) 'Cannabis use is quantitatively associated with nucleus accumbens and amygdala abnormalities in young adult recreational users', *Journal of Neuroscience*, 34(16): 5529–5538.

Gilmore, J.H., Lin, W., Prastawa, M.W., Looney, C.B., Vetsa, Y.S.K., Knickmeyer, R.C., Evans, D.D., Smith, J.K., Hamer, R.M. and Lieberman, J.A. (2007) 'Regional gray matter growth, sexual dimorphism, and cerebral asymmetry in the neonatal brain', *Journal of Neuroscience*, 27(6): 1255–1260.

Golden, M.H. (2009) 'Proposed recommended nutrient densities for moderately malnourished children', *Food and Nutrition Bulletin*, 30(3 suppl): S267–S342.

Goldman, S.R. (2012) 'Adolescent literacy: Learning and understanding content', *The Future of Children*, 22(2): 89–116.

Goldman, S.R. and Snow, C. (2015) 'Adolescent literacy: Development and instruction', in A. Pollatsek and R. Treiman (eds) *The Oxford Handbook of Reading*, Oxford: Oxford University Press, pp 463–478.

Gonzalez, R. and Swanson, J.M. (2012) 'Long-term effects of adolescent-onset and persistent use of cannabis', *Proceedings of the National Academy of Sciences*, 109(40): 15970–15971.

Gorey, C., Kuhns, L., Smaragdi, E., Kroon, E. and Cousijn, J. (2019) 'Age-related differences in the impact of cannabis use on the brain and cognition: A systematic review', *European Archives of Psychiatry and Clinical Neuroscience*, 269(1): 37–58.

Goscha, A. and Pankau, R. (1994) 'Social-emotional and behavioral adjustment in children with Williams-Beuren syndrome', *American Journal of Medical Genetics*, 53(4): 335–339.

Goswami, U. (2002) 'Phonology, reading development, and dyslexia: A cross-linguistic perspective', *Annals of Dyslexia*, 52(1): 139–163.

Goswami, U. (2004) 'Neuroscience and education', *British Journal of Educational Psychology*, 74(1): 1–14.

Goswami, U. (2006) 'Neuroscience and education: From research to practice?', *Nature Reviews Neuroscience*, 7(5): 406–413.

Goswami, U. (2008) *Cognitive Development: The Learning Brain,* Hove: Psychology Press.

Goswami, U. (2019) *Cognitive Development and Cognitive Neuroscience: The Learning Brain* (2nd edn), London: Routledge.

Goswami, U. and Bryant, P. (2007) 'Children's cognitive development and learning: primary review research survey', in Alexander, R., Doddington, C., Gray, J., Hargreaves, L., and Kershner, R. (eds) *The Cambridge Primary Review Research Surveys*, London: Routledge.

Gouin, K., Murphy, K. and Shah, P.S. (2011) 'Effects of cocaine use during pregnancy on low birthweight and preterm birth: Systematic review and metaanalyses', *American Journal of Obstetrics and Gynecology*, 204(4): 340e1–340e12.

Gould, F., Clarke, J., Heim, C., Harvey, P.D., Majer, M. and Nemeroff, C.B. (2012) 'The effects of child abuse and neglect on cognitive functioning in adulthood', *Journal of Psychiatric Research*, 46(4): 500–506.

Graf, P. and Schacter, D.L. (1985) 'Implicit and explicit memory for new associations in normal and amnesic subjects', *Journal of Experimental Psychology: Learning, Memory, and Cognition*, 11(3): 501.

Greco, C., Hayne, H. and Rovee-Collier, C. (1990) 'Roles of function, reminding, and variability in categorization by 3-month-old infants', *Journal of Experimental Psychology: Learning, Memory, and Cognition*, 16(4): 617.

Greenough, W.T., Black, J.E. and Wallace, C.S. (2002) 'Experience and brain development', in M.H. Johnson, Y. Munakata and R.O. Gilmore (eds) *Brain Development and Cognition: A Reader*, Hoboken, NJ: Wiley-Blackwell. pp 539–559

Griffin, A. (2017) 'Adolescent neurological development and implications for health and well-being', *Healthcare (Basel, Switzerland)*, 5(4): 62.

Grossman, K., Grossman, K.E., Spangler, G., Suess, G. and Unzner, L. (1985) 'Maternal sensitivity and newborn's orientation as related to quality of attachment in northern Germany', *Monographs of the Society for Research in Child Development*, 50(1/2): 233–256.

Guinness World Records. (2023) 'Most pi places memorized', Available from: https://www.guinnessworldrecords.com/world-records/most-pi-places-memorised [Accessed 31 January 2023].

Gunnar, M.R. and Donzella, B. (2002) 'Social regulation of the cortisol levels in early human development', *Psychoneuroendocrinology*, 27(1): 199–220.

Guthrie, R. and Susi, A. (1963) 'A simple phenylalanine method for detecting phenylketonuria in large populations of newborn infants', *Pediatrics*, 32(3): 338–343.

Guyer, A.E., Silk, J.S. and Nelson, E.E. (2016) 'The neurobiology of the emotional adolescent: From the inside out', *Neuroscience & Biobehavioral Reviews*, 70: 74–85.

Gweon, H., Dodell-Feder, D., Bedny, M. and Saxe, R. (2012) 'Theory of mind performance in children correlates with functional specialization of a brain region for thinking about thoughts', *Child Development*, 83(6): 1853–1868.

Hair, N.L., Hanson, J.L., Wolfe, B.L. and Pollak, S.D. (2015) 'Association of child poverty, brain development, and academic achievement', *JAMA Pediatrics*, 169(9): 822–829.

Haith, M.M. and Benson, J.B. (1998) 'Infant cognition', in W. Damon (ed) *Handbook of Child Psychology*, Vol. 2: *Cognition, Perception, and Language*, Hoboken, NJ: John Wiley & Sons, pp 199–254.

Halgamuge, M.N., Skafidas, E. and Davis, D. (2020) 'A meta-analysis of in vitro exposures to weak radiofrequency radiation exposure from mobile phones (1990–2015)', *Environmental Research*, 184: 109227.

Hamilton, J.L., Nesi, J. and Choukas-Bradley, S. (2020) 'Teens and social media during the COVID-19 pandemic: Staying socially connected while physically distant', *PsyArXiv*. Available from: https://psyarxiv.com/5stx4/ [Accessed 31 January 2023].

Hamner, T., Udhnani, M.D., Osipowicz, K.Z. and Lee, N.R. (2018) 'Pediatric brain development in Down syndrome: A field in its infancy', *Journal of the International Neuropsychological Society*, 24(9): 966–976.

Harlow, H.F. and Zimmerman, R.R. (1959) 'Affectional response in the infant monkey', *Science*, 130(3373): 422–432.

Harnishfeger, K.K. and Bjorklund, D.F. (1993) 'The ontogeny of inhibition mechanisms: A renewed approach to cognitive development', in M.L. Howe and R. Pasnak (eds) *Emerging Themes in Cognitive Development*, New York: Springer, pp 28–49.

Harris, S. (2011) 'Too much internet use "can damage teenagers' brains"', *Mail Online*, 18 July, Available from: https://www.dailymail.co.uk/sciencetech/article-2015196/Too-internet-use-damage-teenagers-brains.html [Accessed 26 August 2020].

Hartley-Parkinson, R. (2019) 'Vegan diets "risk lowering nutrient critical for unborn babies' brains"', *Metro*, 29 August, Available from: https://metro.co.uk/2019/08/29/vegan-diets-starve-brain-of-critical-nutrients-especially-for-unborn-babies-10649018/ ([Accessed 29 September 2021].

Hazlett, H.C., Gu, H., Munsell, B.C., Kim, S.H., Styner, M., Wolff, J.J., Elison, J.T., Swanson, M.R., Zhu, H., Botteron, K.N., Collins, D.L., Constantino, J.N., Dager, S.R., Estes, A.M., Evans, A.C., Fonov, V.S., Gerig, G., Kostopoulos, P., McKinstry, R.C., Pandey, J., Paterson, S., Pruett, J.R., Schultz, R.T., Shaw, D.W., Zwaigenbaum, L., and Piven, J. (2017) 'Early brain development in infants at high risk for autism spectrum disorder', *Nature*, 542(7641): 348–351.

Hebb, D.O. (1949) *The Organization of Behavior: A Neuropsychological Theory*, New York: John Wiley & Sons.

Hein, T.C. and Monk, C.S. (2017) 'Research review: Neural response to threat in children, adolescents, and adults after child maltreatment – a quantitative meta-analysis', *Journal of Child Psychology and Psychiatry*, 58(3): 222–230.

Hepper, P.G., Shahidullah, S. and White, R. (1991) 'Handedness in the human fetus', *Neuropsychologia*, 29(11): 1107–1111.

Hepper, P.G., Wells, D.L. and Lynch, C. (2005) 'Prenatal thumb sucking is related to postnatal handedness', *Neuropsychologia*, 43(3): 313–315.

Herculano-Houzel, S. (2017) *The Human Advantage: A New Understanding of How Our Brain Became Remarkable*, Cambridge, MA: MIT Press.

Hickok, G. (2009) 'Eight problems for the mirror neuron theory of action understanding in monkeys and humans', *Journal of Cognitive Neuroscience*, 21(7): 1229–1243.

Hill, E.L. and Frith, U. (2003) 'Understanding autism: Insights from mind and brain', *Philosophical Transactions of the Royal Society of London. Series B: Biological Sciences*, 358(1430): 281–289.

Hillis, S., Mercy, J., Amobi, A. and Kress, H. (2016) 'Global prevalence of past-year violence against children: A systematic review and minimum estimates', *Pediatrics*, 137(3): 1–22.

Himes, S.K., Stroud, L.R., Scheidweiler, K.B., Niaura, R.S. and Huestis, M.A. (2013) 'Prenatal tobacco exposure, biomarkers for tobacco in meconium, and neonatal growth outcomes', *Journal of Pediatrics*, 162(5): 970–975.

Hirsh-Pasek, K., Treiman, R. and Schneiderman, M. (1984) 'Brown & Hanlon revisited: Mothers' sensitivity to ungrammatical forms', *Journal of Child Language*, 11(1): 81–88.

Holland, D., Chang, L., Ernst, T.M., Curran, M., Buchthal, S.D., Alicata, D., Skranes, J., Johansen, H., Hernandez, A. and Yamakawa, R. (2014) 'Structural growth trajectories and rates of change in the first 3 months of infant brain development', *JAMA Neurology*, 71(10): 1266–1274.

Honey, P. and Mumford, A. (1982) *The Manual of Learning Styles*, Maidenhead: Peter Honey.

Horta, B.L., de Mola, C.L. and Victora, C.G. (2015) 'Breastfeeding and intelligence: A systematic review and meta-analysis', *Acta Paediatrica*, 104(S467): 14–19.

Howard, S. (2017) *Skills in Psychodynamic Counselling & Psychotherapy*, London: SAGE.

Hruby, G.G., Goswami, U., Frederiksen, C.H. and Perfetti, C.A. (2011) 'Neuroscience and reading: A review for reading education researchers', *Reading Research Quarterly*, 46(2): 156–172.

Huijbregts, S.C.J., De Sonneville, L.M.J., Licht, R., Van Spronsen, F.J., Verkerk, P.H. and Sergeant, J.A. (2002) 'Sustained attention and inhibition of cognitive interference in treated phenylketonuria: Associations with concurrent and lifetime phenylalanine concentrations', *Neuropsychologia*, 40(1): 7–15.

Hüppi, P.S., Warfield, S., Kikinis, R., Barnes, P.D., Zientara, G.P., Jolesz, F.A., Tsuji, M.K. and Volpe, J.J. (1998) 'Quantitative magnetic resonance imaging of brain development in premature and mature newborns', *Annals of Neurology*, 43(2): 224–235.

Hurdal, M.K., Kurtz, K.W. and Banks, D.C. (2001) 'Case study: Interacting with cortical flat maps of the human brain', *Proceedings of the IEEE Conference on Visualization, VIZ'01*: 469–472.

Huttenlocher, P.R. (1979) 'Synaptic density in human frontal cortex: Developmental changes and effects of aging', *Brain Research*, 163(2): 195–205.

Hwang, K., Ghuman, A.S., Manoach, D.S., Jones, S.R. and Luna, B. (2016) 'Frontal preparatory neural oscillations associated with cognitive control: A developmental study comparing young adults and adolescents', *NeuroImage*, 136: 139.

Hyatt, K.J. (2007) 'Brain Gym® building stronger brains or wishful thinking?', *Remedial and Special Education*, 28(2): 117–124.

iLiveHere. (2019) 'Socio-economic statistics for Bognor Regis, West Sussex', iLiveHere—Britain's worst places to live, Available from: https://www.ilivehere.co.uk/statistics-bognor-regis-west-sussex-4295.html [Accessed 31 January 2023].

Inchley, J., Currie, D., Vieno, A., Torsheim, T., Ferreira-Borges, C., Weber, M.M. and Breda, J. (2018) *Adolescent Alcohol-Related behaviours: Trends and Inequalities in the WHO European Region, 2002–2014*, Copenhagen: WHO Regional Office for Europe.

Ingalhalikar, M., Smith, A., Parker, D., Satterthwaite, T.D., Elliott, M.A., Ruparel, K., Hakonarson, H., Gur, R.E., Gur, R.C. and Verma, R. (2014) 'Sex differences in the structural connectome of the human brain', *Proceedings of the National Academy of Sciences*, 111(2): 823–828.

Ionta, S. (2021) 'Visual neuropsychology in development: Anatomo-functional brain mechanisms of action/perception binding in health and disease', *Frontiers in Human Neuroscience*, 15: 282.

Izard, C.E. (2007) 'Basic emotions, natural kinds, emotion schemas, and a new paradigm', *Perspectives on Psychological Science*, 2(3): 260.

Jacobs, R.A., Jordan, M.I. and Barto, A.G. (1991) 'Task decomposition through competition in a modular connectionist architecture: The what and where vision tasks', *Cognitive Science*, 15: 219–250.

Jaddoe, V.W., Verburg, B.O., De Ridder, M.A.J., Hofman, A., Mackenbach, J.P., Moll, H.A., … and Witteman, J.C. (2007) 'Maternal smoking and fetal growth characteristics in different periods of pregnancy: The generation R study', *American Journal of Epidemiology*, 165(10): 1207–1215.

James, O. (2011) *How not to F*** Them up: The First Three Years*. London: Vermilion.

Johnson, M.H. (2005) 'Subcortical face processing', *Nature Reviews Neuroscience*, 6(10): 766–774.

Johnson, M.H. and de Haan, M. (2010) *Developmental Cognitive Neuroscience* (3rd edn), Hoboken, NJ: Wiley-Blackwell.

Johnson, M.H., Dziurawiec, S., Ellis, H. and Morton, J (1991) 'Newborns' preferential tracking of face-like stimuli and its subsequent decline', *Cognition*, 40(1–2): 1–19.

Johnson, M.H., Mareschal, D. and Csibra, G. (2008) 'The development and integration of the dorsal and ventral pathways in object processing', in C.A. Nelson and M. Luciana (eds) *Handbook of Developmental Cognitive Neuroscience*, Cambridge, MA: MIT Press, pp 467–478.

Johnson, S.P. and Aslin, R.N. (1995) 'Perception of object unity in 2-month-old infants', *Developmental Psychology*, 31: 739–745.

Johnstone, L. and Boyle, M. (2018) *The Power Threat Meaning Framework: Towards the Identification of Patterns in Emotional Distress, Unusual Experiences and Troubled or Troubling Behaviour, as an Alternative to Functional Psychiatric Diagnosis*, Leicester: British Psychological Society.

Jones, K.L. and Smith, D.W. (1973) 'Recognition of the fetal alcohol syndrome in early infancy', *The Lancet*, 302(7836): 999–1001.

Jordan-Young, R. and Rumiati, R.I. (2012) 'Hardwired for sexism? Approaches to sex/gender in neuroscience', *Neuroethics*, 5(3): 305–315.

Joshi, S.A., Duval, E.R., Kubat, B. and Liberzon, I. (2020) 'A review of hippocampal activation in post-traumatic stress disorder', *Psychophysiology*, 57(1): e13357.

Jutras-Aswad, D., DiNieri, J.A., Harkany, T. and Hurd, Y.L. (2009) 'Neurobiological consequences of maternal cannabis on human fetal development and its neuro-psychiatric outcome', *European Archives of Psychiatry and Clinical Neuroscience*, 259(7): 395–412.

Kaldy, Z. and Sigala, N. (2004) 'The neural mechanisms of object working memory: what is where in the infant brain?', *Neuroscience Biobehavioral Review*, 28: 113–121.

Kandel, E. (2007) *In Search of Memory: The Emergence of a New Science of Mind*, New York: W. W. Norton.

Kanwisher, N., McDermott, J. and Chun, M.M. (1997) 'The fusiform face area: A module in human extrastriate cortex specialized for face perception', *Journal of Neuroscience*, 17(11): 4302–4311.

Kaplan, L.C., Wharton, R., Elias, E., Mandell, F., Donlon, T., Latt, S.A., Opitz, J.M. and Reynolds, J.F. (1987) 'Clinical heterogeneity associated with deletions in the long arm of chromosome 15: Report of 3 new cases and their possible genetic significance', *American Journal of Medical Genetics*, 28(1): 45–53.

Kaufman, J. (1991) 'Depressive disorders in maltreated children', *Journal of the American Academy of Child & Adolescent Psychiatry*, 30(2): 257–265.

Kaufman, J., Csibra, G. and Johnson, M.H. (2003) 'Representing occluded objects in the human infant brain', *Proceedings of the Royal Society of London, Series B: Biological Sciences*, 270(2): 140–143.

Kaufman, J., Csibra, G. and Johnson, M.H. (2005) 'Oscillatory activity in the infant brain reflects object maintenance', *Proceedings of the National Academy of Sciences of the United States of America*, 102(42): 15271–15274.

Kaufman, J., Mareschal, D. and Johnson, M.H. (2003) 'Graspability and object processing in infants', *Infant Behavior and Development*, 26(4): 516–528.

Kaushanskaya, M. and Marian, V. (2009) 'The bilingual advantage in novel word learning', *Psychonomic Bulletin & Review*, 16(4): 705–710.

Kawabata, H., Gyoba, J., Inoue, H. and Ohtsubo, H. (1999) 'Visual completion of partly occluded grating in infants under 1 month of age', *Vision Research*, 39(21): 3586–3591.

Keating, D.P. (1980) 'Thinking processes in adolescence', in J. Adelson (ed) *Handbook of Adolescent Psychology*, New York: Wiley, pp 211–246.

Keating, D.P. and Bobbitt, B.L. (1978) 'Individual and developmental differences in cognitive-processing components of mental ability', *Child Development*, 49(1): 155–167.

Kellman, P.J. and Spelke, E. (1983) 'Perception of partly occluded objects in infancy', *Cognitive Psychology*, 15: 483–524.

Kelly, Y., Sacker, A., Gray, R., Kelly, J., Wolke, D. and Quigley, M.A. (2009) 'Light drinking in pregnancy, a risk for behavioural problems and cognitive deficits at 3 years of age?', *International Journal of Epidemiology*, 38(1): 129–140.

Kessler, R.C., Amminger, G.P., Aguilar-Gaxiola, S., Alonso, J., Lee, S. and Ustun, T.B. (2007) 'Age of onset of mental disorders: A review of recent literature', *Current Opinion in Psychiatry*, 20(4): 359.

Khakh, B.S., Beaumont, V., Cachope, R., Munoz-Sanjuan, I., Goldman, S.A. and Grantyn, R. (2017) 'Unravelling and exploiting astrocyte dysfunction in Huntington's disease', *Trends in Neurosciences*, 40(7): 422–437.

Kiess, W., Meidert, A., Dressendörfer, R.A., Schriever, K., Kessler, U., Köunig, A., Schwarz, H.P. and Strasburger, C.J. (1995) 'Salivary cortisol levels throughout childhood and adolescence: Relation with age, pubertal stage, and weight', *Pediatric Research*, 37(4): 502–506.

King, J.C. (2000) 'Physiology of pregnancy and nutrient metabolism', *The American Journal of Clinical Nutrition*, 71(5): 1218S–1225S.

Kintsch, W. and Rawson, K.A. (2007) 'Comprehension', in C. Hulme and M.J. Snowling (eds) *The Science of Reading: A Handbook*, Hoboken, NJ: Blackwell, pp 206–209.

Kintsch, W., Patel, V.L. and Ericsson, K.A. (1999) 'The role of long-term working memory in text comprehension', *Psychologia*, 42(4): 186–198.

Kirkham, N.Z., Slemmer, J.A. and Johnson, S.P. (2002) 'Visual statistical learning in infancy: Evidence for a domain general learning mechanism', *Cognition*, 83(2): B35–B42.

Klein, R.M., Christie, J. and Parkvall, M. (2016) 'Does multilingualism affect the incidence of Alzheimer's disease? A worldwide analysis by country', *SSM – Population Health*, 2: 463–467.

Klingberg, T. (2006) 'Development of superior frontal-intraparietal network for visuospatial working memory', *Neuropsychologia*, 44(11): 2171–2177.

Klingberg, T., Forssberg, H. and Westerberg, H. (2002) 'Increased brain activity in frontal and parietal cortex underlies the development of visuospatial working memory capacity during childhood', *Journal of Cognitive Neuroscience*, 14: 1–10.

Klingberg, T., Vaidya, C.J., Gabrieli, J.D., Moseley, M.E. and Hedehus, M. (1999) 'Myelination and organization of the frontal white matter in children: a diffusion tensor MRI study', *Neuroreport*, 10(13): 2817–2821.

Knopik, V.S., Maccani, M.A., Francazio, S. and McGeary, J.E. (2012) 'The epigenetics of maternal cigarette smoking during pregnancy and effects on child development', *Development and Psychopathology*, 24(4): 1377–1390.

Kovács, Á.M. and Mehler, J. (2009) 'Cognitive gains in 7-month-old bilingual infants', *Proceedings of the National Academy of Sciences*, 106(16): 6556–6560.

Kraemer, D.J.M., Rosenberg, L.M. and Thompson-Schill, S.L. (2009) 'The neural correlates of visual and verbal cognitive styles', *The Journal of Neuroscience*, 29(12): 3792–3798.

Kuhl, P.K. (1991) 'Human adults and human infants show a "perceptual magnet effect" for the prototypes of speech categories, monkeys do not', *Attention, Perception, & Psychophysics*, 50(2): 93–107.

Kuhl, P.K., Andruski, J.E., Chistovich, I.A., Chistovich, L.A., Kozhevnikova, E.V., Ryskina, V.L., Stolyarova, E.I., Sundberg, U. and Lacerda, F. (1997) 'Cross-language analysis of phonetic units in language addressed to infants', *Science*, 277(5326): 684.

Kuhl, P.K., Tsao, F.M. and Liu, H.M. (2003) 'Foreign-language experience in infancy: Effects of short-term exposure and social interaction on phonetic learning', *Proceedings of the National Academy of Sciences of the United States of America*, 100(15): 9096.

Kuhl, P.K., Williams, K.A., Lacerda, F., Stevens, K.N. and Lindblom, B. (1992) 'Linguistic experience alters phonetic perception in infants by 6 months of age', *Science*, 255(5044): 606.

Lakhanpaul, M. (2020) 'Down syndrome medical interest group/demography', Available from: https://www.dsmig.org.uk/information-resources/by-topic/demography/ [Accessed 22 June 2021].

Larson, R.W., Moneta, G., Richards, M.H. and Wilson, S (2002) 'Continuity, stability, and change in daily emotional experience across adolescence', *Child Development*, 73(4): 1151–1165.

Lebel, C., Mattson, S.N., Riley, E.P., Jones, K.L., Adnams, C.M., May, P.A. and Kan, E. (2012) 'A longitudinal study of the long-term consequences of drinking during pregnancy: Heavy in utero alcohol exposure disrupts the normal processes of brain development', *Journal of Neuroscience*, 32(44): 15243–15251.

Lenneberg, E.H. (1967) *Biological Foundations of Language*, New York: John Wiley & Sons.

Leonard, L.B., Chapman, K., Rowan, L.E. and Weiss, A.L. (1983) 'Three hypotheses concerning young children's imitations of lexical items', *Developmental Psychology*, 19(4): 591.

Lerner, R.M. and Steinberg, L. (2009) *Handbook of Adolescent Psychology*, Vol. 1: *Individual Bases of Adolescent Development*. New York: John Wiley & Sons.

Leslie, A.M. (1987) 'Pretense and representation: The origins of "theory of mind"', *Psychological Review*, 94(4): 412–426.

Liang, J., Matheson, B.E., Kaye, W.H. and Boutelle, K.N. (2014) 'Neurocognitive correlates of obesity and obesity-related behaviors in children and adolescents', *International Journal of Obesity*, 38(4): 494–506.

Libertus, M.E. and Brannon, E.M. (2010) 'Stable individual differences in number discrimination in infancy', *Developmental Science*, 13(6): 900–906.

Lindell, A.K. and Kidd, E. (2011) 'Why right-brain teaching is half-witted: A critique of the misapplication of neuroscience to education', *Mind, Brain, and Education*, 5(3): 121–127.

Lindquist, K.A. (2013) 'Emotions emerge from more basic psychological ingredients: A modern psychological constructionist model', *Emotional Review*, 4(5): 356– 368.

Lindquist, K.A., Wager, T.D., Kober, H., Bliss-Moreau, E. and Barrett, L.F. (2012) 'The brain basis of emotion: A meta-analytic review', *The Behavioral and Brain Sciences*, 35(3): 121–143.

Lipsky, L.M., Nansel, T.R., Haynie, D.L., Liu, D., Li, K., Pratt, C. A., … and Simons-Morton, B. (2017) 'Diet quality of US adolescents during the transition to adulthood: Changes and predictors', *The American Journal of Clinical Nutrition*, 105(6): 1424–1432.

Lloyd-Fox, S., Begus, K., Halliday, D., Pirazzoli, L., Blasi, A., Papademetriou, M., Darboe, M.K., Prentice, A.M., Johnson, M.H., Moore, S.E. and Elwell, C.E. (2017) 'Cortical specialisation to social stimuli from the first days to the second year of life: A rural Gambian cohort', *Developmental Cognitive Neuroscience*, 25: 92–104.

Lloyd-Fox, S., Blasi, A., Volein, A., Everdell, N., Elwell, C.E. and Johnson, M.H. (2009) 'Social perception in infancy: a near infrared spectroscopy study', *Child Development*, 80(4): 986–999.

Loane, M., Morris, J.K., Addor, M.-C., Arriola, L., Budd, J., Doray, B., Garne, E., Gatt, M., Haeusler, M. and Khoshnood, B. (2013) 'Twenty-year trends in the prevalence of Down syndrome and other trisomies in Europe: Impact of maternal age and prenatal screening', *European Journal of Human Genetics*, 21(1): 27–33.

Lord, C., Elsabbagh, M., Baird, G. and Veenstra-Vanderweele, J. (2018) 'Autism spectrum disorder', *The Lancet*, 392(10146): 508–520.

Lorenz, K. (2002) *King Solomon's Ring: New Light on Animal Ways*, London: Routledge.

Lovegrove, W., Martin, F. and Slaghuis, W. (1986) 'A theoretical and experimental case for a visual deficit in specific reading disability', *Cognitive Neuropsychology*, 3(2): 225–267.

Luby, J., Belden, A., Botteron, K., Marrus, N., Harms, M. P., Babb, C., ... and Barch, D. (2013) 'The effects of poverty on childhood brain development: The mediating effect of caregiving and stressful life events', *JAMA Pediatrics*, 167(12): 1135–1142.

Luciana, M. and Collins, P.F. (2012) 'Incentive motivation, cognitive control, and the adolescent brain: Is it time for a paradigm shift?', *Child Development Perspectives*, 6(4): 392–399.

Luciana, M., Bjork, J.M., Nagel, B.J., Barch, D.M., Gonzalez, R., Nixon, S.J. and Banich, M.T. (2018) 'Adolescent neurocognitive development and impacts of substance use: Overview of the adolescent brain cognitive development (ABCD) baseline neurocognition battery', *Developmental Cognitive Neuroscience*, 32: 67–79.

Luciana, M., Conklin, H.M., Cooper, C.J. and Yarger, R.S. (2005) 'The development of nonverbal working memory and executive control processes in adolescents', *Child Development*, 76: 697–712.

Lumian, D.S., Dmitrieva, J., Mendoza, M.M., Badanes, L.S. and Watamura, S.E. (2016) 'The impact of program structure on cortisol patterning in children attending out-of-home child care', *Early Childhood Research Quarterly*, 34: 92–103.

Luna, B. (2017) 'Neuroimaging and the adolescent brain: A period of plasticity for vulnerabilities and opportunities', in, R. Dahl, A. Suleiman, B. Luna, S. Choudhury, K. Noble, S.J. Lupien, E. Ward, Y.-Y. Tang and M.R. Uncapher (eds) *The Adolescent Brain: A Second Window of Opportunity*, Florence: UNICEF Office of Research – Innocenti, pp 29–34.

Luna, B., Garver, K.E., Urban., T., Lazar, N.A. and Sweeney, J.A. (2004) 'Maturation of cognitive processes from late childhood to adulthood', *Child Development*, 75(5): 1357–1372.

Lupien, S.J., McEwen, B.S., Gunnar, M.R. and Heim, C. (2009) 'Effects of stress throughout the lifespan on the brain, behaviour and cognition', *Nature Reviews Neuroscience*, 10(6): 434.

Lyall, A.E., Shi, F., Geng, X., Woolson, S., Li, G., Wang, L., Hamer, R.M., Shen, D. and Gilmore, J.H. (2015) 'Dynamic development of regional cortical thickness and surface area in early childhood', *Cerebral Cortex*, 25(8): 2204–2212.

Lyon, G.R., Shaywitz, S.E. and Shaywitz, B.A. (2003) 'A definition of dyslexia', *Annals of Dyslexia*, 53(1): 1–14.

Maccoby, E.E. and Jacklin, C.N. (1978) *The Psychology of Sex Differences*, Stanford, CA: Stanford University Press.

Main, M. and Cassidy, J. (1988) 'Categories of response to reunion with the parent at age 6: Predictable from infant attachment classifications and stable over a 1-month period', *Developmental Psychology*, 24(3): 415.

Main, M. and Solomon, J. (1990) 'Procedures for identifying infants as disorganized/disoriented during the Ainsworth Strange Situation', in M.T. Greenberg, D. Cicchetti and E.M. Cummings (eds) *Attachment in the Preschool Years*, Chicago: University of Chicago Press, pp 121–160.

Mammarella, I.C., Toffalini, E., Caviola, S., Colling, L. and Szűcs, D. (2021) 'No evidence for a core deficit in developmental dyscalculia or mathematical learning disabilities', *Journal of Child Psychology and Psychiatry*, 62(6): 704–714.

Mandler, J.M. (1988) 'How to build a baby: On the development of an accessible representational system', *Cognitive Development*, 3(2): 113–136.

Marek S. and Dosenbach, N. (2018) 'The frontoparietal network: Function, electrophysiology, and importance of individual precision mapping', *Dialogues in Clinical Neuroscience*, 20(2): 133–140.

Mareschal, D., Johnson, M.H., Sirois, S., Spratling, M., Thomas, M.S. and Westermann, G. (2007) *Neuroconstructivism: How the Brain Constructs Cognition*, Vol. 1, Oxford: Oxford University Press.

Mareschal, D., Plunkett, K. and Harris, P. (1999) 'A computational and neuro-psychological account of object-oriented behaviours in infancy', *Developmental Science*, 2(3): 306–317.

Marsh, B. (2019) 'Teenage drinking has doubled', *Daily Mail*, 21 October, Available from: https://www.dailymail.co.uk/health/article-84445/Teenage-drinking-doubled.html [Accessed 21 October 2019].

Marshall, P.J. and Fox, N.A. (2004) 'A comparison of the electroencephalogram between institutionalized and community children in Romania', *Journal of Cognitive Neuroscience*, 16(8): 1327–1338.

Marshall, P.J. and Meltzoff, A.N. (2011) 'Neural mirroring systems: Exploring the EEG mu rhythm in human infancy', *Developmental Cognitive Neuroscience*, 1(2): 110–123.

Martin, A., Koenig, K., Schultz, R., Dykens, E.M., Cassidy, S.B. and Leckman, J.F. (1998) 'Prader-Willi syndrome', *American Journal of Psychiatry*, 155(9): 1265–1273.

Maurer, D. (1993) 'Neonatal synesthesia: Implications for the processing of speech and faces', in B. de Boysson-Bardies, S. de Schonen, P. Jusczyk, P. McNeilage and J. Morton (eds) *Developmental Neurocognition: Speech and Face Processing in the First Year of Life*, New York: Springer, pp 109–124.

McCarthy, D.M., Kabir, Z.D., Bhide, P.G. and Kosofsky, B.E. (2014) 'Effects of prenatal exposure to cocaine on brain structure and function', in M. Diana, G. Di Chiara and P. Spano (eds) *Progress in Brain Research: Dopamine* (Vol. 211), Amsterdam: Elsevier, pp 277–289.

McCaskey, U., von Aster, M., O'Gorman, R. and Kucian, K. (2020) 'Persistent differences in brain structure in developmental dyscalculia: A longitudinal morphometry study', *Frontiers in Human Neuroscience*, 14: 272.

McCauley, E., Ito, J. and Kay, T. (1986) 'Psychosocial functioning in girls with Turner's syndrome and short stature: Social skills, behavior problems, and self-concept', *Journal of the American Academy of Child Psychiatry*, 25(1): 105–112.

McCormick, D.A., Clark, G.A., Lavond, D.G. and Thompson, R.F. (1982) 'Initial localization of the memory trace for a basic form of learning', *Proceedings of the National Academy of Sciences*, 79(8): 2731–2735.

McCrory, E., De Brito, S.A. and Viding, E. (2011) 'The impact of childhood maltreatment: A review of neurobiological and genetic factors', *Frontiers in Psychiatry*, 2: 48.

McEvoy, C.T., Temple, N. and Woodside, J.V. (2012) 'Vegetarian diets, low-meat diets and health: A review', *Public Health Nutrition*, 15(12): 2287–2294.

McKone, E., Crookes, K., Jeffery, L. and Dilks, D.D. (2012) 'A critical review of the development of face recognition: Experience is less important than previously believed', *Cognitive Neuropsychology*, 29(1–2): 174–212.

McKone, E., Wan, L., Pidcock, M., Crookes, K., Reynolds, K., Dawel, A., Kidd, E. and Fiorentini, C. (2019) 'A critical period for faces: Other-race face recognition is improved by childhood but not adult social contact', *Scientific Reports*, 9(1): 12820.

McKone, E., Crookes, K. and Kanwisher, N. (2009) 'The cognitive and neural development of face recognition in humans', in M. Gazzaniga (ed) *The Cognitive Neurosciences*, Cambridge, MA: MIT Press, pp 467–482.

Medland, S.E., Duffy, D.L., Wright, M.J., Geffen, G.M., Hay, D.A., Levy, F., Van-Beijsterveldt, C.E., Willemsen, G., Townsend, G.C. and White, V. (2009) 'Genetic influences on handedness: Data from 25,732 Australian and Dutch twin families', *Neuropsychologia*, 47(2): 330–337.

Meltzoff, A.N. (1985) 'Immediate and deferred imitation in fourteen-and twenty-four-month-old infants', *Child Development*, 56(1): 62–72.

Meltzoff, A.N. (1988a) 'Imitation of televised models by infants', *Child Development*, 59(5): 1221–1229.

Meltzoff, A.N. (1988b) 'Infant imitation after a 1-week delay: Long-term memory for novel acts and multiple stimuli', *Developmental Psychology*, 24(4): 470–476.

Meltzoff, A.N. (1988c) 'Infant imitation and memory: Nine-month-olds in immediate and deferred tests', *Child Development*, 59(1): 217–225.

Meltzoff, A.N. (1995) 'What infant memory tells us about infantile amnesia: Long-term recall and deferred imitation', *Journal of Experimental Child Psychology*, 59(3): 497–515.

Meltzoff, A.N. and Borton, R.W. (1979) 'Intermodal matching by human neonates', *Nature*, 282: 403–404.

Meltzoff, A.N., Kuhl, P.K., Movellan, J. and Sejnowski, T.J. (2009) 'Foundations for a new science of learning', *Science*, 325: 284–288.

Meltzoff, A.N. and Marshall, P.J. (2018) 'Human infant imitation as a social survival circuit', *Current Opinion in Behavioral Sciences*, 24: 130–136.

Meltzoff, A.N. and Moore, M.K. (1983) 'Newborn infants imitate adult facial gestures', *Child Development*, 54(3): 702–709.

Meltzoff, A.N. and Moore, M.K. (1995) 'A theory in the role of imitation in the emergence of self', in P. Rochat (ed) *The Self in Infancy: Theory and Research*, Amsterdam: Elsevier, pp 73–94.

Mendel, G. (1967) 'Experiments on plant hybrids', in C. Stern and E.R. Sherwood (eds) *The Origin of Genetics: A Mendel Source Book*, San Francisco: W. H. Freeman, pp 1–48.

Merzenich, M.M., Wright, B.A., Jenkins, W., Xerri, C., Byl, N., Miller, S. and Tallal, P. (2002) 'Cortical plasticity underlying perceptual, motor, and cognitive skill development: Implications for neurorehabilitation', in M.H. Johnson, Y. Munakata and R. Gilmore (eds) *Brain Development and Cognition: A Reader* (2nd edn), Oxford: Blackwell, pp 292–304.

Meyer, K.D. and Zhang, L. (2009) 'Short- and long-term adverse effects of cocaine abuse during pregnancy on the heart development', *Therapeutic Advances in Cardiovascular Disease*, 3(1): 7–16.

Mills, K.L., Goddings, A.-L., Clasen, L.S., Giedd, J.N. and Blakemore, S.-J (2014) 'The developmental mismatch in structural brain maturation during adolescence', *Developmental Neuroscience*, 36(3–4): 147–160.

Milner, B. (1982) 'Some cognitive effects of frontal-lobe lesions in man', *Philosophical Transactions of the Royal Society of London, Series B, Biological Sciences*, 298: 211–226.

Minagawa-Kawai, Y., Matsuoka, S., Dan, I., Naoi, N., Nakamura, K. and Kojima, S. (2009) 'Prefrontal activation associated with social attachment: Facial-emotion recognition in mothers and infants', *Cerebral Cortex*, 19(2): 284–292.

Minagawa-Kawai, Y., van der Lely, H., Ramus, F., Sato, Y., Mazuka, R. and Dupoux, E. (2011) 'Optical brain imaging reveals general auditory and language-specific processing in early infant development', *Cerebral Cortex*, 21(2): 254–261.

Molfese, D.L. and Molfese, V.J. (1979) 'Hemisphere and stimulus differences as reflected in the cortical responses of newborn infants to speech stimuli', *Developmental Psychology*, 15(5): 505.

Molfese, D.L. and Molfese, V.J. (1980) 'Cortical response of preterm infants to phonetic and nonphonetic speech stimuli', *Developmental Psychology*, 16(6): 574.

Moore, C.J. and Price, C.J. (1999) 'Three distinct ventral occipitotemporal regions for reading and object naming', *Neuroimage*, 10(2): 181–192.

Mota, B. and Herculano-Houzel, S. (2015) 'Cortical folding scales universally with surface area and thickness, not number of neurons', *Science*, 349(6243): 74–77.

Munakata, Y. and Yerys, B.E. (2001) 'All together now: When dissociations between knowledge and action disappear', *Psychological Science*, 12(4): 335–337.

Munawar, K., Kuhn, S.K. and Haque, S. (2018) 'Understanding the reminiscence bump: A systematic review', *PloS One*, 13(12): e0208595.

Murphy, F.C., Nimmo-Smith, I.A.N. and Lawrence, A.D. (2003) 'Functional neuroanatomy of emotions: A meta-analysis', *Cognitive, Affective, & Behavioral Neuroscience*, 3(3): 207–233.

Murray, M.L., Hsia, Y., Glaser, K., Simonoff, E., Murphy, D.G.M., Asherson, P.J., Eklund, H. and Wong, I.C.K. (2014) 'Pharmacological treatments prescribed to people with autism spectrum disorder (ASD) in primary health care', *Psychopharmacology*, 231(6): 1011–1021.

Murty, N.A.R., Teng, S., Beeler, D., Mynick, A., Oliva, A. and Kanwisher, N. (2020) 'Visual experience is not necessary for the development of face-selectivity in the lateral fusiform gyrus', *Proceedings of the National Academy of Sciences*, 117(37): 23011–23020.

Mussolin, C., De Volder, A., Grandin, C., Schlögel, X., Nassogne, M.-C. and Noël, M.-P. (2010) 'Neural correlates of symbolic number comparison in developmental dyscalculia', *Journal of Cognitive Neuroscience*, 22(5): 860–874.

National Center for Children in Poverty. (2019) 'Child poverty', Available from: http://nccp.org/topics/childpoverty.html [Accessed 16 September 2019].

National Fragile X Foundation. (2021) 'Fragile X prevalence and statistics, National Fragile X Foundation', Available from: https://fragilex.org/understanding-fragile-x/fragile-x-101/prevalence/ [Accessed 7 June 2021].

National Institute on Drug Abuse. (2019) 'Monitoring the future', Available from: https://www.drugabuse.gov/related-topics/trends-statistics/monitoring-future. [Accessed 21 October 2019].

National Library of Medicine (2021) 'Phenylketonuria: MedlinePlus genetics', Available from: https://medlineplus.gov/genetics/condition/phenylketonuria/ [Accessed 29 June 2021].

Nelson, C.A. (1995) 'The ontogeny of human memory: A cognitive neuroscience perspective', *Developmental Psychology*, 31(5): 723.

Nelson, C.A. (1999) 'Neural plasticity and human development', *Current Directions in Psychological Science*, 8(2): 42–45.

Nelson, M.D. and Tumpap, A.M. (2017) 'Posttraumatic stress disorder symptom severity is associated with left hippocampal volume reduction: A meta-analytic study', *CNS Spectrums*, 22(4): 363–372.

Nelson, C.A., Zeanah, C.H., Fox, N.A., Marshall, P.J., Smyke, A.T. and Guthrie, D. (2007) 'Cognitive recovery in socially deprived young children: The Bucharest Early Intervention Project', *Science*, 318(5858): 1937–1940.

NHS (National Health Service). (2017a) 'Benefits of breastfeeding', Available from: https://www.nhs.uk/conditions/baby/breastfeeding-and-bottle-feeding/breastfeeding/benefits/ [Accessed 16 September 2019].

NHS (National Health Service). (2017b) 'Post-traumatic stress disorder (PTSD) – complex PTSD', Available from: https://www.nhs.uk/conditions/post-traumatic-stress-disorder-ptsd/complex/ [Accessed 17 January 2020].

NICE (National Institute for Health and Care Excellence). (2018) 'Recommendations: Attention deficit hyperactivity disorder: Diagnosis and management', Available from: https://www.nice.org.uk/guidance/ng87/chapter/Recommendations#diagnosis [Accessed 1 June 2021].

Nicolson, R.I. and Fawcett, A.J. (1995) 'Dyslexia is more than a phonological disability', *Dyslexia: An International Journal of Research and Practice*, Available from: https://citeseerx.ist.psu.edu/document?repid=rep1&type=pdf&doi=d561c3f9c35e78e666845da40954afa49ed886fe [Accessed 31 January 2023].

Nicolson, R.I. and Fawcett, A.J. (2019) 'Development of dyslexia: The delayed neural commitment framework', *Frontiers in Behavioral Neuroscience*, 13: 112.

Nippold, M.A. (2000) 'Language development during the adolescent years: Aspects of pragmatics, syntax, and semantics', *Topics in Language Disorders*, 20(2): 15–28.

Nippold, M.A. (2004) 'Research on later language development International perspectives', in R.A. Berman (ed) *Language Development Across Childhood and Adolescence*, Vol. 3 Trends in Language Acquisition Research. Amsterdam: John Benjamins, pp 1–9.

Nowakowski, R.S. and Hayes, N.L. (2002) 'General principles of CNS development', in M.H. Johnson, Y. Munakata and R.O. Gilmore (eds) *Brain Development and Cognition: A Reader*, Hoboken, NJ: Wiley-Blackwell, pp 57–82.

NSPCC (National Society for the Prevention of Cruelty to Children). (2019) 'Statistics on child abuse', Available from: https://learning.nspcc.org.uk/statistics-child-abuse/ [Accessed 9 December 2019].

NSPCC (National Society for the Prevention of Cruelty to Children). (2020) 'Effects of child abuse', Available from: http://www.nspcc.org.uk/what-is-child-abuse/effects-of-child-abuse/ [Accessed 11 May 2020].

Núñez-Jaramillo, L., Herrera-Solís, A. and Herrera-Morales, W.V. (2021) 'ADHD: Reviewing the causes and evaluating solutions', *Journal of Personalized Medicine*, 11(3): 166.

Nutbrown, P.C. (2006) *Threads of Thinking: Young Children Learning and the Role of Early Education* (3rd edn), London: SAGE.

Nyaradi, A., Li, J., Hickling, S., Foster, J. and Oddy, W.H. (2013) 'The role of nutrition in children's neurocognitive development, from pregnancy through childhood', *Frontiers in Human Neuroscience*, 7: 97.

O'Dea, S. (2021) 'Smartphone users 2026', Statista, Available from: https://www.statista.com/statistics/330695/number-of-smartphone-users-worldwide/ [Accessed 27 September 2021].

O'Doherty, J.P. (2004) 'Reward representations and reward-related learning in the human brain: Insights from neuroimaging', *Current Opinion in Neurobiology*, 14(6): 769–776.

Office for Health and Improvement Disparities (2022) 'Childhood obesity: applying All Our Health', Available from: https://www.gov.uk/government/publications/childhood-obesity-applying-all-our-health/ [Accessed 30 January 2023].

Ogura, K., Fujii, T., Abe, N., Hosokai, Y., Shinohara, M., Takahashi, S. and Mori, E. (2011) 'Small gray matter volume in orbitofrontal cortex in Prader-Willi syndrome: A voxel-based MRI study', *Human Brain Mapping*, 32(7): 1059–1066.

Ohnishi, T., Moriguchi, Y., Matsuda, H., Mori, T., Hirakata, M., Imabayashi, E., Hirao, K., Nemoto, K., Kaga, M. and Inagaki, M. (2004) 'The neural network for the mirror system and mentalizing in normally developed children: An fMRI study', *Neuroreport*, 15(9): 1483–1487.

Olesen, P.J., Westerberg, H. and Klingberg, T. (2004) 'Increased prefrontal and parietal activity after training of working memory', *Nature Neuroscience*, 7(1): 75–79.

Onishi, K.H. and Baillargeon, R. (2005) 'Do 15-month-old infants understand false beliefs?', *Science*, 308(5719): 255.

Osso, L.A. and Chan, J.R. (2019) 'A surprising role for myelin in Williams syndrome', *Nature Neuroscience*, 22(5): 681–683.

Ouattara, D.N. (2018) 'Combatting infant mortality: A priority for Africa', *International Policy Digest*, 21 November, Available from: https://intpolicydigest.org/2018/11/21/combatting-infant-mortality-a-priority-for-africa/ [Accessed 28 September 2021].

Palmer, A. (2012) 'These two brains both belong to three-year-olds, so why is one so much bigger?', *The Telegraph*, 28 October, Available from: https://www.telegraph.co.uk/news/0/two-brains-belong-three-year-olds-one-much-bigger/ [Accessed 13 April 2020].

Parker, L.A., Rock, E.M. and Limebeer, C.L. (2011) 'Regulation of nausea and vomiting by cannabinoids', *British Journal of Pharmacology*, 163(7): 1411–1422.

Parsons, S. and Bynner, J. (2005) *Does Numeracy Matter More?* London: National Research and Development Centre for Adult Literacy and Numeracy.

Pascalis, O., de Schonen, S., Morton, J., Deruelle, C. and Fabre-Grenet, M. (1995) 'Mother's face recognition by neonates: A replication and an extension', *Infant Behavior and Development*, 18(1): 79–85.

Pascual-Leone, J. (1970) 'A mathematical model for the transition rule in Piaget's developmental stages', *Acta Psychologica, Amsterdam*, 32(4): 301–345.

Pashler, H., McDaniel, M., Rohrer, D. and Bjork, R. (2008) 'Learning styles concepts and evidence', *Psychological Science in the Public Interest*, 9(3): 105–119.

Pasquinelli, E. (2012) 'Neuromyths: Why do they exist and persist?', *Mind, Brain, and Education*, 6(2): 89–96.

Paulsen, D., Platt, N., Scott, H. and Brannon, E. (2011) 'Decision-making under risk in children, adolescents, and young adults', *Frontiers in Psychology*, 2: 72.

Pelton, L.H. (2015) 'The continuing role of material factors in child maltreatment and placement', *Child Abuse & Neglect*, 41: 30–39, Available from: https://doi.org/10.1016/j.chiabu.2014.08.001 [Accessed 31 January 2023].

Peng, P., Wang, C. and Namkung, J. (2018) 'Understanding the cognition related to mathematics difficulties: A meta-analysis on the cognitive deficit profiles and the bottleneck theory', *Review of Educational Research*, 88(3): 434–476.

Pennington, B.F., Gilger, J.W., Pauls, D., Smith, S.A., Smith, S.D. and DeFries, J.C. (1991) 'Evidence for major gene transmission of developmental dyslexia', *JAMA*, 266(11): 1527–1534.

Pereira, C. and Reddy, J.S.K. (2018) 'The boy who grew a new brain: Understanding this miracle from a neuro-quantum perspective', *NeuroQuantology*, 16(7): 39–48.

Perez, L.A., Peynircioğlu, Z.F. and Blaxton, T.A. (1998) 'Developmental differences in implicit and explicit memory performance', *Journal of Experimental Child Psychology*, 70(3): 167–185.

Perfetti, C.A. and Bolger, D.J. (2004) 'The brain might read that way', *Scientific Studies of Reading*, 8(3): 293–304.

Perlini, C., Bellani, M., Rossetti, M.G., Zovetti, N., Rossin, G., Bressi, C. and Brambilla, P. (2019) 'Disentangle the neural correlates of attachment style in healthy individuals', *Epidemiology and Psychiatric Sciences*, 28(4): 371–375.

Perry, B.D. (2002) 'Childhood experience and the expression of genetic potential: What childhood neglect tells us about nature and nurture', *Brain and Mind*, 3(1): 79–100.

Perry, B.D. (2019) [@BDPerry], tweet, 18 February, Available from: https://twitter.com/BDPerry/status/1097642666983079938 [Accessed 24 October 2022].

Perry, B.D. and Pollard, R. (1997) 'Altered brain development following global neglect in early childhood', in *Proceedings from the Society for Neuroscience Annual Meeting* (New Orleans).

Perry, C.J. and Fallah, M. (2014) 'Feature integration and object representations along the dorsal stream visual hierarchy', *Frontiers in Computational Neuroscience*, 8: 84.

Perone, S., Madole, K.L., Ross-Sheey, S., Carey, M. and Oakes, L.M. (2008) 'The relation between infants' activity with objects and attention to object appearance', *Developmental Psychology*, 44(5): 1242–1248.

Peters, L. and De Smedt, B. (2018) 'Arithmetic in the developing brain: A review of brain imaging studies', *Developmental Cognitive Neuroscience*, 30: 265–279.

Peterson, R.L. and Pennington, B.F. (2012) 'Seminar: Developmental dyslexia', *The Lancet*, 379(9830): 1997–2007.

Phan, K.L., Wager, T., Taylor, S.F. and Liberzon, I. (2002) 'Functional neuro-anatomy of emotion: A meta-analysis of emotion activation studies in PET and fMRI', *Neuroimage*, 16(2): 331–348.

Phan, S. (2014) 'Cell phones improve literacy rates', The Borgen Project, Available from: https://borgenproject.org/cell-phones-improve-literacy-rates/ [Accessed 27 September 2021].

Piaget, J. and Inhelder, B. (1969) *The Psychology of the Child*, London: Routledge & Kegan Paul.

Pinel, J.P.J. (2011) *Biopsychology* (8th edn), London: Pearson Education.

Pinker, S. (1994) *The Language Instinct: How the Mind Creates Language*, London: Penguin.

Pinkstone, J. (2017) 'How smartphone addiction in teenagers can lead to depression', *Mail Online*, 30 November, Available from: http://www.dailymail.co.uk/~/article-5129401/index.html [Accessed 26 August 2020].

Pinti, P., Tachtsidis, I., Hamilton, A., Hirsch, J., Aichelburg, C., Gilbert, S. and Burgess, P.W. (2020) 'The present and future use of functional near-infrared spectroscopy (fNIRS) for cognitive neuroscience', *Annals of the New York Academy of Sciences*, 1464(1): 5–29.

Popova, S., Lange, S., Probst, C., Gmel, G. and Rehm, J. (2017) 'Estimation of national, regional, and global prevalence of alcohol use during pregnancy and fetal alcohol syndrome: A systematic review and meta-analysis', *The Lancet Global Health*, 5(3): e290–e299.

Poulin-Dubois, D., Blaye, A., Coutya, J. and Bialystok, E. (2011) 'The effects of bilingualism on toddlers' executive functioning', *Journal of Experimental Child Psychology*, 108(3): 567–579.

Poulsen, C., Picton, T.W. and Paus, T. (2009) 'Age-related changes in transient and oscillatory brain responses to auditory stimulation during early adolescence', *Developmental Science*, 12(2): 220–235.

Prader, A., Labhart, A. and Willi, H. (1956) 'Syndrom von Adipositas, kleinwuchs, kryptochismus und oligophrenie nach myotoniertgem zustand im neugeborenalter', *Schweizerische medizinische Wochenschrift*, 86: 1260–1261.

Prado, E.L. and Dewey, K.G. (2014) 'Nutrition and brain development in early life', *Nutrition Reviews*, 72(4): 267–284.

Prashnig, B. (2004) *The Power of Diversity: New Ways of Learning and Teaching through Learning Styles* (revd edn), Stafford: Network Educational Press Ltd.

Pratte, M.S. (2018) 'Iconic memories die a sudden death', *Psychological Science*, 29(6): 877–887.

Price, C.J. and McCrory, E. (2007) 'Functional brain imaging studies of skilled reading and developmental dyslexia', in C. Hulme and M.J. Snowling (eds) *The Science of Reading: A Handbook*, Oxford: Blackwell, pp 473–496.

Public Health England. (2020) 'Anencephaly: Information for parents', Available from: https://www.gov.uk/government/publications/anencephaly-description-in-brief/anencephaly-information-for-parents [Accessed 2 July 2021].

Quadri, S. and Matthews, S. (2018) 'British teenage girls are among the heaviest drinkers in Europe – and have overtaken boys', *The Telegraph*, 26 September, Available from: https://www.telegraph.co.uk/news/2018/09/26/british-teen age-girls-among-heaviest-drinkers-europe-have/ [Accessed 28 September 2021].

Quinn, P.C. and Slater, A. (2003) 'Face perception at birth and beyond', in O. Pascalis and A. Slater (eds) *Development of Face Processing in Infancy and Early Childhood*, New York: Nova Science Publishers, pp 3–11.

Quirin, M., Gillath, O., Pruessner, J.C. and Eggert, L.D. (2009) 'Adult attachment insecurity and hippocampal cell density', *Social Cognitive and Affective Neuroscience*, 5(1): 39–47.

Rapin, I. (2016) 'Dyscalculia and the calculating brain', *Pediatric Neurology*, 61: 11–20.

Rauschecker, J. and Scott, S.K. (2015) 'Pathways and streams in the auditory cortex: An update on how work in nonhuman primates has contributed to our understanding of human speech processing', in G. Hickok and S.L. Small (eds) *Neurobiology of Language*, London: Academic Press, pp 287–298.

Rayner, K. (1998) 'Eye movements in reading and information processing: 20 years of research', *Psychological Bulletin*, 124: 372–422.

Rees, J.L. (2003) 'Genetics of hair and skin color', *Annual Review of Genetics*, 37(1): 67–90.

Reichelt, A.C. and Rank, M.M. (2017) 'The impact of junk foods on the adolescent brain', *Birth Defects Research*, 109(20): 1649–1658.

Reilly, J.S., Bates, E.A. and Marchman, V.A. (1998) 'Narrative discourse in children with early focal brain injury', *Brain and Language*, 61(3): 335–375.

Reiss, A.L., Mazzocco, M.M., Greenlaw, R., Freund, L.S. and Ross, J.L. (1995) 'Neurodevelopmental effects of X monosomy: A volumetric imaging study', *Annals of Neurology*, 38(5): 731–738.

Reiss, A.L., Eliez, S., Schmitt, J.E., Straus, E., Lai, Z., Jones, W. and Bellugi, U. (2006) 'Neuroanatomy of Williams syndrome: A high-resolution MRI study', in U. Bellugie and M. St. George (eds) *Journey from Cognition to Brain to Gene*, Cambridge, MA: MIT Press, pp 105–122.

Reissland, N. (1988) 'Neonatal imitation in the first hour of life: Observations in rural Nepal', *Developmental Psychology*, 24(4): 464–469.

Repacholi, B.M. and Gopnik, A. (1997) 'Early reasoning about desires: Evidence from 14-and 18-month-olds', *Developmental Psychology*, 33(1): 12–21.

Rippon, G. (2019) *The Gendered Brain: The New Neuroscience that Shatters the Myth of the Female Brain*, London: Penguin.

Robinson, M. (2008) *Child Development from Birth to Eight: A Journey through the Early Years*, Maidenhead: Open University Press and McGraw-Hill Education.

Rose, H. and Rose, S. (2016) *Can Neuroscience Change Our Minds?* Bristol: Polity Press.

Rose, J. (2006) 'Independent review of the teaching of early reading: Final report', Department for Education and Skills, Available from: https://dera.ioe.ac.uk/5551/2/report.pdf [Accessed 28 September 2021].

Rose, S.A., Feldman, J.F. and Jankowski, J.J. (2001) 'Visual short-term memory in the first year of life: Capacity and recency effects', *Developmental Psychology*, 37(4): 539–549.

Ross, J., Roeltgen, D. and Zinn, A. (2006) 'Cognition and the sex chromosomes: Studies in Turner syndrome', *Hormone Research in Paediatrics*, 65(1): 47–56.

Rossion, B. (2013) 'The composite face illusion: A whole window into our understanding of holistic face perception', *Visual Cognition*, 21(2): 139–253.

Roza, S.J., Verburg, B.O., Jaddoe, V.W., Hofman, A., Mackenbach, J.P., Steegers, E. A., … and Tiemeier, H. (2007) 'Effects of maternal smoking in pregnancy on prenatal brain development: The Generation R study', *European Journal of Neuroscience*, 25(3): 611–617.

Rubia, K. (2018) 'Cognitive neuroscience of attention deficit hyperactivity disorder (ADHD) and its clinical translation', *Frontiers in Human Neuroscience*, 12: 100.

Rubia, K., Smith, A.B., Woolley, J., Nosarti, C., Heyman, I., Taylor, E. and Brammer, M. (2006) 'Progressive increase of frontostriatal brain activation from childhood to adulthood during event-related tasks of cognitive control', *Human Brain Mapping*, 27(12): 973–993.

Rubia, K.H., Coplan, R.J., Chen, X., Buskirk, A. and Wojslawowicz, J. (1999) 'Peer relationships in childhood', in M.H. Bornstein and M. Lamb (eds) *Developmental Psychology: An Advanced Textbook* (4th edn), Mahwah, NJ: Erlbaum, pp 451–501.

Russo, R., Nichelli, P., Gibertoni, M. and Cornia, C. (1995) 'Developmental trends in implicit and explicit memory: A picture completion study', *Journal of Experimental Child Psychology*, 59(3): 566–578.

Ryan, S.A. and Kokotailo, P. (2019) 'Policy statement: Committee on substance use and prevention: Alcohol use by youth', *American Academy of Pediatrics*, Available from: www.pediatrics.org/cgi/doi/10.1542/peds.2010-0438 [Accessed 31 January 2023].

Sachdev, H.P.S., Gera, T. and Nestel, P. (2005) 'Effect of iron supplementation on mental and motor development in children: Systematic review of randomised controlled trials', *Public Health Nutrition*, 8(2): 117–132.

Samea, F., Soluki, S., Nejati, V., Zarei, M., Cortese, S., Eickhoff, S.B., Tahmasian, M. and Eickhoff, C.R. (2019) 'Brain alterations in children/adolescents with ADHD revisited: A neuroimaging meta-analysis of 96 structural and functional studies', *Neuroscience & Biobehavioral Reviews*, 100: 1–8.

Sanchez, M.M., Ladd, C.O. and Plotsky, P.M. (2001) 'Early adverse experience as a developmental risk factor for later psychopathology: Evidence from rodent and primate models', *Development and Psychopathology*, 13(3): 419–449.

Santiago, L.B., Jorge, S.M. and Moreira, A.C. (1996) 'Longitudinal evaluation of the development of salivary cortisol circadian rhythm in infancy', *Clinical Endocrinology*, 44(2): 157–161.

Sapolsky, R.M., Uno, H., Rebert, C.S. and Finch, C.E. (1990) 'Hippocampal damage associated with prolonged glucocorticoid exposure in primates', *Journal of Neuroscience*, 10(9): 2897–2902.

Sauseng, P., Bergmann, J. and Wimmer, H. (2004) 'When does the brain register deviances from standard word spellings? An ERP study', *Cognitive Brain Research*, 20(3): 529–532.

Sayal, K., Prasad, V., Daley, D., Ford, T. and Coghill, D. (2018) 'ADHD in children and young people: Prevalence, care pathways, and service provision', *The Lancet Psychiatry*, 5(2): 175–186.

Schachner, A. and Hannon, E.E. (2011) 'Infant-directed speech drives social preferences in 5-month-old infants', *Developmental Psychology*, 47(1): 19.

Schacter, D.L. (1995) 'Introduction: Memory distortion: History and current status', in D. Schacter (ed) *Memory Distortion: How Minds, Brains, and Societies Reconstruct the Past*, Cambridge, MA: Harvard University Press, pp 1–43.

Schacter, D.L. and Moscovitch, M. (1984) 'Infants, amnesics, and dissociable memory systems', in M. Moscovitch (ed) *Infant Memory*, New York: Plenum, pp 173–216.

Schapiro, A. and Turk-Browne, N. (2015) 'Statistical learning', in A.W. Toga (ed) *Brain Mapping: An Encyclopedic Reference*, London: Academic Press, pp 501–506.

Scher, L.J. and Shyman, E. (2019). 'Challenging weak central coherence: A brief exploration of neurological evidence from visual processing and linguistic studies in autism spectrum disorder', *Annals of Behavioral Neuroscience*, 2(2): 136–143.

Schlaggar, B.L., Brown, T.T., Lugar, H.M., Visscher, K.M., Miezin, F.M. and Petersen, S.E. (2002) 'Functional neuroanatomical differences between adults and school-age children in the processing of single words', *Science*, 296(5572): 1476.

Schneider-Hassloff, H., Straube, B., Nuscheler, B., Wemken, G. and Kircher, T. (2015) 'Adult attachment style modulates neural responses in a mentalizing task', *Neuroscience*, 303: 462–473.

Schneider-Hassloff, H., Straube, B., Jansen, A., Nuscheler, B., Wemken, G., Witt, S. H., Rietschel, M. and Kircher, T. (2016) 'Oxytocin receptor polymorphism and childhood social experiences shape adult personality, brain structure and neural correlates of mentalizing', *Neuroimage*, 134: 671–684.

Schore, A. (1994) *Affect Regulation and the Origin of the Self: The Neurobiology of Emotional Development*, Philadelphia, PA: Erlbaum.

Schore, A. (2000) 'Attachment and the regulation of the right brain', *Attachment & Human Development*, 2(1): 23–47.

Schore, A. (2003a) *Affect Dysregulation and Disorders of the Self*, New York: W. W. Norton.

Schore, A. (2003b) 'The human unconscious: The development of the right brain and its role in early emotional life', in V. Green (ed) *Emotional Development in Psychoanalysis, Attachment Theory and Neuroscience: Creating Connections*, London: Routledge, pp 23–54.

Schore, A. (2012) *The Science of the Art of Psychotherapy*, New York: W. W. Norton.

Schulz, K.M. and Sisk, C.L. (2016) 'The organizing actions of adolescent gonadal steroid hormones on brain and behavioral development', *Neuroscience and Biobehavioral Reviews*, 70: 148–158.

Schwartz, M.F. (2006) 'The cognitive neuropsychology of everyday action and planning', *Cognitive Neuropsychology*, 23(1): 202–221.

Schwartzkroin, P.A. and Wester, K. (1975) 'Long-lasting facilitation of a synaptic potential following tetanization in the in vitro hippocampal slice', *Brain Research*, 89(1): 107–119.

Schwieter, J.W. (2019) *The Handbook of the Neuroscience of Multilingualism*, Chichester: John Wiley.

Scoville, W.B. and Milner, B. (2000) 'Loss of recent memory after bilateral hippocampal lesions', *Journal of Neuropsychiatry and Clinical Neurosciences*, 12(1): 103–113.

Sebastiani, G., Herranz Barbero, A., Borrás-Novell, C., Alsina Casanova, M., Aldecoa-Bilbao, V., Andreu-Fernández, V., Pascual Tutusaus, M., Ferrero Martínez, S., Gómez Roig, M.D., and García-Algar, O. (2019) 'The effects of vegetarian and vegan diet during pregnancy on the health of mothers and offspring', *Nutrients*, 11(3): 557.

Sebire, N.J., Jolly, M., Harris, J.P., Wadsworth, J., Joffe, M., Beard, R.W., Regan, L., and Robinson, S. (2001) 'Maternal obesity and pregnancy outcome: A study of 287,213 pregnancies in London', *International Journal of Obesity and Related Metabolic Disorders: Journal of the International Association for the Study of Obesity*, 25(8): 1175.

Semple, W.E., Goyer, P.F., McCormick, R., Donovan, B., Muzic Jr, R.F., Rugle, L., McCutcheon, K., Lewis, C., Liebling, D. and Kowaliw, S. (2000) 'Higher brain blood flow at amygdala and lower frontal cortex blood flow in PTSD patients with comorbid cocaine and alcohol abuse compared with normals', *Psychiatry*, 63(1): 65–74.

Shalev, R.S., Manor, O., Kerem, B., Ayali, M., Badichi, N., Friedlander, Y. and Gross-Tsur, V. (2001) 'Developmental dyscalculia is a familial learning disability', *Journal of Learning Disabilities*, 34(1): 59–65.

Shallice, T. (1982) 'Specific impairments of planning', *Philosophical Transactions of the Royal Society London Biological Sciences*, 298: 199–209.

Shaywitz, B.A., Shaywitz, S.E., Pugh, K.R., Constable, R.T., Skudlarski, P., Fulbright, R.K., Bronen, R.A., Fletcher, J.M., Shankweiler, D.P. and Katz, L. (1995) 'Sex differences in the functional organization of the brain for language', *Nature*, 373(6515): 607–609.

Shen, M.D. and Piven, J. (2017) 'Brain and behavior development in autism from birth through infancy', *Dialogues in Clinical Neuroscience*, 19(4): 325–334.

Shen, M.D., Nordahl, C.W., Young, G.S., Wootton-Gorges, S.L., Lee, A., Liston, S.E., Harrington, K.R., Ozonoff, S. and Amaral, D.G (2013) 'Early brain enlargement and elevated extra-axial fluid in infants who develop autism spectrum disorder', *Brain*, 136(9): 2825–2835.

Sherman, L.E., Payton, A.A., Hernandez, L.M., Greenfield, P.M. and Dapretto, M. (2016) 'The power of the like in adolescence', *Psychological Science*, 27(7): 1027–1035.

Shoraka, H.R., Haghdoost, A.A., Baneshi, M.R., Bagherinezhad, Z. and Zolala, F (2020) 'Global prevalence of classic phenylketonuria based on neonatal screening program data: Systematic review and meta-analysis', *Clinical and Experimental Pediatrics*, 63(2): 34–43.

Siegal, M. (1997) *Knowing Children* (2nd edn), Hove: Psychology Press.

Sims, M., Guilfoyle, A. and Parry, T.S. (2006) 'Children's cortisol levels and quality of child care provision', *Child: Care, Health and development*, 32(4): 453–466.

Skinner, B.F. (1953) *Science and Human Behavior*, New York: Macmillan.

Skinner, B.F. and Frederic, B. (1957) *Verbal Behavior*, New York: Appleton-Century-Crofts.

Slater, A., Mattock, A. and Brown, E. (1990) 'Size constancy at birth: Newborn infants' responses to retinal and real size', *Journal of Experimental Child Psychology*, 49(2): 314–322.

Slotnick, S. (2013) *Controversies in Cognitive Neuroscience*, Basingstoke: Palgrave Macmillan.

Smith, E.E., Jonides, J., Marshuetz, C. and Koeppe, R.A. (1998) 'Components of verbal working memory: Evidence from neuroimaging', *Proceedings of the National Academy of Sciences of the United States of America*, 95(3): 876–882.

Sommer, I.E., Aleman, A., Bouma, A. and Kahn, R.S. (2004) 'Do women really have more bilateral language representation than men? A meta-analysis of functional imaging studies', *Brain*, 127(8): 1845–1852.

Song, Y., Zhu, Q., Li, J., Wang, X. and Liu, J. (2015) 'Typical and atypical development of functional connectivity in the face network', *Journal of Neuroscience*, 35(43): 14624–14635.

Sowell, E.R., Thompson, P.M., Leonard, C.M., Welcome, S.E., Kan, E., and Toga, A.W. (2004) 'Longitudinal mapping of cortical thickness and brain growth in normal children', *Journal of Neuroscience*, 24(38): 8223–8231.

Sparrevohn, R. and Howie, P.M. (1995) 'Theory of mind in children with autistic disorder: Evidence of developmental progression and the role of verbal ability', *Journal of Child Psychology and Psychiatry*, 36(2): 249–263.

Squire, L.R. and Zola-Morgan, S. (1991) 'The medial temporal lobe memory system', *Science*, 253(5026): 1380–1386.

Sroufe, L.A. (1979) 'Socioemotional development', in J. Osofsky (ed) *Handbook of Infant Development*, New York: Wiley, pp 462–516.

Sroufe, L.A. (1997) *Emotional Development: The Organization of Emotional Life in the Early Years*, Cambridge: Cambridge University Press.

Stanovich, K.E. (1985) 'Explaining the variance in reading ability in terms of psychological processes: What have we learned?', *Annals of Dyslexia*, 35(1): 67.

Stanovich, K.E. (1988) 'Explaining the differences between the dyslexic and the garden-variety poor reader: The phonological-core variable-difference model', *Journal of Learning Disabilities*, 21(10): 590–604.

Stats Team, NHS Digital. (2018) 'Statistics on drugs misuse' [Power Point], Health and Social Care Information Centre.

Stein, J. and Walsh, V. (1997) 'To see but not to read: The magnocellular theory of dyslexia', *Trends in Neurosciences*, 20(4): 147–152.

Steinberg, L. (2005) 'Cognitive and affective development in adolescence', *Trends in Cognitive Science*, 9(2): 69–74.

Steinberg, L. (2010) 'A dual systems model of adolescent risk-taking', *Developmental Psychobiology: The Journal of the International Society for Developmental Psychobiology*, 52(3): 216–224.

Steinberg, L., Icenogle, G., Shulman, E.P., Breiner, K., Chein, J., Bacchini, D., Chang, L., Chaudhary, N., Giunta, L.D. and Dodge, K.A. (2018) 'Around the world, adolescence is a time of heightened sensation seeking and immature self-regulation', *Developmental Science*, 21(2): e12532.

Stern, D.N. (2000) *The Interpersonal World of the Infant: A View from Psychoanalysis and Development Psychology* (revd edn), London: Basic Books.

Stiles, J., Bates, E.A., Thal, D., Trauner, D.A. and Reilly, J. (2002) 'Linguistic and spatial cognitive development in children with pre and perinatal focal brain injury: A ten-year overview from the San Diego longitudinal project', in M.H. Johnson, Y. Munakata and R. Gilmore (eds) *Brain Development and Cognition: A Reader*, Oxford: Blackwell, pp 272–291.

Stirling, J., Amaya-Jackson, L. and Amaya-Jackson, L. (2008) 'Understanding the behavioral and emotional consequences of child abuse', *Pediatrics*, 122(3): 667–673.

Strange, B.A., Fletcher, P.C., Henson, R.N.A., Friston, K.J. and Dolan, R.J. (1999) 'Segregating the functions of human hippocampus', *Proceedings of the National Academy of Sciences*, 96(7): 4034–4039.

Strømme, P., Bjørnstad, P.G. and Ramstad, K. (2002) 'Prevalence estimation of Williams syndrome', *Journal of Child Neurology*, 17(4): 269–271.

Strouse, G.A. and Samson, J.E. (2021) 'Learning from video: A meta-analysis of the video deficit in children ages 0 to 6 years', *Child Development*, 92(1): e20–e38.

Sujan, A.C., Öberg, A.S., Quinn, P.D. and D'Onofrio, B.M. (2019) 'Annual research review: Maternal antidepressant use during pregnancy and offspring neurodevelopmental problems–a critical review and recommendations for future research', *Journal of Child Psychology and Psychiatry*, 60(4): 356–376.

Swaab, D.F. (1997) 'Prader-Willi syndrome and the hypothalamus', *Acta Paediatrica – International Journal of Paediatrics – Supplements Only*, 423: 50–54.

Swaab, D.F., Purba, J.S. and Hofman, M.A. (1995) 'Alterations in the hypothalamic paraventricular nucleus and its oxytocin neurons (putative satiety cells) in Prader-Willi syndrome: A study of five cases', *Journal of Clinical Endocrinology & Metabolism*, 80(2): 573–579.

Sybert, V.P. and McCauley, E. (2004) 'Turner's syndrome', *New England Journal of Medicine*, 351(12): 1227–1238.

Szűcs, D. (2016) 'Subtypes and comorbidity in mathematical learning disabilities: Multidimensional study of verbal and visual memory processes is key to understanding', *Progress in Brain Research*, 227: 277–304.

Tager-Flusberg, H. (2003) 'Developmental disorders of genetic origin', in M. de Haan and M.H. Johnson (eds) *The Cognitive Neuroscience of Development*, Hove: Psychology Press, pp 237–261.

Tallon-Baudry, C., Bertrand, O., Peronnet, F. and Pernier, J. (1998) 'Induced-band activity during the delay of a visual short-term memeory task in humans', *Journal of Neuroscience*, 18(11): 4244–4254.

Tamnes, C.K., Herting, M.M., Goddings, A.-L., Meuwese, R., Blakemore, S.-J., Dahl, R.E., Güroğlu, B., Raznahan, A., Sowell, E.R., Crone, E.A. and Mills, K.L. (2017) 'Development of the cerebral cortex across adolescence: A multisample study of inter-related longitudinal changes in cortical volume, surface area, and thickness', *Journal of Neuroscience*, 37(12): 3402–3412.

Tamura, T., Goldenberg, R.L., Hou, J., Johnston, K.E., Cliver, S.P., Ramey, S.L. and Nelson, K.G. (2002) 'Cord serum ferritin concentrations and mental and psychomotor development of children at five years of age', *Journal of Pediatrics*, 140(2): 165–170.

Teffer, K. and Semendeferi, K. (2012) 'Human prefrontal cortex: Evolution, development, and pathology', *Progress in Brain Research*, 195: 191–218.

Telegraph. (2013) 'Why women are the talkative sex', 21 February, Available from: https://www.telegraph.co.uk/news/science/science-news/9884652/Why-women-are-the-talkative-sex.html [Accessed 28 September 2021].

Temple, E. and Posner, M.I. (1998) 'Brain mechanisms of quantity are similar in 5-year-old children and adults', *Proceedings of the National Academy of Sciences*, 95(13): 7836–7841.

Teyler, T.J. and Fountain, S.B. (1987) 'Neuronal plasticity in the mammalian brain: Relevance to behavioral learning and memory', *Child Development*, 58(3): 698–712.

Thomas, K.M., Hunt, R.H., Vizueta, N., Sommer, T., Durston, S., Yang, Y. and Worden, M.S. (2004) 'Evidence of developmental differences in implicit sequence learning: An fMRI study of children and adults', *Journal of Cognitive Neuroscience*, 16(8): 1339–1351.

Thompson, B.L., Levitt, P. and Stanwood, G.D. (2009) 'Prenatal exposure to drugs: Effects on brain development and implications for policy and education', *Nature Reviews Neuroscience*, 10(4): 303–312.

Thornton, S. (2002) *Growing Minds: An Introduction to Cognitive Development*, Basingstoke: Palgrave Macmillan.

Tick, B., Bolton, P., Happé, F., Rutter, M. and Rijsdijk, F. (2016) 'Heritability of autism spectrum disorders: A meta-analysis of twin studies', *Journal of Child Psychology and Psychiatry*, 57(5): 585–595.

Tizard, B. (2009) 'The making and breaking of attachment theory', *The Psychologist*, 23: 902–903.

Tokuhama-Espinosa, T. (2018) *Neuromyths: Debunking False Ideas about the Brain*, New York: W. W. Norton.

Tomasello, M. (2019) *Becoming Human: A Theory of Ontogeny*, Cambridge, MA: Belknap Press.

Tottenham, N., Hare, T.A., Quinn, B.T., McCarry, T.W., Nurse, M., Gilhooly, T., Millner, A., Galvan, A., Davidson, M.C. and Eigsti, I.-M. (2010) 'Prolonged institutional rearing is associated with atypically large amygdala volume and difficulties in emotion regulation', *Developmental Science*, 13(1): 46–61.

Turkeltaub, P.E., Gareau, L., Flowers, D.L., Zeffiro, T.A. and Eden, G.F. (2003) 'Development of neural mechanisms for reading', *Nature Neuroscience*, 6(7): 767–773.

Turner, H.H. (1938) 'A syndrome of infantilism, congenital webbed neck, and cubitus valgus', *Endocrinology*, 23: 566–574.

United Nations. (nd) 'Ending poverty', Available from: https://www.un.org/en/global-issues/ending-poverty [Accessed 26 September 2022].

Van Dyke, D.L., Wiktor, A., Roberson, J.R. and Weiss, L. (1991) 'Mental retardation in Turner syndrome', *Journal of Pediatrics*, 118(3): 415–417.

Van Soelen, I.L.C., Brouwer, R.M., van Baal, G.C.M., Schnack, H.G., Peper, J.S., Collins, D.L., Evans, A.C., Kahn, R.S., Boomsma, D.I. and Pol, H.H. (2012) 'Genetic influences on thinning of the cerebral cortex during development', *Neuroimage*, 59(4): 3871–3880.

Van Tieghem, M.R. and Tottenham, N. (2018) 'Neurobiological programming of early life stress: Functional development of amygdala–prefrontal circuitry and vulnerability for stress-related psychopathology', in E. Vermetten, D. Baker and V. Risbrough (eds) *Behavioral Neurobiology of PTSD*, Cham: Springer, pp 117–136.

Vargha-Khadem, F., Isaacs, E. and Muter, V. (1994) 'A review of cognitive outcome after unilateral lesions sustained during childhood', *Journal of Child Neurology*, 9: 2S67–2S73.

Verkerk, A.J.M.H., Pieretti, M., Sutcliffe, J.S., Fu, Y.-H., Kuhl, D.P.A., Pizzuti, A., Reiner, O., Richards, S., Victoria, M.F., Zhang, F., Eussen, B.E., van Ommen, G.-J.B., Blonden, L.A.J., Riggins, G.J., Chastain, J. L., Kunst, C.B., Galjaard, H., Thomas Caskey, C., Nelson, D. L.Oostra, B., Warren, S.T (1991) 'Identification of a gene (FMR-1) containing a CGG repeat coincident with a breakpoint cluster region exhibiting length variation in fragile X syndrome', *Cell*, 65(5): 905–914.

Volle, E., Gilbert, S.J., Benoit, R.G. and Burgess, P.W. (2010) 'Specialization of the rostral prefrontal cortex for distinct analogy processes', *Cerebral Cortex*, 20(11): 2647–2659.

Von Aster, M.G. and Shalev, R.S. (2007) 'Number development and developmental dyscalculia', *Developmental Medicine & Child Neurology*, 49(11): 868–873.

Von Der Heide, R., Vyas, G. and Olson, I.R. (2014) 'The social network-network: Size is predicted by brain structure and function in the amygdala and paralimbic regions', *Social Cognitive and Affective Neuroscience*, 9(12): 1962–1972.

Vondra, J.I., Shaw, D.S., Swearingen, L., Cohen, M. and Owens, E.B. (2001) 'Attachment stability and emotional and behavioral regulation from infancy to preschool age', *Development and Psychopathology*, 13(1): 13–33.

Vytal, K. and Hamann, S. (2010) 'Neuroimaging support for discrete neural correlates of basic emotions: A voxel-based meta-analysis', *Journal of Cognitive Neuroscience*, 22(12): 2864–2885.

Wada, J.A., Clarke, R. and Hamm, A. (1975) 'Cerebral hemispheric asymmetry in humans: Cortical speech zones in 100 adult and 100 infant brains', *Archives of Neurology*, 32(4): 239.

Wadhwa, D. (2019) 'Understanding poverty', World Bank, Available from: https://www.worldbank.org/en/understanding-poverty [Accessed 28 September 2021].

Wagner, R.K., Zirps, F.A., Edwards, A.A., Wood, S.G., Joyner, R.E., Becker, B.J., Liu, G. and Beal, B. (2020) 'The prevalence of dyslexia: A new approach to its estimation', *Journal of Learning Disabilities*, 53(5): 354–365.

Wakeley, A., Rivera, S. and Langer, J. (2000) 'Can young infants add and subtract?', *Child Development*, 71(6): 1525–1534.

Walsh, B. and Smith, A. (2002) 'Articulatory movements in adolescents', *Journal of Speech, Language, and Hearing Research*, 45(6): 1119–1133.

Walsh, D., McCartney, G., Smith, M. and Armour, G. (2019) 'Relationship between childhood socioeconomic position and adverse childhood experiences (ACEs): A systematic review', *Journal of Epidemiology and Community Health*, 73(12): 1087–1093.

Wang, B., Zhan, S., Gong, T. and Lee, L. (2013) 'Iron therapy for improving psychomotor development and cognitive function in children under the age of three with iron deficiency anaemia', *Cochrane Database of Systematic Reviews*, Available from: https://www.cochranelibrary.com/cdsr/doi/10.1002/14651858.CD001444.pub2/epdf/full [Accessed 31 January 2023].

Ward, J. (2010) *The Student's Guide to Cognitive Neuroscience* (2nd edn), Hove: Psychology Press.

Ward, J. (2012) *The Student's Guide to Social Neuroscience*, Hove: Psychology Press.

Wason, P.C. and Johnson-Laird, P.N. (1972) *Psychology of Reasoning: Structure and Content*, Cambridge, MA: Harvard University Press.

Watamura, S.E., Coe, C.L., Laudenslager, M.L. and Robertson, S.S. (2010) 'Effect of child care on salivary cortisol, SIgA, and specific antibody secretion in young children', *Psychoneuroendocrinology*, 35(8): 1156–1166.

Watamura, S.E., Donzella, B., Alwin, J. and Gunnar, M.R. (2003) 'Morning-to-afternoon increases in cortisol concentrations for infants and toddlers at child care: Age differences and behavioral correlates', *Child Development*, 74(4): 1006–1020.

Watson, J. (2019) *Drop the Disorder! Challenging the Culture of Psychiatric Diagnosis*, Monmouth: PCCS Books.

Weiland, B.J., Thayer, R.E., Depue, B.E., Sabbineni, A., Bryan, A.D. and Hutchison, K.E. (2015) 'Daily marijuana use is not associated with brain morphometric measures in adolescents or adults', *Journal of Neuroscience*, 35(4): 1505–1512.

Weir, K. (2014) 'The lasting impact of neglect', *Monitor*, 45(6), Available from: https://www.apa.org/monitor/2014/06/neglect [Accessed 4 May 2020].

Weisz, D.J., Clark, G.A. and Thompson, R.F. (1984) 'Increased responsivity of dentate granule cells during nictitating membrane response conditioning in rabbit', *Behavioural Brain Research*, 12(2): 145–154.

Wellman, H.M. (2017) 'Learning a theory of mind', in V. Slaughter and M. de Rosnay (eds) *Theory of Mind Development in Context*, Abingdon: Routledge, pp 1–22.

Werker, J.F. and Tees, R.C. (1984) 'Cross-language speech perception: Evidence for perceptual reorganization during the first year of life', *Infant Behavior and Development*, 7(1): 49–63.

Wernicke, C. (1977) 'Der aphasische symptomenkomplex eine psychologische studie auf anatomischer basis', in G.H. Eggert (ed) *Wernicke's Works on Aphasia: A Sourcebook and Review*, Berlin: Mouton de Gruyter, pp 91–145.

Westermann, G. and Mareschal, D. (2004) 'Mechanisms of development in infant visual object processing', *Infancy*, 5(2): 131–151.

Whitaker, K.J., Vendetti, M.S., Wendelken, C. and Bunge, S.A. (2018) 'Neuroscientific insights into the development of analogical reasoning', *Developmental Science*, 21(2): e12531.

White, D. and Rabago-Smith, M. (2010) 'Genotype–phenotype associations and human eye color', *Journal of Human Genetics*, 56(1): 5–7.

WHO (World Health Organization). (2008) 'Worldwide prevalence of anaemia 1993–2005', Available from: https://www.who.int/vmnis/publications/anaemia_prevalence/en/ [Accessed 30 September 2021].

WHO (World Health Organization). (2016) 'WHO recommendations on antenatal care for a positive pregnancy experience', Available from: https://apps.who.int/iris/bitstream/handle/10665/250800/WHO-RHR-16.12-eng.pdf?sequence=1&isAllowed=y [Accessed 30 September 2021].

WHO (World Health Organization). (2017) '10 facts on breastfeeding', Available from: http://www.who.int/features/factfiles/breastfeeding/en/ [Accessed 28 September 2021].

Wilke, M., Krägeloh-Mann, I. and Holland, S.K. (2007) 'Global and local development of gray and white matter volume in normal children and adolescents', *Experimental Brain Research*, 178(3): 296–307.

Wilson, M. (2017) *Resource-Focused Counselling and Psychotherapy: An Introduction*, London: Routledge.

Wing, L. and Gould, J. (1979) 'Severe impairments of social interaction and associated abnormalities in children: Epidemiology and classification', *Journal of Autism and Developmental Disorders*, 9(1): 11–29.

Winnicott, D.W. (1964) *The Child, the Family and the Outside World*, London: Penguin.

Wolf, M. and Bowers, P.G. (1999) 'The double-deficit hypothesis for the developmental dyslexias', *Journal of Educational Psychology*, 91(3): 415.

Wolf, M., Ullman-Shade, C. and Gottwald, S. (2016) 'Lessons from the reading brain for reading development and dyslexia', *Australian Journal of Learning Difficulties*, 21(2): 143–156.

Wolf, S.A., Boddeke, H. and Kettenmann, H. (2017) 'Microglia in physiology and disease', *Annual Review of Physiology*, 79: 619–643.

Wolff, J.J., Gerig, G., Lewis, J.D., Soda, T., Styner, M.A., Vachet, C., Botteron, K.N., Elison, J.T., Dager, S.R., Estes, A.M., Hazlett, H.C., Schultz, R.T., Zwaigenbaum, L. and Piven, J. (2015) 'Altered corpus callosum morphology associated with autism over the first 2 years of life', *Brain*, 138(7): 2046–2058.

Woon, F.L., and Hedges, D.W. (2008) 'Hippocampal and amygdala volumes in children and adults with childhood maltreatment-related posttraumatic stress disorder: A meta-analysis', *Hippocampus*, 18(8): 729–736.

World Bank. (2019) 'Poverty headcount ratio at $1.90 a day', Available from: https://data.worldbank.org/indicator/SI.POV.DDAY [Accessed 28 September 2021].

World Poverty Clock. (2018) Available from: https://worldpoverty.io [Accessed 28 September 2021].

Wren, S. (2002) 'Ten myths of reading instruction', *SEDL Letter*, 14(3), Available from: https://files.eric.ed.gov/fulltext/ED467299.pdf [Accessed 28 September 2021].

Wright, J. (2019) 'Genetic testing for autism, explained', *Spectrum | Autism Research News*, 10 April, Available from: https://www.spectrumnews.org/news/genetic-testing-autism-explained/ [Accessed 21 June 2021].

Wu, C.-S., Jew, C.P. and Lu, H.-C. (2011) 'Lasting impacts of prenatal cannabis exposure and the role of endogenous cannabinoids in the developing brain', *Future Neurology*, 6(4): 459–480.

Wymbs, N.F., Orr, C., Albaugh, M.D., Althoff, R.R., O'Loughlin, K., Holbrook, H., Garavan, H., Montalvo-Ortiz, J.L., Mostofsky, S. and Hudziak, J. (2020) 'Social supports moderate the effects of child adversity on neural correlates of threat processing', *Child Abuse & Neglect*, 102: 104413.

Wynn, K. (1990) 'Children's understanding of counting', *Cognition*, 36(2): 155–193.

Wynn, K. (1992) 'Addition and subtraction by human infants', *Nature*, 358(6389): 749–750.

Yan, X., Zhao, X., Li, J., He, L. and Xu, M. (2018) 'Effects of early-life malnutrition on neurodevelopment and neuropsychiatric disorders and the potential mechanisms', *Progress in Neuro-Psychopharmacology and Biological Psychiatry*, 83: 64–75.

Yasuda, H., Barth, A.L., Stellwagen, D. and Malenka, R.C. (2003) 'A developmental switch in the signaling cascades for LTP induction', *Nature Neuroscience*, 6(1): 15–16.

Yoshino, D., Idesawa, M., Kanazawa, S. and Yamaguchi, M.K. (2010) 'Infant perception of the rotating Kanizsa square', *Infant Behavior and Development*, 33: 196–208.

Yurgelun-Todd, D. (2007) 'Emotional and cognitive changes during adolescence', *Current Opinions in Neurobiology*, 17(2): 251–257.

Zeki, S. (2004) 'The neurology of ambiguity', *Consciousness and Cognition*, 13(1): 173–196.

Zelazo, P.D. and Carlson, S.M. (2012) 'Hot and cool executive function in childhood and adolescence: Development and plasticity', *Child Development Perspectives*, 6(4): 354–360.

Zelazo, P.D. and Frye, D. (1997) 'Cognitive complexity and control: A theory of the development of deliberate reasoning and intentional action', in M.I. Stamenov (ed) *Language Structure, Discourse, and the Access to Consciousness*, Amsterdam: John Benjamins, pp 113–153.

Zelazo, P.D., Muller, U., Frye, D. and Marcovitch, S. (2003) 'The development of executive function in early childhood', *Monographs of the Society for Research on Child Development*, 68(3): vii–137.

Zhang, X., Deng, M., Ran, G., Tang, Q., Xu, W., Ma, Y. and Chen, X. (2018) 'Brain correlates of adult attachment style: A voxel-based morphometry study', *Brain Research*, 1699: 34–43.

Zhou, X.-H., Li, Y.-J., Ou, J.-J. and Li, Y.-M. (2018) 'Association between maternal antidepressant use during pregnancy and autism spectrum disorder: An updated meta-analysis', *Molecular Autism*, 9(1): 21.

Zuckerman, B., Frank, D.A. and Mayes, L. (2002) 'Cocaine-exposed infants and developmental outcomes: Crack kids revisited', *JAMA*, 287(15): 1990–1991.

Index

Note: References to figures appear in *italic* type; those in **bold** type refer to tables.